Photograph by Bert Stern

JACOB K. JAVITS has been in Congress for fourteen years as Representative and, since 1956, Senator from New York. He is a Republican member of the Senate Rules and Administration Committee, and his party's leader in the campaign for civil-rights legislation.

Senator Javits was born on the lower East Side of New York City in 1904. He studied at Columbia University and is a graduate of New York University Law School. He was admitted to the bar in 1927. Immediately prior to his election as Senator, he served as Attorney General of New York. He is a veteran of World War II and has traveled extensively in this country and abroad. He is also active as a lecturer and as a contributor to national magazines.

Discrimination—U.S.A.

Discrimination—U.S.A.

by Jacob K. Javits ▣ NEW YORK

HARCOURT, BRACE AND COMPANY

B.1.61

To my wife, Marion, with love

Preface

The struggle against the remaining racial and religious discrimination in the United States engaged my interest and action long before I entered public life. I cannot emphasize too strongly the primary importance of this struggle to the tranquility of our country and its moral leadership of the free world. Patience and determination are basic qualities for success, law is the necessary equipment but most essential of all is the support of a well-informed public opinion. This book is my contribution to the effort to provide information and to stimulate discussion and study of one of the major issues of our time.

This book could not have been written without the valued and expert assistance of many devoted colleagues, friends, and helpers. Any errors of fact and judgment are my own, of course, but I would like to express my deep appreciation and acknowledgment to those who helped me in preparing this book.

First, to Allen Lesser, without whose invaluable and indefatigable assistance as compiler and editor I would have been unable to write this book. To my wife, Marion, I am grateful for her burning indignation, which moved me first to undertake the task of this book at all. And, to my brother, Benjamin, I am grateful; he has been my lifelong inspiration to the "good fight" on momentous public issues. Finally, to my devoted staff—my dear friends as well.

I would like to mention also those who helped with particular chapters or subjects or reviewed the manuscript, Eric F. Goldman, Professor of History, Princeton University; Bill Goode, Director, Michigan Labor Committee for Human Rights; Phineas Indritz, Washington attorney; Frances Levenson, director, National Committee against Discrimination in Housing; Frank Pohlhaus, counsel, National Association for the Advancement of Colored People; Sol Rabkin, director, law department, Anti-Defamation League of the B'nai B'rith; Richard M. Scammon, director of elections research for the Governmental Affairs Institute; Marvin S. Shapiro and William L. Taylor, Washington attorneys.

To Roy Millenson, my assistant for many years and currently Washington representative for the American Jewish Committee; to Robert Kaufman, my brilliant legislative assistant, and to Herbert Blitz, my gifted research assistant, to all these I give my thanks and much appreciation.

Contents

Discrimination—U.S.A.

"Let us then turn this government back into the channel in which the framers of the Constitution originally placed it. Let us discard all this quibbling about this man and the other man— this race and that race and the other race being inferior ... and unite as one people throughout this land, until we shall once more stand up declaring that all men are created equal."

—ABRAHAM LINCOLN

Chapter One

Prospect and Retrospect

I was born in 1904, and I remember vividly my life as a small boy, the son of Jewish immigrants, in a janitor's flat on Orchard and Stanton Streets on the lower East Side of New York City. My father made pants and doubled as janitor of the tenement, then later worked full-time as the janitor for $30 a month, plus rooms. My mother sold crockery and dry goods from a pushcart. In school I read about democracy and about the equality of all in America, but to a poor Jewish boy, running errands for a candy shop, scratching for a penny, watching my father get out the vote for two dollars a head paid by a saloonkeeper who was a Tammany Hall captain, the words "democracy" and "equality" seemed just so many distant, high-sounding phrases. I had little thought that I could win social acceptance, not to speak of being permitted to serve in the high public offices of congressman, attorney general of New York State, and United States senator.

My own experience is symptomatic of the social revolution which has marked American life since the turn of the twentieth century. The United States of the early 1900's was a "white, Protestant, Anglo-Saxon" country, as people used to say. Millions of citizens were not white or Protestant or "Anglo-Saxon" (meaning descended from western European stock), but the dominant assumption was that they should be satisfied with the skimpier educations, the dirtier jobs, and a severely limited right to advance in the economic or political world. In 1900 the top-ranking colleges admitted only a handful of students from minority families, and most of these came from decidedly exceptional circumstances. It was difficult for a Catholic of Irish or southern European background, and still harder for an eastern European Jew, to rise high in the basic industries, in the professions, or in the realm of arts and letters. No realistic person would have thought of proposing anyone but an old-stock white Protestant for the presidency or the vice-presidency of the United States. As for the average Negro, in either the North or the South, he was lucky to find a livelihood that kept him in ramshackle housing and grubby food.

Over the whole of minority America hung the aura of "caste." One vaudevillian would ask, "Why is the wheelbarrow the greatest of all inventions?" The other vaudevillian would answer, "Because it taught Irishmen to walk on their hind legs," and the audience roared. Polite Americans thought nothing of using phrases filled with derision—"bohunk" for the Hungarian, "grease-ball" for the Greek, "kike" for the Jew. In this atmosphere a member of a Congressional Committee, questioning a railroad-construction boss, asked: "You don't call . . . an Italian a white man?" "No, Sir," the construction boss replied. "An Italian is a Dago."

The walls were high but they were not impregnable. In the early 1900's, the minorities, by their talents, their dawn-to-dusk labors, and their use of the ballot, were making themselves felt. The general situation was propitious; America was hurrying into its "progressive" period, an era that was highly susceptible to arguments for social change. The lanterns of reform were lighting up all over the country, and the minorities moved ahead in the general glow. Catholic leaders reported sharply decreasing discrimination in colleges and in jobs. In 1906 a product of the New York aristocracy, President Theodore Roosevelt, named the first Jew to an American cabinet, Secretary of Commerce and Labor Oscar Straus. In 1916 the former Ivy League professor, President Woodrow Wilson, appointed the first American of the Jewish faith to the United States Supreme Court, Justice Louis Brandeis. In between, in 1910, a new group appeared in New York City. It was tiny in membership and operated largely with borrowed office furniture and borrowed funds, but it represented the beginnings of the organization which was to prove so effective a spokesman for the Negro—the National Association for the Advancement of Colored People.

During the decades after World War I, the United States went on chipping away at the crust of caste. Progress was sometimes swift, sometimes slow, and there were years when the nation seemed to turn backward, but over-all it headed toward the elimination of discrimination on the basis of race, creed, or color. After World War II the slow, zigzag movement turned into an avalanche of change.

By the late 1950's, the highest prestige colleges were competing with each other to enroll outstanding students regardless of family background. More miles of trim suburbia were stretching out, now inhabited not only by the old-stock executive group but by the middle-class and working-class sons of immigrants. The only federal civil rights law since Reconstruction days was passed in 1957, and was followed three years later by further civil rights legislation. In one area of American life after another, Negroes scored more "firsts." A particularly striking event occurred in 1958. For decades the top echelon of the American diplomatic service had been considered a special preserve of the wellborn. On January 23, 1958, President Eisenhower appointed Clifton R. Wharton United States Minister to Romania, the first Negro to be named an American chief-of-mission to a country of predominantly white population.

All the while, the 1954 Supreme Court decision ordering the end of the color line in public schools was doing its work. Desegregation was resisted by efforts ranging from the portentous to the ridiculous. In Arkansas, Governor Orval Faubus so brazenly defied the Supreme Court that President Eisenhower ordered federal troops into Little Rock. In Florida, Henry Balch, columnist for the *Orlando Sentinel,* thundered that a children's book telling about the marriage of a white and a black rabbit was a plot of the "integrating desegregationists," and hounded the volume off the shelves of the public libraries. (The author, Garth Williams, mused sadly: "It was written for children from two to five who will understand it perfectly. It was not written for adults, who will not understand it because it is only about a soft furry love and has no hidden message of hate.") Under the circumstances, desegregation moved ahead slowly. In 1960, on the anniversary of the Court decision, the statistics showed that only 6 per cent of the Negro students in the southern and border states were attending integrated schools —and the percentage was zero in Alabama, Georgia, Louisiana, Mississippi, and South Carolina. Yet, whatever the rate of speed, whatever the obstacles, the nation *was* going ahead desegregating its schools.

It is my firm belief that history will rank the Supreme Court decision of 1954 with the Emancipation Proclamation and the Fourteenth Amendment to the Constitution as landmarks in the fight for equality of opportunity for all Americans. The Court decision goes to the heart of the situation; education always has been and always will be the boulevard of opportunity, and this applies to all schooling, whether the third grade or the most advanced graduate work. I had this driven home to me by an incident that took place when I was the representative from New York City's Twenty-first Congressional District. It had been called to my attention that few Negroes were serving in our State Department's Foreign Service. A query to the Department disclosed that there was no objection to Negroes; they simply lacked the specialized training needed for the Foreign Service. I arranged a conference between leading Negro college presidents and representatives of the Department, and, as a result, Negro colleges began to institute the courses that would permit their students to pass Foreign Service examinations.

Today, I am confident, the United States is entering a period when the walls of discrimination will go on tumbling—and being tumbled—down. The nomination of a Catholic for the presidency is already an acceptable fact. The next decade or two may well bring the appointment of a Negro to a cabinet post. By the year 2000, it is conceivable that we may see the election of a Negro to the presidency or the vice-presidency. The appointment of a Negro secretary of state does not seem farfetched when a man like Ralph Bunche is considered. A former assistant secretary of state, this distinguished American Negro is second only to Secretary General Dag Hammarskjöld at the United Nations; he has, and has richly earned, an international reputation as a peace negotiator and statesman. Negro leaders have told me that they feel it will be politically feasible to name a Negro to the Supreme Court within the next ten years.

In the proximate future we may well see a marked increase in the number of Negroes in Congress. The National Association for the Advancement of Colored People, spurred on by the passage of the Civil Rights Acts of 1957 and 1960, has launched a drive to triple Negro registration in the South and thus to put it on a par with the present 60 per cent registration of eligible white voters. I believe that the number of Negroes in the House of Representatives (four in 1958)* is likely to grow steadily, and that, from the Negro 10 per cent of our population, between thirty and forty qualified persons may be elected as representatives to the 106th Congress by the year 2000. Long before then, I expect to see the first Negro since the Reconstruction era taking his place in the United States Senate.

By 1965, public school integration should be well on its way even in the Deep South. The next two Congresses, those which convene in 1961 and 1963, will probably bring an end to the archaic Senate Rule XXII and therefore to the filibuster, which has been the special and stubborn hurdle on the road to civil rights legislation. I make this prediction on the strength of my own experience in the Senate and on the basis of my observation of the mood of the country during the civil rights debates of 1957 and 1960. There is a new generation of Americans—and of Americans who live below the Mason-Dixon line. Today the South is producing an ever increasing number of enlightened citizens who, while still opposed to general civil rights legislation, do not carry over the ancient southern opposition, indeed revulsion, to the idea of accepting Negroes as the equals of whites in public affairs. For example, during the civil rights discussions of recent years, a notable number of southern leaders conceded that the full enjoyment of the ballot belongs to the Negro as well as to the white man.

Some students of minority problems in the United States will argue that I am overly optimistic. They believe that the anti-discrimination movement in the United States has reached, or will soon reach, a plateau; that its very successes are piling up resentments and fears which will slow it down more and more

* For their names, see p. 254.

and perhaps even reverse the trend. They stress, too, that civil rights advocates, in dealing with discrimination based on color, are trying to do the impossible—trying to make continuing progress against deep-seated human instincts.

I am positive that these commentators are wrong. They overlook the fact that the American democracy has its own inner dynamic—a dynamic that consists of an inherent drive to become more democratic. The history of the United States, in essence, is the story of the extension of full rights and of greater opportunities to a larger and larger part of the population. Each major period of the national life brought more people into the general current; each period aroused more intensively the ambitions of those who were still left outside. To predict that the process will not go on is to predict that American history will suddenly veer to a new and drastically different direction, a direction totally foreign to itself.

If the American past argues for a continuing social upsurge, the American present certainly does not gainsay it. The Negro group, latest of the American groups to make its bid for equal rights and equal opportunities, is certain to increase in political power and certain to use that power to win more opportunities. Since 1950, it has been estimated, the potential nonwhite vote has catapulted 25 per cent in New York, 50 per cent in Chicago, 62 per cent in Los Angeles. By the year 2000, one out of every three voters in New York and Chicago, and one out of two voters in Los Angeles, may well be nonwhite. Population shifts of minority groups to urban centers are creating a tide that could elect a nonwhite mayor in New York, Chicago, Philadelphia, or Los Angeles before many years. In the South, as a result of the civil rights legislation already passed and the additional laws that are almost certain to come, the Negro will vote more and more. And, as all American groups have done, he will use the vote to broaden opportunities for himself.

Outside the South, the antidiscrimination forces can count on a hard reality of modern American life: prejudice has proved to be ineffective politics. In the past, bigotry and hate may have had some success, but today they simply do not work. In my own career in politics, I have had no little experience with religious smear campaigns. In the late part of the senatorial campaign of 1956, literature appeared in New York City—which has a large Jewish population—carrying the innuendo that I had forsaken the Jewish faith. The matter was brought out into the open during a television interview when viewers telephoned in the question: "Is it true that you changed your Jewish faith?" Questions such as this, as every public figure knows, are like that old verbal trap which calls for a yes or no answer to the question: "Have you stopped beating your wife yet?" Air time ran out before I could reply that I had not changed my religion. Yet, according to my analysis of the 1956 results, the question had little or no effect on the voters of New York State.

Equally clearly, other attempts to use bigotry did not pay off. In Connecticut, Abraham Ribicoff won election for governor despite the injection of anti-Semitism into the campaign. The late Senator Richard L. Neuberger of Oregon scored an upset victory in a campaign marred by many expressions of bigotry, one of which openly urged voters to elect candidates who were "Christian." Senators Paul Douglas of Illinois and Hubert Humphrey of Minnesota won despite strenuous efforts to label them as recipients of special support from Communist sympathizers and Jews.

The most spectacular proof that appeals to religious prejudice do not work in modern American politics came in the West Virginia presidential primary battle of 1960 between Senator John Kennedy, a Catholic, and Senator Hubert Humphrey, a Protestant. Although Senator Humphrey made it ringingly plain that he wanted no votes gained from religious bias, anti-Catholicism was a blatant part of the campaign. Seasoned observers thought the prejudice might well have a decisive effect: West Virginia is 95 per cent Protestant and was supposed to have a strong anti-Catholic tradition. But when the votes were counted, Kennedy had won a thumping three-to-two victory. He was hurt little or not at all by the anti-Catholic campaign. On the contrary, apparently he was actually helped by it. Heavily Protestant West Virginia seemed the more determined to give the Senator, a Catholic, a victory as a way of showing that it wanted no part of elections determined by irrelevant questions of religion.

The antidiscrimination forces can count on still another fact —that there are, after all, such things as facts. The simple truth is that prejudice and discrimination grow out of men's primitive fear of the strange and the unknown. They are nourished on the tensions and uncertainties of modern civilization. They affect every home and institution, undermining respect for law and order, weakening our defenses, and corrupting the moral fiber of our nation. The moral and material costs of discrimination to our country are so enormous that they can only be approximated. The money damage alone has been estimated by a former cabinet official to be as high as thirty billion dollars a year.[1] A recent project at Columbia University reported that denial of equal educational opportunities deprived America each year of about 158,000 Negro high school graduates and 14,000 Negro college graduates. These are totally needless losses, and we cannot afford them.

There are approximately 18,000,000 Negroes in the United States, one-half of whom live in the South, and another third in five urban centers in the North. Statistics offer a dramatic picture of how meagerly they share in our expanding economy. In 1939, the median income for white workers was $1,112 a year; for nonwhite workers, it was $460. In 1955, white workers had a median income of $3,986, contrasted with $2,342 for nonwhite workers. These figures make plain that while the nonwhite population has shared in our general prosperity and reduced the difference between incomes, the Negro nevertheless continues to pay a severe price solely because of the color of his skin. Today, two out of every five Negro families earn less than $2,000 a year. Average Negro incomes are still only 52 per cent as large as white incomes.[2]

There is a final fact about the results of discrimination, the most important of all. The future of our nation—indeed, its very existence—may well depend upon whether nonwhites living in the underdeveloped countries choose Communism or freedom. The great contest revolves around the one billion two hundred million people—largely Negro and Oriental—who live in the Far East, the Middle East, and Africa. This global picture is crucially related to our domestic struggle over civil rights and the ending of discrimination. It is so importantly related because the nonwhites are watching closely to see whether we practice what we preach about equality and justice.

This truth was brought home to me forcibly on my trip around the world in 1956. In India, I talked with Prime Minister Jawaharlal Nehru, and he could not have been more emphatic in his point that our handling of the color question could be a serious handicap—or a great asset—to the United States among the people of Asia, the Middle East, and Africa. In Taipei, the Nationalist Chinese leader, Chiang Kai-shek, expressed the same opinion.

No American domestic situation gives the Soviet Union and the international Communist party more fuel for their propaganda machines than America's two faces on civil rights. In terms of world prestige, Little Rock cost us more in one day of violent prejudice than the launching of all the Russian space satellites. The Soviet press had a field day with statements like: "The United States monopolies train the murderers of tomorrow in such barbarous actions as the recent outbreaks of racism in the United States. Racial discrimination is an integral part of the United States policy, and the white people in the United States want to annihilate the Negroes." A Russian picture magazine could play up the Little Rock story, featuring one particularly ghastly four-color photograph, showing a group of white-hooded figures beating one Negro while another Negro hung naked from a tree. In the background a Klansman held aloft a large American flag.

Even more damaging to our prestige was the reaction of the press in the uncommitted areas of Asia, the Middle East, and Africa. Typically, the *Times of Indonesia* declared: "It is hard to realize that this is taking place in a country proclaiming its democratic liberties for all to hear." We simply cannot hope to win the nonwhite peoples of the world conclusively to our side if they doubt that we will consider them equals. They will continue to doubt just as long as we wave our Constitution at them with one hand, and with the other tolerate the denial to a substantial part of our citizens in a broad region of our own country of their rights under that Constitution.

The disastrous effects of American racism on American policy abroad, the price we pay for it at home, the naked injustice of barring 10 per cent of our population from full participation in the national life—all of these things are tragic facts, and the people of the United States are daily becoming more aware of them. In 1943, when Wendell Willkie proclaimed "one world" and warned against "our imperialisms at home," he was striking a note that was new and strange to many in the United States. Today, the thought is becoming commonplace, and the more commonplace it is, the more powerful a weapon is placed in the hands of the antidiscrimination forces. The growing knowledgeability and maturity of the American people are another strong indication that the onrushing decades will be an era of rapidly expanding rights and opportunities for those who have had to wait so very long.

As the United States hurries along the road toward genuine democracy, all kinds of efforts will help. The agitations of organizations will have their importance; so, too, will the labors of dedicated individuals and the studies of psychologists, sociologists, economists, and historians. But the prime need is law—more firm, carefully formulated legislation on the federal, state, and municipal levels directed toward making equal rights and equal opportunities ultimate realities. Law is the indispensable advance guard of social change. It gives well-intentioned men a standard to which they can repair. It nudges the indifferent and it tames the hostile.

In this connection, too little attention has been paid to the fact that the federal government now spends more than thirty billion dollars a year on contracts with private firms. This means that hundreds of thousands of jobs are placed where the government has the power—indeed, the responsibility—to see that they are filled without regard to religion or color, but the Congress has to help. In 1953, by Executive Order, President Eisenhower established the Federal Committee on Government Contracts, the main purpose of which is to combat discriminatory practices in industries fulfilling government contracts. The Committee has done some good work, but it is hampered by inadequate funds and staff and especially by the fact that it does not have the authority of an institution established by Congress. (Since 1953, it has investigated only 837 complaints, and settled to its satisfaction only 245.) [3]

In 1959, as part of his package civil rights proposals, President Eisenhower recommended the establishment of a statutory Federal Commission on Equal Opportunity Under Government Contracts. New York State pioneered in this field with the formation of the State Commission Against Discrimination. This agency's experience and its success—which are discussed in a later chapter—fully justify the President's recommendation. The Eisenhower proposal was lost in the Senate compromises, but its ultimate enactment is of prime importance. For the first time, it would set up an agency that could be sweepingly effective. Of equal significance, it would provide an unmistakable symbol—at home and abroad—that the United States not only seeks a national policy of nondiscrimination in employment but enforces it.

The disgraceful and dangerous housing situation urgently calls for legislative action at both the federal and state levels. An estimated 27,000,000 Americans are members of minority groups, and, of these, 60 per cent are believed to be living in substandard dwellings because of discrimination. The situation not only means grimy, unhealthy, crime-breeding living; it is preserving educational segregation in the North. The heavy concentration of racial groups in certain schools of New York City, for example, is dictated by segregated patterns of living.

Action is needed to bring, in all fifty states, the enactment of legislation already existing in five states, which forbids discrimination in any housing aided by federally guaranteed mortgages under the Federal Housing Administration (FHA) or the Veterans Administration (VA). The existing state laws authorize agencies or commissions to deal with discrimination on a basis of conciliation and mediation and, if these fail, by civil action in the courts. But a big share of the responsibility for driving Jim Crow out of the housing field must be assumed by the federal government—and it could do a great deal more than it is presently attempting. It should be fundamental federal policy for all agencies connected with housing to push vigorously for equal opportunity to a decent home. Every effort should be made—particularly every administrative effort—to bring about compliance by builders who seek the aid of FHA and VA mortgages. The Urban Renewal program shows that this can be done. Its administration has stated and largely enforced the following blunt instruction: "Such contracts or instruments for sale or lease of land shall contain, among other things, provisions that will . . . provide that there shall not be effected an execution by the purchaser or lessee or their successors in interest any agreement, lease or conveyance or other instrument whereby the project land is restricted upon the basis of race, creed or color in the sale, lease or occupancy thereof."

The Commission on Race and Housing, functioning under a grant from the private foundation The Fund for the Republic has urged that the president appoint a special committee to determine what specific further help the federal government can give. This is a sound recommendation. There is an analogy between such a body and the special committee which some years ago did so much to eliminate segregation in the armed forces. The new commission should not inquire into facts; that can be left to the Federal Commission on Civil Rights. Its responsibility should be to ferret out new, hardheaded ways that can be used to end racial discrimination in all federally aided housing.

We need Executive action, we need laws, federal and state, and we need, in the North as well as in the South, a touch of humility and more than a touch of self-criticism about what our own communities have done and not done. In the closing weeks of the 86th Congress, Senator Olin B. Johnston of South Carolina, an all-out opponent of civil rights and of school desegregation, had some tart words to speak about conditions outside the South. New York City, he charged, had "the worst racial unrest and the worst prejudice and the worst police problem of any city in the world." The Senator continued: "I only wish the racial relations in the city of New York were on the high plane and peaceful level that they are in the state of South Carolina and in other southern states which so often come under attack from the New York press and the other liberal newspapers of the North." [4] Southerners in last-ditch efforts to continue the caste system for the Negro cannot be prevented from making this kind of argument, however exaggerated it may be. What can be done is to make the argument more and more ineffective by making it more and more untrue.

Those of us who live in states like New York, where public sentiment and every responsible governmental agency are on record against any inequality of opportunity, have a special responsibility to practice, and practice in highly positive terms, what we preach. If southern segregationists are to be deprived of their most cherished distortion—that racial or religious discrimination which persists in the North gives a license for Jim Crowism in the South—then none among us can be a mere bystander in the fight.

It is a fight filled with its ups and downs, its nagging complexities, its shocking desertions, as I am only too well aware from my years in public office. It is also a fight peculiarly appropriate to the only nation in all of man's long history that ever dared mix so many different races, nationalities, and religions, and, having mixed them, dared to declare that the end product could be equal rights and equal opportunity for all. That Americans have the desire, the strength, and the faith to go on pushing toward this goal has been said many times, but it was once said in a way that carries its special force over all the intervening decades.

In 1880, United States Senator B. K. Bruce rose to support a pending bill. His remarks moved to the subject of the general meaning of the American experience, and he said: "As a people, our history is full of surmounted obstacles. We have been scaling difficult problems for more than a hundred years. We have been (and will continue to be) settling material, moral and great political questions that before our era had been unsolved. . . ."

B. K. Bruce was a Negro, born into human slavery, elected to the United States Senate from Mississippi amid all the anti-Negro bitterness and violence of Reconstruction days. His speech was in support of a bill protecting the civil rights and extending the opportunities of—the American Indian.

Chapter Two

Promise and Fulfillment

In our relatively brief history, America has meant many things to many men. To the rival kingdoms of seventeenth-century Europe, it was a place abounding in natural resources and the promise of opportunities for vast wealth; it was a continent worth fighting for. To the European, America was a harsh, primitive land, full of savages and unknown dangers, a place where a man would go only if he were desperately seeking to escape and find freedom for himself and his family. But most of the early settlers came here seeking a peaceful haven in the wilderness where a man could worship God in his own fashion without fear of persecution and death, and make his own way free of the considerations of birth and the social stratum to which he belonged. To the debtors, the ex-convicts, the indentured servants, the adventurers, the disillusioned and the dispossessed as well, America was a second chance at life, liberty, and the pursuit of happiness. What was the promise and what is its fulfillment?

Our villages, towns, and cities bear the names of men who came from all parts of the world and who founded them—this was the compact of the promise. One such town is Aaronsburg in Pennsylvania, founded by Aaron Levy, a Jewish settler of the Revolutionary period. He donated the land on which the Salem Evangelical Lutheran Church was built. When the 150th anniversary of the founding of this church was celebrated on October 23, 1949, Felix Frankfurter, associate justice of the United States Supreme Court, in a speech at the site, paid the following tribute to the colonists:

> The saga of our republic is the story of the most significant racial and religious admixture in history. The fifty-six signers of the Declaration of Independence were men of varying religious outlook and eighteen of them of non-English stock. It cannot be too often recalled that when the Continental Congress chose John Adams, Franklin and Jefferson as a committee to devise the national emblem, they recommended a seal containing the national emblems of England, Scotland, Ireland, France, Germany and Holland as representing "the countries from which these States have been peopled." [1]

Pulaski, the name of towns in New York, Indiana, Michigan, and several other states, memorializes the famous Polish nobleman and Revolutionary War hero, Count Casimir Pulaski. The Bronx in New York City derives its name from a Scandinavian who arrived with the early Dutch settlers. McLeod in Minnesota betrays its Scottish ancestry, and Bamberg in South Carolina bears the name of a German family. The list of examples fills a book.[2]

What made these Americans of the seventeenth and eighteenth centuries different from the religiously intolerant Europe from which they came? What was it that changed the souls of provincial Englishmen, stolid Dutchmen, isolationist Swedes, haughty Frenchmen, and other Europeans who helped to found and settle the colonies? These early settlers came here with all the prejudices of their native lands. It was the adequate living space for all, the contiguity to those who were "different," the social and political needs of a new society, and the patriotic leadership that changed these people.

Religion was the prime issue, and the touchstone of liberty was religious toleration, but the early colonists were not prepared to share with each other the liberty they sought for themselves, and the history of the colonies is studded with intolerance and even persecution in matters of religion. Almost without exception they hated and feared Catholics, and tried to bar them from their midst. Religious motives were reinforced by the fear of conquest and subsequent expulsion or subjection at the hands of the French Catholics, who held Canada to the north, or the Spanish Catholics, who held Florida to the south. Thus Catholics were believed dangerous not only on grounds of religious aggression but also as spies and agents for a political enemy. The colonists, therefore, imposed head taxes to discourage Catholic immigrants, persecuted priests, created constitutional barriers to citizenship, and set up disqualifications of every description. They left an evil tradition of bigotry which has bedeviled every succeeding generation of Americans.

Only in the early years in Maryland, which was founded by English Catholics, and in Rhode Island was there toleration for Catholics, though not for others. A law decreeing death for anyone who denied the divinity of Jesus was put on the Maryland statute books but never enforced. But the Papists, as they were called, were soon outnumbered in Maryland by the Puritans who settled there and ousted them from control. Under Puritan rule, tolerance in Maryland came to an end. In no colony at the time of the Revolution did Catholics have the right to vote or hold office.[3]

The colonists feared each other, too, and Protestants felt the lash of intolerance. Puritan Massachusetts tried to set up a Congregational church state and in order to keep out dissident voices hanged four Quakers in 1658, including a woman named Mary

Dyer.[4] Three hundred years later, in a unique demonstration of America's progress in eliminating religious intolerance, a Catholic, Mrs. Foster Furcolo, wife of the governor of Massachusetts, dedicated a statue honoring the martyred Quaker heroine.

The Puritans also drove out such nonconformist liberal voices as Anne Hutchinson and Roger Williams. A Baptist preacher, Williams founded Rhode Island as an idealistic oasis of religious liberty for all men. By the law of 1655 "all men of competante estates, and of civill conversation" were allowed to vote and hold office. But the letter of the law ran contrary to the spirit of the settlers in Rhode Island, and before long Catholics and Jews were disfranchised.

The Quakers were subject to discrimination in more than one colony because they refused to bear arms and because they insisted on their own form of worship. In the early days of New York as a royal colony, the governors tried to strengthen the Church of England, and therefore compelled Quakers, Presbyterians, Moravians, and other nonconformists to submit to their whims, or land in jail. The Quakers had their own colony in Pennsylvania, and William Penn, who founded the colony, was a leader in the fight for toleration, but Pennsylvania, like the other colonies, excluded Catholics, Jews, and atheists from voting and holding office.

The Puritans in turn found themselves unwelcome in several colonies. Anglican Virginia persecuted them. Johan Printz, the governor of Delaware, used every power he possessed to drive them out and keep his colony safe for the Swedish Lutheran church.

A short-lived Mennonite settlement near the Delaware River in 1662 tried to bar from its midst all Jews, Catholics, and "English stiff-necked Quakers, Puritans, fool-hardy believers in the Millenium, and obstinate modern pretenders to revelation." [5] Peter Stuyvesant, the Dutch governor of New Amsterdam, succinctly summed up the colonial dilemma in a letter of October 30, 1655, in which he said: "To give liberty to the Jews will be very detrimental there, because the Christians there will not be able at the same time to do business. Giving them liberty, we cannot refuse the Lutherans and Papists."

One of the brighter spots in the early colonial period was South Carolina, where the Huguenots, who had settled there from France in considerable numbers, fought and won religious freedom for themselves and all other groups except the Catholics. They held the balance in the struggle between members of the Church of England and dissenting Protestant groups over the right to vote, and as a result of this fight, in the Berkeley County election of November, 1701, aliens, indentured servants, and even free Negroes were allowed to vote. Two years later, in the election for the South Carolina Assembly, a contemporary account said: "Jews, Strangers, Sailors, Servants, Negroes, & almost every *French* Man in Craven & Berkly County came down to elect, & Votes were taken." [6] In later years, however, ownership of property and real estate were made qualifications for voting privileges.

Fortunately, the laws on the books of the colonies were far worse in their language than in their enforcement. It was as a matter of fact almost impossible to build a fence around a colony. If a man wanted to free himself from colonial restrictions and had the courage of his convictions, he had only to go out into the vast wilderness beyond the seacoast settlements and clear a home for himself out of the forest. This freedom served to restrain any dictatorial tendencies in colonial governments.

For, in so many other respects, America was a radically different world from Europe. Primitive conditions in the colonies weakened class distinctions and promoted a sense of equality.

There was constant danger from marauding Indians and from aggression by France from the north and Spain from the south. Therefore, the colonists were compelled to tolerate each other and to recognize that religious differences could be tolerated and were not a bar to collective political and social action. The growing intercolonial and overseas trade brought the colonies close together on political and economic issues.

Thus, in time, a kind of religious tolerance developed in all the colonies despite harsh laws and occasional reversion to earlier intolerant patterns. Restrictions upon voting and holding office based on religion gradually gathered dust on the statute books.

The Revolutionary War and the establishment of the United States brought civil and religious liberty to Catholics, but in many states there was no complete emancipation for Jews for many decades, although in most colonies Jews had enjoyed liberty of conscience. North Carolina was an exception, and Jews did not acquire the right to vote there until 1868. In Maryland, Christianity was a prerequisite to holding office until 1825, when Thomas Kennedy, an Irishman, won a determined fight to amend the law.[7] In Connecticut, the state-supported Congregational church was not disestablished until 1818, when members of other Christian congregations were exempted from paying taxes toward the support of that church. Jewish congregations, however, were not recognized for similar tax exemption until 1843. Jews and Catholics could not hold office in New Hampshire until 1876, and its constitution still does not recognize Jews as proper subjects for legal protection. The New Hampshire constitution to this day says only: "Every denomination of Christians . . . shall be equally under the protection of the law."[8] Many states also disqualify nonbelievers in any religion from holding office.

To the nineteenth-century European immigrant, America was

a land of opportunity and liberty, of expanding frontiers, of untapped wealth in the vast lands to the west and in the great cities that were developing along the eastern seaboard. The mass emigration of these "poor, homeless and oppressed" forms one of the epochal stories of all times. Those who came hoped to find a better future for themselves and for their children in the land of democracy and liberty. They were the humble people, the peasants and the laborers; and they built farms and great cities on the prairie. They swept out the dark corners of the eastern cities, established vital industries, developed our natural resources, and became captains of commerce. These millions of immigrants gave the final endorsement to the proposition that one judges a man not by his faith or the color of his skin but by what he says and does with his fellows.

The potato famine in Ireland, the Napoleonic Wars on the Continent, and the political upheavals in Germany had sent over a million immigrants from these countries to our shores before 1840. Other Europeans came in the same period—Jews, Lutherans, Scandinavians, Englishmen, Frenchmen, Italians, Russians, and Poles. Protestant America viewed with increasing dismay the problem of absorbing them along with the huge mass of Catholic immigrants from Ireland and Germany. The Germans and the Scandinavians settled far away on the new farm lands in the Midwest, but the Irish, packed into the slums of Boston, New York, and Philadelphia, alarmed the older Americans and revived suppressed fears of Catholic domination.[9]

The teachings of Thomas Jefferson, James Madison, and other American leaders had placed bigotry and prejudice beyond the pale of respectability, but the feeling against Catholics continued to grow. Before long it erupted in nineteenth-century America into a new kind of nativism which struck out at all the foreign born. American one-hundred-percenters blamed the Irish in the cities for all kinds of corruption and crime as well as for the slums they lived in and all the other evils attributed to newcomers, but which actually exist because these people are disoriented and poor—often exploited. Economic, cultural, and antiforeign feelings became compounded with religious prejudices which had never entirely died down, and served to stimulate majority-versus-minority thinking in the United States based on national origin as well as religion.

When depression made jobs scarce, the Irish laborers had to go on poor relief, and soon demagogic nativist organizations under high-sounding patriotic names began to spread vicious reports and rumors about them. The Irish were accused of taking jobs from native Americans and of lowering moral and cultural standards. Word passed around that the Irish had brought disease and poverty into the country, that they were clannish and could not become the right kind of Americans, and that they were disloyal because their first allegiance was to the Pope.

As economic pressures mounted, resentment grew and the mob became inflamed against the Irish. In Boston, clashes began to develop as early as 1829 and led to mob attacks on Irish homes, churches, and convents. Mobs rioted in Charleston, Massachusetts, and in 1830, for the first time in our history, Americans witnessed the ugly sight of an angry mob burning a religious edifice—the Ursuline Convent. Anti-Irish riots also broke out in New York; and in Philadelphia in 1844, churches were damaged, thirteen people were killed, and fifty were wounded in a mob fight against the Irish before order was restored. The self-appointed nativist guardians of Protestant America indulged in the most lurid stories of plots and corruption, spiced with a touch of sex and adultery, against the Catholics, and made the name of Rome a fighting word.[10]

This is an appalling chapter in American history, but a good one to remember as we assess the problems today of Puerto

Ricans in New York and Negroes in Chicago. It reached its climax in the decade before the Civil War with the formation of the Native American Party in 1845, and the United American, or Know-Nothing Party. The Know-Nothings assumed a pose of secrecy, hence the name. They spread many false stories about the Irish-Catholics, and as a result many men and women lost their jobs. The Know-Nothings made politics out of their prejudices, and were successful in electing a governor in Massachusetts. They reached their peak in the national campaign of 1856, when they put up Millard Fillmore for president, but he carried only one state, Maryland. The party rapidly disintegrated after this in the heat of the slavery controversy.

The strong public reaction to the Know-Nothings and to other nativist exhibitions of intolerance and prejudice is a testimonial to the American sense of democracy and justice. Indignation meetings were held in Boston after the burning of the Ursuline Convent, and throughout the country people denounced the violence that had taken place. In Philadelphia, funds were raised to repair the damaged Church of St. Augustine. The sale of pornographic, anti-Catholic literature was stopped, and its vendors arrested.

The strength of the American spirit of democracy is seen in the fact that half a century of anti-Catholic propaganda failed to produce much more than a few elected officials, a few speeches in Congress, and two state laws establishing literacy tests for voting. The Know-Nothings proved that prejudice makes bad politics; they failed completely in their efforts to write into American law any of their proposals for restrictions upon Catholics and the foreign born.

The nativist movement vanished in the crucible of the War between the States. A strong sense of dedication to individual dignity and civil rights and liberties swept the country; anti-

Catholic prejudice continued to plague the American political scene for many decades thereafter, but it never again became so blatant a factor in our political or social lives.

The prejudices stirred up by the nativist movement affected other groups besides the Catholics. The tensions aroused by the Civil War and the Reconstruction period provided fertile soil for demagogues, who exploited problems created by unrestricted immigration, low wages, and competition with Negroes for jobs and housing, and encouraged discrimination against newcomers. In New York, resentment against military conscription resulted in riots in which the mob took over the city from Union Square to Central Park. Its anger turned against Negroes, many of whom were beaten and some hanged from lamp posts. From July 13 to July 16, 1863, when an army of soldiers, police, and citizens restored order, about one thousand persons had been killed.

In the seventies and eighties, the Bavarians and Swabians packed into the lower East Side of New York, the Poles into Buffalo, Pittsburgh and Chicago, the Italians into Boston and Philadelphia, each for a time becoming targets of agitation, prejudice, and discrimination. In New Orleans, on March 14, 1891, a mob stormed the jail and lynched eleven Italian immigrants.

Demagogues found their easiest victims in the Chinese laborers who had been brought into the country in increasing numbers after 1849 as a source of cheap labor in the East as well as on the West Coast. The agitators were responsible for numerous acts of violence, and in 1871, a riot in San Francisco resulted in the killing of twenty-one Chinese. Reflecting this pressure, the California legislature passed several bills restricting the rights of labor and residence of the Chinese, but these were struck down by the federal courts as unconstitutional.

Eventually the pressure for limiting Chinese immigration

reached Washington, and Congress passed a bill restricting their immigration. It was vetoed in 1879 by President Rutherford B. Hayes because it exposed Americans living in China to retaliation. Subsequent negotiations with the Chinese government, however, led to an agreement which formed the basis of the Chinese Exclusion Act of 1882. It denied the entry of Chinese laborers for ten years, but allowed students, teachers, and merchants to enter. The ban was later made permanent.[11] During World War II, when China became our ally, the Exclusion Act was repealed and replaced by a quota of 105 annually on the immigration of those who had been born Chinese nationals.

Anti-Japanese feeling was also strong on the Pacific coast, and popular agitation was fed by excited warnings against the "yellow peril." Japan was a powerful, rising country, and when San Francisco in 1906 tried to segregate Japanese children in an "Oriental" school, Tokyo sent a vigorous protest to President Theodore Roosevelt. We had a treaty with Japan under which its citizens were guaranteed the rights of the most favored nation, and despite defiant voices in California, calmer counsels prevailed.[12]

Under the agreement reached in 1907, San Francisco admitted to its schools Japanese children under sixteen years of age, and Japan promised rigid enforcement of a law forbidding the emigration of laborers. These exclusion acts provided a precedent for subsequent measures restricting immigration, which led to the Immigration Act of 1924. This Act introduced a new pattern of discrimination into American democracy by establishing quotas based on national origin—country of birth.

As a result of Civil War tensions, discrimination against Jews, which had always persisted on a religious basis, now took on economic and social patterns. Several incidents during the war itself attracted nationwide attention. One issue arose in 1861 over the appointment of a Jewish chaplain to the armed forces.

Although there were many thousands of Jewish servicemen in the Union ranks, the application was denied on the grounds that the Act of Congress required chaplains to be "of a Christian denomination." Strong protests were registered from various parts of the country, but it took the personal intervention of President Abraham Lincoln himself to settle the problem amicably and satisfactorily. Subsequently, Lincoln appointed several rabbis as army chaplains.[13]

A much greater storm of controversy and protest was created when General Ulysses S. Grant issued General Orders, No. 11, expelling "the Jews as a class" within twenty-four hours from the Department of Tennessee under his command. Despite the war in 1862, considerable trade was being carried on legally in the sale of Confederate cotton, which the northern industries needed, for gold, which the South needed. Many soldiers as well as civilians were involved in this speculation, which the military leaders vigorously opposed. Grant had made several efforts to stop it, and his previously issued instructions indicate that he blamed Jewish traders exclusively.[14]

Grant never explained his General Orders, in spite of considerable pressure. It created extreme hardships and aroused a furor across the country because of its sweeping anti-Jewish prejudice. The General Orders were issued on December 17, 1862, and revoked on direct command from President Lincoln by General in Chief of the Army Henry W. Halleck on January 4, 1863.

The controversy was revived in the presidential campaign of 1868, and several Jewish supporters of General Grant defended him against the charge of prejudice. During his term in office, General Grant never showed any sign of prejudice, and appointed Jews to high as well as minor offices on their merits.

The fact that one of the leaders of the Confederacy was Judah P. Benjamin, himself Jewish, provided an easy way to defame all Jews in the South as well as in the North. He became the butt of many jokes, derogatory cartoons, and newspaper reports. Allegations that Jews controlled the money of the country by speculating in gold, and were seeking to control its economy, were made in some of the most respectable newspapers of the time. Jews were held to be responsible for every ill—for high prices, for shortages, for inflation, and for many of the problems of the country produced by the war. In the Union army and in the army of the Confederacy, Jewish officers suffered because of the fact that they were Jewish. The multiplicity of anti-Semitic incidents during the war, however, should not obscure the fact that Jews were only one of the many scapegoats who were blamed for wartime evils and hardships.[15]

There had been earlier anti-Semitic episodes involving men like Mordecai Manuel Noah and Commodore Uriah P. Levy, but the wartime anti-Semitism brought aroused awareness to American Jews for the first time that this evil could exist in the United States. It led to the establishment of the Board of American Israelites to help combat anti-Semitism. But, most important, it also led to the realization among some Jews that civil rights could not be denied to any one group, such as Negroes, without affecting the rights of all other groups.

Most intense interest was aroused in the summer of 1877 when Joseph Seligman, a prominent New York banker and a man who had rendered distinguished service in helping the North finance the Civil War, was refused accommodations for himself and his family at the Grand Union Hotel in Saratoga Springs, New York. Seligman's custom had been to spend his vacations at this hotel for many years prior to this incident. In 1877, however, the hotel had been sold to Judge Henry Hilton, a prominent New York political figure, and A. T. Stewart, a New York department store merchant and himself an Irish immigrant. Like Seligman, Stewart had come to the United

States penniless, and subsequently had risen to a position of wealth and prominence.

It was Judge Hilton, with Stewart's acquiescence, who actually issued the order denying Seligman accommodations at the hotel. Indignation over the occurrence was widespread, and many articles were written and sermons preached on this subject. The fact that a man of such national prominence as Joseph Seligman had been the victim of this kind of discrimination aroused the indignation of Oliver Wendell Holmes, Henry Ward Beecher, Mark Twain, and many others.[16]

The Seligman case had its counterpart in many other areas of America's social life, and exposed a pattern of discrimination against Jews which still persists in some quarters. It is interesting to note that the large immigration from the 1880's to 1910 was not responsible for the outbreak of anti-Semitism, although agitators exploited the alien customs and mannerisms of the immigrants. Most Americans looked upon the newcomers with sympathy, and sincerely tried to be helpful in making it possible for them to become settled and productive Americans. Here, too, is an object lesson in how to deal better with the immigration of Puerto Ricans and Negroes to the great cities of the North.

Anti-Semitism did not become a serious danger to American liberty until the second decade of the twentieth century. Three outstanding instances highlight its rise as a social evil. The first was the lynching of Leo Frank in August, 1913, by a Georgia mob. Frank was a graduate of Cornell University and part owner and manager of a pencil factory in Marietta, Georgia. He was accused of assaulting and killing a fourteen-year-old girl who worked in the factory, and his trial was made the subject of some of the most vicious anti-Semitic propaganda ever heard in America up to that time. The unfortunate man, beaten by other prisoners, was taken from the prison hospital by a mob and hanged. Frank's innocence was established by careful investigation, but in the heated period of his trial, the sensational charges and the violence of language—and action—shocked the world.[17]

The aftermath of the First World War likewise saw widespread incidence of anti-Semitism. The revival of the Ku Klux Klan with its anti-Catholic, anti-Jewish prejudices was responsible in part, but perhaps most damaging was the vicious anti-Semitic campaign waged by Henry Ford through his newspaper the *Dearborn Independent*. For over seven years, beginning in 1920, this paper carried on a relentless campaign against Jews, in which it publicized numerous slanders and scurrilities. Among them was the "Protocols of the Elders of Zion," a notorious forgery which British, Russian, and German anti-Semites had used extensively. Jews had to expose this fabricated document and formally deny its lies. Henry Ford, after being sued for libel, made a complete retraction and apologized for the false accusations made in his newspaper.[18] His sons, led by Edsel and Henry Ford II, have shown their outstanding patriotism and freedom from any vestige of prejudice in countless outstanding public services which have helped to bring about greater respect and justice for minorities in our country.

In the 1930's, under the impact of the rise of Hitlerism in Germany and the economic depression in the United States, anti-Semitism reached a frightening peak of virulence. Its manifestations touched every avenue of American activity and affected Jews in all walks of life. New barriers against Jews were raised in employment, housing, education, and social relations. A whole new breed of hatemongers was developed on the American scene who thrived on the spread of hate propaganda against Jews, then later against Catholics, Negroes, and other minority groups.

From 1933 onward, the word "Jew" appeared with increasing

frequency—in the American press, over the radio, and on the speaker's platform. German propaganda had succeeded in making the United States more "Jew-conscious" than it had ever been. The radio sermons and publications of Father Charles E. Coughlin in 1939 whipped up emotions to fever pitch. Anti-Semitic groups multiplied all over the country, and the demagogues had a field day. Anti-Semitism became a factor in the American political scene, and there were dramatic scenes of attack and denunciation on the floor of Congress.[19]

But Americans reacted strongly against this uncontrolled outburst of bigotry and prejudice. Responsible American leaders issued sharp warnings against the consequences of hatemongering, and the good sense of the American people quickly asserted itself. They realized that these evils were being spread deliberately by the Nazis and by their agents in this country as a means of dividing and weakening our country. This led to the rapid decline of the anti-Semitic groups and the recognition that the fight against religious and racial prejudice and discrimination affected not only specific minority groups but the whole national interest.

Neither anti-Semitism nor racial prejudice has ever been considered a respectable activity in the United States. It has always been something of which the people were ashamed and which was indulged in surreptitiously when it could not be suppressed entirely. Our country's political maturity and its rise to the leadership of the free world have intensified the fight against bigotry and the manifestations of discrimination wherever they may appear. In our history, we have tried in many ways to overcome this weakness in our democracy, and there may be no one formula which can cure it. But it is a fact that our country has fought and generally overcome much of the grave prejudice against Quakers, Catholics, Jews, and other religious nonconformists, against Irishmen, Poles, Chinese, Japanese, Greeks, Italians, Levantines, and others of different national origins. It is still fighting serious prejudice against Negroes and those of Puerto Rican and Mexican extraction. That fight will go on until all Americans enjoy equally the opportunities and responsibilities of our democracy without regard to race, creed, or national origin. This is the assurance of our freedom: that the denial of equality of opportunity will not be accepted as the norm in fact or in law.

Chapter Three

What the Law Says

From the earliest times, the American spirit in its devotion to the principles of democracy has never been comfortable with the concept of second-class citizenship. The American spirit has often been tempted to set one man above another because of his color, his creed, or his ancestry, but it has never succeeded in silencing its conscience. The noted sociologist Gunnar Myrdal described this conflict as the American dilemma:

> At bottom, our problem is the moral dilemma of the American —the conflict between his moral valuations on various levels of consciousness and generality. The "American Dilemma" . . . is the ever-raging conflict between . . . the valuations . . . which we shall call the "American Creed" . . . of high national and Christian precepts, and, on the other hand, the valuations . . . where personal and local interests; economic, social, and sexual jealousies; considerations of community prestige and conformity; group prejudices against particular persons or types of people; and all sorts of miscellaneous wants, impulses, and habits dominate his outlook.[1]

The struggle against slavery and prejudice began in the earliest colonial decades; it was a national consequence of the American spirit. The struggle has continued without pause throughout our history, but progress has been sporadic rather than steady. Human liberty has been achieved in sorties impelled by historical events—and often after long periods of retreat—rather than as the result of successive victories or brilliant leadership.

But it is significant that the greatest progress has been made when the law has given the opportunity to, and support for, the efforts of education and conciliation. Respect for law as the expression of the conscience of the community has been a dominant factor in American life. As the final arbiter in our living together, it is the essential frame of reference for other efforts to establish the principle that the civil status of each individual should be equal to that of every other.

The American conscience was manifest in the prohibition against slavery proclaimed by the trustees of the colony of Georgia.[2] Though only briefly enforced, it was the forerunner of a series of laws in other colonies which successfully attempted to limit and restrict the slave trade. George Washington and Thomas Jefferson were leaders in the fight which led to the end of the slave trade in the states long before Congress made it illegal in 1808. Slavery itself was outlawed in all the northern states, except Delaware, as well as in the Northwest lands north of the Ohio decades before the Emancipation Proclamation.[3]

The conscience of the nation was aroused to its highest pitch in the Reconstruction period after the War between the States, when Congress sought by law to extend to the Negro all the rights enjoyed by white citizens of the United States. The obstacles that confronted the Congress were many, but its leaders were determined men, and they began by amending the Constitution. Now, the Constitution of 1787 contemplated a system of dual sovereignties, each of which was to be free from undue restraint by the other. No power was delegated to the federal government to protect the rights of its citizens to equal treatment under state laws not dealing with matters then entrusted by the Constitution to the central government. The states alone had authority over the personal status of their citizens. The Bill of Rights was interpreted at an early date to apply exclusively to the federal government and not to the states.[4] There was, therefore, no constitutional basis for Congress or the Supreme Court to attempt to bring about equal opportunity for all citizens in education, voting, housing, jobs, places of public use, or before the law.

That basis was provided by the amendments to the Constitution enacted during the Reconstruction period and by the civil rights laws adopted to aid in their enforcement. The Thirteenth Amendment declares that "neither slavery nor involuntary servitude, except as a punishment for crime whereof the party shall have been duly convicted, shall exist within the United States. . . ." Approved by Congress in February, 1865, and formally adopted at the end of the year, it was one of Lincoln's last political victories.

The Fourteenth Amendment provides that "no state shall make or enforce any law which shall abridge the privileges or immunities of citizens of the United States; nor shall any state deprive any person of life, liberty, or property, without due process of law; nor deny to any person within its jurisdiction the equal protection of the laws." And the Fifteenth Amendment states that "the right of citizens of the United States to vote shall not be denied or abridged by the United States or by any state on account of race, color, or previous condition of servitude." Both were adopted in a period of great political turmoil and bitterness highlighted by the impeachment and trial of President Andrew Johnson.

Almost simultaneous with the passage of these constitutional amendments, overwhelmingly Republican Congresses—the Senate in 1866 was Republican by 42 to 11; the House by 143 to 49—under the leadership of men devoted to the cause of equal rights for all Americans—men like Thaddeus Stevens, leader of the House of Representatives, and Charles Sumner, senator from Massachusetts—enacted a series of statutes constituting a comprehensive program for the protection of civil rights. The first of the statutes was passed in 1866 after the Senate Republicans united to override President Johnson's veto. It was entitled "An Act to protect all Persons in the United States in their Civil Rights and furnish the Means of their Vindication." [5] Known as the Civil Rights, or Enforcement Act, it was designed to outlaw the Black Codes which the southern states had enacted to restrict the occupation and movement of Negroes. This Act, still in full force and effect, placed all citizens on an equal basis, giving each the same right "as is enjoyed by white citizens . . . to inherit, purchase, lease, sell, hold, and convey real and personal property." Violations of the Act were punishable by imprisonment for one year, or a fine of $1,000, or both.

Two other statutes were of a limited nature, and were intended to help enforce the Thirteenth Amendment. They were the Slave Kidnapping Act, "An Act to prevent and punish Kidnapping"; [6] and the Peonage Abolition Act, "An Act to abolish and forever prohibit the System of Peonage in the Territory of New Mexico and other parts of the United States." [7] The first made it a crime to kidnap with the intent to enslave; and the second defined "involuntary servitude" and provided penalties for violations of the Thirteenth Amendment.

Acrimonious debate and strong southern opposition preceded passage of the Act of May 31, 1870—"An Act to enforce the Right of Citizens of the United States to vote in the several States of this Union, and for other Purposes." This statute and the Act of February 28, 1871, which supplemented it, were passed to protect the Negroes' right to vote by providing federal supervision of elections.[8] Conspiracy to interfere with the rights and privileges guaranteed by the United States Constitution was punishable by imprisonment up to ten years, or a fine of $5,000, or both.

During the elections of 1870, activity by the Ku Klux Klan increased, to great public indignation. To curb their outrages, Congress in 1871 passed the Ku Klux Klan Act.[9] It allowed the president to suspend the writ of habeas corpus, increased the power of the federal courts, and prohibited actions under cover of law which deprived persons of their constitutional rights.[10] Interference was punishable by imprisonment up to six years at hard labor. It led to the dissolution of the Klan, but in the South other means of intimidating Negroes and depriving them of the franchise arose to take its place.

The final piece of civil rights legislation went less far than Senator Sumner would have wished; he died a year before its adoption. The "Act to protect all citizens in their civil and legal rights," the Civil Rights Act of 1875, which may be regarded as a tribute to his devotion to the cause, secured for Negroes the right to equal accommodations in hotels, public transportation such as railroads and trolleys, theaters, other places of amusement, and public facilities.[11] Congress refused to include schools, churches, and cemeteries. Denial of those accommodations referred to in the Act by private persons was punishable as a misdemeanor, and injured persons were given the right to sue for damages.

Thousands of criminal proceedings, primarily in the South, were brought under these various statutes. Between 1871 and 1876 more than 3,500 cases were brought before federal courts in the South, and convictions were obtained in about 20 per cent of the cases. Popular sentiment at this time, in the North at least, was strongly in favor of strict enforcement of Negro rights.

But enforcement of these statutes was considerably qualified or canceled out entirely by several decisions of the Supreme

Court. In 1883, in the civil rights cases, the Court declared that the Fourteenth Amendment prohibited only "State action of a particular character. . . . Individual invasion of individual rights is not the subject matter of the amendment." [12] The Court therefore concluded that "no legislation of the United States . . . can be called into activity . . . until some State law has been passed, or some State action through its officers or agents has been taken, adverse to the rights of citizens, sought to be protected by the Fourteenth Amendment. . . ." [13] The Court also struck down most of the Civil Rights Act of 1875, holding that the provisions under which hotel and theater owners in New York and San Francisco had been indicted for refusing to accommodate Negroes were unconstitutional. The change between this view and decisions of the Supreme Court since World War II is very marked.

Several cases brought by Negroes gave the Court this opportunity to rule that state action, not individual action, against the rights of a citizen had been specified in the Fourteenth Amendment, and that no state action was alleged in the cases brought before the Court. The Court ruled further that the statute of 1875 could likewise be concerned only with state action because Congress had no authority over the rights of private persons in hotels and theaters. Any related clauses in the Civil Rights Act were therefore void. The Court did indicate in its decision, however, that in interstate travel and in the District of Columbia, Congress had the authority to regulate the accommodations of Negroes. The Court upheld the provision in the 1875 statute guaranteeing to Negroes the right to serve on juries, the only section which survived this decision.

Associate Justice John M. Harlan, a Kentuckian, argued in dissent that the law was constitutional. He reasoned that "railroad corporations, keepers of inns, and managers of places of public amusement are agents or instrumentalities of the State because they are charged with duties to the public, and are amenable, in respect of their duties and functions, to governmental regulation." [14]

Following this line of logic, the Court held in *United States v. Cruikshank* that Congress lacked the power to punish private individuals for conspiring to hinder Negroes in the exercise of their constitutional rights.[15] But in *Ex parte Virginia,* the Court upheld the indictment of a Virginia judge charged with excluding Negroes from state juries.[16] It declared that such actions by a judicial officer of a state constituted state action prohibited under the Fourteenth Amendment. And in *Ex parte Yarbrough,* the Court sustained the conviction, under the civil rights acts, of private individuals who had attacked a Negro for voting in a congressional election.[17] Federal authority to legislate in this area was found in the federal power to control federal elections.[18]

In the years after Reconstruction, congressional and popular enthusiasm for the protection of the rights of Negroes waned considerably. In 1877, an attempt by the Democratic Congress to repeal many of the civil rights acts would have succeeded but for the veto of President Rutherford B. Hayes. In 1894, however, during the second Cleveland Administration, Congress was successful in its efforts to eliminate federal supervision of the rights of Negroes; [19] most of the provisions dealing with protection of the right to vote were repealed.[20] Several other provisions were eliminated in the Criminal Code of 1909, at a time when civil liberties did not appear to be the concern of a majority of Americans.[21]

The two major pieces of criminal legislation in the civil rights area that remained in effect at the time when the Civil Rights Act of 1959 was being debated and which could be enforced were Sections 51 and 52 of the United States Code.[22] The first, a conspiracy statute, may be used to prosecute private persons as well as public servants. It declares:

> If two or more persons conspire to injure, oppress, threaten, or intimidate any citizen in the free exercise or enjoyment of any right or privilege secured to him by the Constitution or laws of the United States, or because of his having so exercised the same; or
>
> If two or more persons go in disguise on the highway, or on the premises of another, with intent to prevent or hinder his free exercise or enjoyment of any right or privilege so secured—
>
> They shall be fined not more than $5,000 or imprisoned not more than ten years, or both.[23]

Section 52 is limited to interference by public officers. It is not a conspiracy statute, carries much lighter penalties than Section 51, and may be used to prosecute one person.

> Whoever, under cover of any law, statute, ordinance, regulation, or custom, willfully subjects any inhabitant of any State . . . to the deprivation of any rights, privileges, or immunities secured or protected by the Constitution or laws of the United States, or to different punishments, pains, or penalties, on account of such inhabitant being an alien, or by reason of his color, or race, than are prescribed for the punishment of citizens, shall be fined not more than $1,000 or imprisoned not more than one year, or both.[24]

The Supreme Court decisions on the civil rights program and the changing temper of the public as reflected in Congress influenced the Department of Justice to drop any real attempt to enforce the civil rights acts after the Reconstruction period. Prosecutions were rare.

Not until 1939, when Attorney General Frank Murphy, later Supreme Court justice, without the benefit of any new legislation created a Civil Rights Section (originally called the Civil Liberties Unit) in the Criminal Division of the Department of Justice, was there any determined effort by the federal government to protect the civil liberties of its citizens. Despite limited personnel and resources (in 1954 it had only eight lawyers and five stenographers), the Section brought many cases in pursuance of its objective to prosecute violations of what was left of the civil rights acts. The success of this effort was limited to a great extent by the reluctance of southern juries to convict those accused of civil rights violations. Indeed, this reluctance to convict was eventually the basis for the historic legislation of 1957.

An effort to apply the remaining civil rights laws to stop lynchings was brought before the Supreme Court by the Civil Rights Section in 1945 in the case of *Screws* v. *United States.*[25] A Georgia sheriff named Screws and two of his associates had arrested a Negro on a petty larceny charge and had beaten him to death. The men were tried and convicted in federal court of having deprived the unfortunate Negro of his rights under the Fourteenth Amendment to be tried by due process of law. Their conviction was set aside by the Supreme Court on the ground that the trial judge had not instructed the jury properly. In the Court's judgment no willful action had been shown by the convicted men to deprive their victim of a federal right, and therefore they could not be prosecuted under Section 52. Subsequently, the defendants were acquitted at their second trial.

The Court did, however, uphold several other cases brought under the same laws in which willful intent to deprive a prisoner of his constitutional rights was clear. Typical of the kind of case brought by the Department of Justice and upheld by the Court in 1951 was *Williams* v. *United States,* in which a policeman had been convicted of beating several men until they confessed guilt to the crime of larceny.[26]

The first major piece of civil rights legislation in more than eighty years was passed by Congress in 1957 after weeks of obstruction, filibuster, and bitter debate.[27] The House vote was 286 to 126; the Senate, 72 to 18. The major emphasis in the Civil Rights Act of 1957 was on securing the right to vote, and toward this end it provided for the establishment of a six-man Federal Commission on Civil Rights, with a term of two years and the power to hold hearings and subpoena witnesses and documents. The Federal Commission is charged with the duty to "investigate allegations . . . that certain citizens . . . are being deprived of their right to vote and have that vote counted by reason of their color, race, religion, or national origin"; to "study and collect information concerning legal developments constituting a denial of equal protection of the laws under the Constitution"; and to "appraise the laws and policies of the Federal Government with respect to equal protection of the laws under the Constitution." [28] It was required to report its findings and recommendations to Congress at the end of two years.

Section 131 (c) of the Act prohibits any person from intimidating another "for the purpose of interfering with the rights of such other person to vote or to vote as he may choose, or of causing such other person to vote for, or not to vote for, any candidate for [any federal elective office] . . . at any general, special, or primary election. . . ." [29] The Section gives the attorney general the power to seek injunctions against violations of this provision and also one of the provisions of the old civil rights acts, amended to read as follows:

All citizens of the United States who are otherwise qualified by law to vote at any election by the people in any State . . . shall be entitled and allowed to vote at all such elections, without distinction of race, color, or previous condition of servitude. . . .[30]

In a move interpreted as a concession to southern sensibilities, Congress included in this Act a provision that repealed a Reconstruction statute of 1866 giving the president power to use troops to enforce civil rights legislation. This is not to be confused with the president's authority to send in troops where needed to enforce the lawfully issued order of a federal court—which was the 1957 situation in Little Rock.

As implementation of the Civil Rights Act of 1957, the Department of Justice organized a Civil Rights Division to replace its Civil Rights Section. The Division is a much larger unit in personnel and resources, and is in a stronger position administratively to enforce federal civil rights statutes. In addition, it conducts research in civil rights matters and makes recommendations to the attorney general regarding proposed policies and legislation.

On September 4, 1958, the first suit under Section 131 (c) of the new 1957 Civil Rights Law was brought in a federal district court by the Civil Rights Division against the election registrars of Terrell County, Georgia, to halt the alleged deprivation of voting rights of Negroes. The Department of Justice sought an injunction against the county registrars for refusing to register qualified voters. The district court, however, held that Section 131 (c) was unconstitutional because it "creates a remedy against purely private, as distinguished from state, deprivation of voting rights on account of color." [31] It ruled further that the fact that the case at hand was against state officials did not derogate from its conclusion that the provision was unconstitutional on its face. The significance of this decision is obvious; it would have severely limited the applicability of the new 1957 law to actions by state officials acting allegedly under their official authority. The Department of Justice appealed it to the Supreme Court, and on February 29, 1960, the Supreme Court reversed the lower court's decision, thus upholding the right of the attorney general to bring suit.

In another suit brought by the Department of Justice under Section 131 (c), the Court of Appeals for the Fifth Circuit construed the statute as inapplicable to a proceeding against the State of Alabama and the resigned members of the Board of Registrars of Macon County, Alabama.[32] On May 16, 1960, the Supreme Court sent back the case for new trial in view of the provisions of the Civil Rights Act of 1960, specifically permitting proceedings against a state.

During the Reconstruction period, Negroes exercised the franchise in great numbers. As long as Union soldiers policed the polls, they could vote. But in 1877, federal troops were withdrawn, and within a short time the southern Negro was widely disfranchised mostly by intimidation and force. In Mississippi, for example, bands of armed men openly threatened to kill any Negro who tried to vote in the elections of 1874, with the result that Democrats carried the legislature by a large majority. Other states promptly copied the "Mississippi Plan," as this form of intimidation came to be known. Few Negroes dared to disregard this "advice."

Between 1890 and 1910, the southern states sought to provide a legal basis for keeping the Negro away from the ballot box. They tried to do this by setting up literacy tests; character, residence, and property qualifications; the "grandfather" clause, making eligibility for voting a hereditary right; the poll tax, which still survives in the states of the "white" primary—Alabama, Arkansas, Mississippi, Texas, and Virginia—and other apparently legal devices. The "grandfather" clause was eliminated by the Supreme Court, but the "white" primary remained. The Democratic primary is the only decisive election in many southern states; by restricting participation in this primary to white citizens only, Negroes were in effect excluded from the election itself. But a series of Supreme Court decisions beginning in 1944 ruled the "white" primary illegal, and despite southern efforts to amend their primary laws, it is today on the way out as a means of depriving the Negro of a voice at the polls.[33]

Another significant Supreme Court opinion affecting civil rights was delivered in 1948 in the case of *Shelley* v. *Kraemer*.[34] The Court held that state courts could not enforce a racially restrictive covenant against a Negro purchaser of land. Until the enactment of local laws against discrimination in housing, this decision provided the only restraint upon such practices.

But, by all odds, the most significant landmark set by the Supreme Court may well be the unanimous 1954 decision in the case of *Brown* v. *Board of Education of Topeka,* holding that segregation in public education violated the equal protection clause of the Fourteenth Amendment.[35] By this interpretation, the Court overruled the "separate but equal" formula expressed in the 1896 decision of *Plessy* v. *Ferguson,* which had declared constitutional a Louisiana statute requiring separate facilities for whites and Negroes in railroad cars, and by analogy, in schools and other public facilities.[36]

The Supreme Court decision in *Cooper* v. *Aaron,* in which it refused to postpone public school integration, was the most recent outgrowth of the Faubus-Little Rock affair at the time this was written.[37] The Court emphasized its rejection of the "claim by the Governor and Legislature of [Arkansas] . . . that there is no duty on state officials to obey Federal court orders resting on . . . the [Supreme] Court's considered interpretation of the United States Constitution." [38]

The doctrine that separate educational facilities are inherently unequal has been extended by the federal courts to strike down discriminatory state action in other areas. It has been held that public facilities such as parks,[39] swimming pools,[40] and golf courses may not be segregated.[41] Injunctions have also been issued against the enforcement of state statutes requiring segregation in intrastate transportation.[42] Indeed, the most striking advances in the fight against discrimination within the last decade have been made by the decisions of the Supreme Court.

Historically, the courts have had the most to do with determining the status of the individual, and it was logical that the judiciary branch should play the greatest role in ending much discrimination. The timing of this line of decisions is most important. These decisions occurred when ferment in the world's social order was as revolutionary as at any period in history, and far more widespread. Everywhere in the free world in the last five years men and women have been seeking individual dignity, the right of self-determination, and the opportunity for greater development. This ferment far more than the Warren Court—the coming of Chief Justice Earl Warren to the Supreme Court bench in 1953—has been the cause of the decisions against discrimination.

The logical corollary is that law can play and will continue to play a vital role in bringing true equality of opportunity for all Americans. At the same time, public education and the processes of mediation, conciliation, and technical assistance must accompany legal action and legislation, lest there be a repetition of the unhappy experience of the post-Reconstruction period when public feeling did a turnabout. Civic groups must continue the work of education through newspapers, pamphlets, broadcast discussions, and other media of community inter-communication, which in turn can lead to the removal of local discriminatory practices. The sanction of the law can provide the atmosphere necessary to make acceptable changes previously regarded as controversial. Law is vital to back up the forces of moderation and to control the "recalcitrant 10 per cent" who exist in any community.

Gordon W. Allport, in his study on *The Nature of Prejudice,* reaches this conclusion on the place of law in the fight against discrimination:

Law is intended only to control the outward expression of intolerance. But outward action, psychology knows, has an eventual effect upon inner habits of thought and feeling. And for this reason we list legislative action as one of the major methods of reducing, not only public discrimination, but private prejudice as well.[43]

Chapter Four

The Challenge and the Rule of Law

The late Benjamin N. Cardozo, associate justice of the United States Supreme Court, and one of our greatest jurists, observed, in a discussion of the judicial process, how strongly a judge was influenced by the prevailing mores of his time, but went on to say:

> This does not mean . . . that a judge is powerless to raise the level of existing conduct. In one field or another of activity, practices in opposition to the sentiments and standards of the age may grow up and threaten to intrench themselves if not dislodged. Despite their temporary hold, they do not stand comparison with accepted norms of morals. Indolence or passivity has tolerated what the considerate judgment of the community condemns. In such cases, one of the highest functions of the judge is to establish the true relation between conduct and profession.

When the Supreme Court in 1954 ruled that racially segregated public schools violated the Fourteenth Amendment, it performed this "highest function" as dramatically and courageously as any judicial body in history. It fulfilled a promise first made 180 years earlier in the Constitution and Declaration of Independence. And, in doing so, it affirmed the truth that law

52

must be faithful to our highest ideals, not merely a reflection of our practices.

In affirming the rights of all citizens to participate as equals in the benefits of a free nation, the Court in effect issued a challenge to southern officials to exercise wise leadership in bringing about the transition, to the people of the South to change patterns of behavior many knew to be wrong, to Congress and the Executive to fulfill the roles entrusted to them by the Constitution, and to federal judges to carry out the Court's mandate with firmness and wisdom. Implicit also in the Court's decision was a challenge to the North to re-examine attitudes and practices which, while perhaps not overtly unconstitutional, nevertheless sometimes led to the same result as state-enforced segregation.

School integration in the South has been very slow, even six years after the Supreme Court's decision. Out of 2,970,000 Negro pupils in 2,896 school districts, only around 407,000 have a chance to go to an integrated school whether they do actually attend or not. But in the great majority of these instances, the transition has been peaceful and has carried the promise of better understanding. This progress refutes the arguments of those who professed little faith in the rule of law, who said that a decision of nine men was powerless to change the customs of an age.

As the pattern of southern resistance to the Supreme Court's school segregation decision became clear, public attention focused increasingly on the legislative and executive branches of government. The president is charged by the Constitution with the duty to protect and defend the Constitution and to "take care that the laws be faithfully executed." The way in which Congress and the Executive carry out their respective responsibilities inevitably exerts a great influence upon the problem of discrimination.

The policy of the Administration has been formulated in a variety of ways and on many levels. It is reflected in the moral pronouncements and leadership provided by the president and his cabinet, in the enforcement of existing laws protecting civil rights by the attorney general, in the investigation into violations of civil rights conducted by the Department of Justice and the Federal Commission on Civil Rights, and in Administration recommendations to Congress for the enactment of new laws. Repeatedly over the years, President Eisenhower has voiced his abhorrence of prejudice and denounced it as immoral, in particular that prejudice which results in denial of the franchise and of equal job opportunity; but lasting progress, he has stressed, must come through education, which brings changes in the hearts and minds of men.

The Administration's civil rights legislative programs, while not going as far as they should to protect these rights, were much stronger than those of the opposition's congressional leadership, and gave recognition and some implementation to the Supreme Court's decision against public school segregation. While the President has spoken softly he has also on occasion carried a big stick. When Governor Orval Faubus of Arkansas called out the National Guard in 1957 in an effort to prevent the enforcement of a federal court order and the entry of nine Negro children into an all-white high school in Little Rock, the President took direct action. Invoking well-established authority, he ordered federalization of the National Guard and authorized the use of United States armed forces to halt the "willful obstruction of justice." Order was restored, the inviolability of federal court decrees preserved, and the nine children were returned to school. The President's unhesitating use of federal authority in Arkansas settled a basic and historic question. Resort to anarchy or the use of force to defy the federal courts would not be tolerated. Southern officials might continue to attempt to nullify the Supreme Court's decision against public school segregation, but it was extremely unlikely that the events of Little Rock would be repeated.

Many looked to the Civil Rights Commission, created by the Civil Rights Act of 1957, as a new source of federal authority. The Commission ran into trouble right at the outset, and its accomplishments as a result were limited. But in fact-finding and recommendations it gave marked promise of considerable achievement. Although three of its six members were southerners, the confirmation of nominations was delayed for months by the Senate Judiciary Committee under the chairmanship of Senator James O. Eastland of Mississippi. Once this hurdle was overcome, the Commission faced the time-consuming task of finding a staff and programing action. More time was lost when its investigations ran head-on into tactics of defiance and evasion by southern officials. Finally it had to limit its inquiry primarily to denials of the right to vote, and to segregation in education and housing.

In spite of these obstructions, the Commission made a definite contribution to the battle for civil rights. In hearings held in Montgomery, Alabama, in December, 1958, the Commission brought to the attention of the country the shameful denial of the voting franchise to Negroes in many parts of the South. Teachers with doctorates, and other professional men who were Negroes had been refused the right to register and vote because registrars (among whom some lacked grade school educations) said they could not pass literacy tests. Other Negro citizens never were given a chance to register. The hearings jarred public complacency and gave southern Negroes a needed indication that the federal government was concerned about their plight. I regard the Commission's 668-page report and its recommendations—discussed in a later chapter—as one of the most significant and progressive documents in the entire civil rights field since the days of Reconstruction.

Other administration agencies and officials have played a role in its antidiscrimination policies. When the governors of Arkansas and Virginia closed their public schools in 1958 to avoid compliance with federal court orders for desegregation, Secretary of Health, Education and Welfare Arthur S. Flemming forcefully pointed out the magnitude of the injustice done to the primary victims of this action, the children. On other occasions, James Mitchell, the secretary of labor, has consistently urged upon labor and management groups the importance of affording equal job opportunity. But the focal point of government action against segregation and discrimination is in the office of the attorney general and the Department of Justice.

Since 1954, the attorney general, first Herbert Brownell and then William Rogers, has used the prestige of his office to seek support from the organized bar and the public for the Supreme Court's desegregation decisions. The Department of Justice has intervened as a friend of the court in a number of school segregation cases brought by private parties, acting either at the request of the court or on its own initiative. When a federal judge in Little Rock suspended the operation of a public school desegregation plan for two years because of mob action, the solicitor general intervened on appeal before the Supreme Court to make a moving and successful plea against allowing the rule of law to be subverted by bowing to violence.

The primary task of the Department of Justice is the enforcement of federal statutes protecting the equal rights of citizens. Where state officials act to deprive persons of rights secured by the Constitution, where private individuals conspire to deny certain constitutional rights, where private individuals cross state lines in the course of committing certain acts of violence, the Department is authorized to bring criminal proceedings. But the law is inadequate, and enforcement of criminal statutes where needed the most is made very difficult by regional considerations. The law does not give a solid enough basis for effective community action.

In recent years, acts of violence have been increasing in the South, especially against Negro citizens seeking to assert newly won rights. A survey published jointly by the Southern Regional Council, the American Friends Service Committee, and the National Council of the Churches of Christ in the U.S.A., entitled *Intimidation, Reprisal and Violence in the South's Racial Crisis,* disclosed 530 such instances from 1955 to 1959. The Department has freely used the facilities of the Federal Bureau of Investigation where federal crimes have been suspected, but actual prosecutions have been almost nonexistent.

The reasons for this are devious. Restrictive court interpretations of the permissible scope of federal jurisdiction have saddled the government with an especially heavy burden of proof to sustain in civil rights cases. Police brutality, for example, is punishable as a federal crime only where an intent can be shown to deprive the victim of a constitutional right. Private citizens may be convicted only if there is proof that they were involved in a conspiracy aimed at interfering with a federal right.

But even where ample evidence of a violation of federal law has been obtained, the Department has hesitated to prosecute. This is traceable to the historic reluctance of southern white juries to convict white men and women for crimes committed against Negroes. In most southern communities, only registered voters may serve on local juries. Disfranchisement therefore carries with it disqualification for jury service.

In any case, the appearance of Negroes on jury panels is still a rarity in the South. The conviction of four white youths in June, 1959, by an all-white jury in Florida for the rape of a

Negro coed was sufficiently unusual to warrant nationwide newspaper coverage. Whether this and similar contemporaneous occurrences indicate that this particular manifestation of prejudice is on the wane remains to be seen. The difficulty is that one juror in twelve is often sufficient to force a dismissal when a jury cannot agree.

Critics say that the Department has shown too great a concern for its won and lost record. In answer, the Department suggests that respect for law is not promoted by prosecutions which continually result in acquittals. Others continue to wonder whether federal law which is rarely invoked in prosecutions can serve as a deterrent.

Since 1957, the Civil Rights Division of the Department of Justice has been authorized to bring equity suits for preventive relief in the federal courts in cases involving discriminatory denials of the right to vote. Equity proceedings do not involve jury trials; though the Department has been seemingly slow to make use of its new authority, it has reasons, too. Here again, there was a long delay by the Senate in confirming S. Wilson White as deputy attorney general to head the Division, which is now headed by Harold Tyler of New York.

Finally, it is the duty of the attorney general and his department to prepare recommendations for legislation for the president to transmit to Congress. In 1959, the Administration placed a seven-point program for civil rights before the Congress.

Of the three co-ordinate branches of the federal government, Congress, until 1957, was the least likely forum for action to enforce civil rights. From 1875 until Congress acted in 1957, no civil rights legislation had ever passed both Houses. Similar bills had been passed by the House nine times since 1953, but before 1957 not one had been permitted to come to a vote in the Senate. In the Congress it has been the Senate, with its rules of debate permitting filibuster, which traditionally has been the chief stumbling block. The Constitution requires that the states be represented equally in the Senate, irrespective of population, and therefore the South is significantly present in the Senate, with 22 senators out of 100. Also most of the important business of the Senate prior to voting is transacted by committees, and committee assignments generally, and chairmanships strictly, are awarded on the basis of seniority. In the absence of a two-party system in much of the South, southern senators tend to keep their seats for longer, to accumulate seniority, and therefore to hold many pivotal committee chairmanships.

The rules of the Senate traditionally have permitted nearly unlimited debate. A small but determined minority has been able often to frustrate the majority by the expedient of talking, or threatening to talk, a bill to death. During this century the filibuster has been employed by various groups with differing degrees of effectiveness, but in the hands of a small group of southern senators the filibuster and even the threat has been used adroitly and has proved notably successful in blocking civil rights legislation.

Up to 1957, not a single civil rights measure in the Senate had survived. Even in 1957, Senator Strom Thurmond carried on a filibuster for a record twenty-four hours and eighteen minutes in an effort to prevent a vote. But the group of southern senators had apparently already decided that the filibuster should not be employed, as the terms of the bill then before the Senate were not so obnoxious to them as to warrant its use. Nineteen fifty-seven marked a new turn in the use of the filibuster by the southern senators; the result is not yet fully discernible. It represented a decision to tolerate some civil rights legislation rather than to risk making the filibuster so unpopular as to eliminate it entirely as a weapon.

In 1917, after a "little group of willful men" had filibustered

President Wilson's proposal for arming United States merchant ships prior to our entry into World War I, the Senate passed a rule enabling it to invoke cloture—that is, to limit and end debate—by a vote of two-thirds of the senators present and voting. This rule stood until 1949 when cloture was made more difficult by increasing the number necessary to limit debate to two-thirds of the entire membership of the Senate.

Neither rule proved effective, and attempts to change it in 1953 and 1957 were unsuccessful. In January, 1959, a bipartisan group led by Senators Paul Douglas, Clinton P. Anderson, and myself moved that the Senate take up its rules, and pass a new rule permitting limitation of debate by a vote of the majority of the membership of the Senate fifteen days after the filing of a motion for cloture. But the leaders of both parties were unwilling to do battle to end the filibuster. The motion was defeated, and the only concession achieved was the return of the Senate, on the motion of majority leader Lyndon Johnson of Texas, to its pre-1949 rule allowing cloture to be imposed by a vote of two-thirds of those present and voting instead of two-thirds of the whole Senate—or 67 of its 100 members.

The realities of party politics have made matters even more difficult. With the Democratic party split into opposing camps on basic issues, unity has always been a major concern of the party. Unyielding southern opposition to civil rights legislation has prompted more northern Democrats than should do so to believe that compromises are necessary in order to prevent further split in their party. Necessarily, the concessions have always been one-sided—when considered on the civil rights issue alone.

The situation has also been bedeviled by the fact that for some Republicans, support for minority rights has had little practical political meaning notwithstanding the fact that the Republican Party is the party of Lincoln. After 1928, and especially during the days of the New Deal, the "Negro vote" was considered unshakably Democratic. Relatively few Republicans represented the large urban areas where minority groups were concentrated, and for the others, especially those from the plains and mountain states, the problems of discrimination seemed rather remote.

By 1957, however, the situation had begun to change. Congress is sensitive to the tides of public opinion, and more members of both political parties came to Congress convinced that segregation was harmful to our society and to the hope of world peace. They were determined to remove it. Moreover, the large popular vote cast by Negroes for President Eisenhower in the 1956 election persuaded many Republicans that their party was called on for leadership. When the President recommended a four-point program for civil rights in 1957, legislation proved feasible first in the House of Representatives, where a bipartisan coalition, led by Representatives Emanuel Celler and Kenneth B. Keating, both of New York, helped to bring a bill through Congress.

Under the Administration's proposal, the attorney general was empowered to seek injunctive relief in the federal courts upon evidence that any person had been deprived or was about to be deprived of his right to vote or of equal treatment otherwise under the state laws. This was the famous Part III of the Civil Rights Bill of 1957. Under this bill, the Civil Rights Section of the Department of Justice became a Division, and a new post of assistant attorney general was created to head it and enforce it. If a federal court order issued as a result were violated, contempt proceedings were to be conducted under the traditional procedures of federal courts—a trial by the judge without a jury but subject to all the usual appeals.

The fight was to be difficult and bitter. The hurdle of the Senate Judiciary Committee, which had so often served as the graveyard for civil rights legislation, was still pending—and so were the additional hurdles of the Senate itself and the filibuster. Also, at southern insistence, a "jury-trial" amendment was attached to the bill. The issue raised was largely a red herring; there exists no constitutional right to a jury trial in such contempt cases. The motivating force of the proposal was the feeling of southern senators that southern juries would tend to be more lenient toward offenders than federal judges would.

In southern state after southern state there is no jury trial for civil or criminal contempt. Actually, it has been the southern states which have led all others in holding that any effort to accord a jury trial in contempt of court cases would be unconstitutional under the constitutions of these states. The popular image of trial by jury as a basic right was exploited successfully, however, and a modified jury-trial provision was finally included in the bill. The fight was long, and bitter debate continued from June to August 29, 1957. The filibuster threat coming late in the session of 1957 hung constantly over the debate. Nevertheless, I do not believe the southern senators proposed to use it unless the bill proved to be a strong one after the amendment stage. The Senate sensed this, but the desire to enact the kind of civil rights bill which was needed was not strong enough to cope with the filibuster threat. First to go out of the House of Representatives bill was Part III— defeated in the Senate 52 to 38—giving the attorney general the needed authority to go into court to sue to protect an individual's civil rights in key cases. With Part III went the effect of this bill on equality of opportunity—in public education, in the use of parks and playgrounds, and in the use of buses and other means of public accommodation. There were other ways to assert these rights, but the remedy lay with the aggrieved individuals who were, too often, by education and by economic and social status unable to sue for themselves. They needed the majesty and authority of the United States to safeguard these rights. Little Rock, which erupted in violence after the end of the session, showed how badly the opportunity had been muffed to assert the determination of the federal government to assure individuals of their civil rights.

Criminal proceedings under civil rights laws on the books before 1957 are punitive rather than preventive and, for reasons already indicated, had often proved ineffective. Civil suits for damages could not give the complaining parties the relief they really sought. Suits by private parties for injunctive relief had been the most effective instrument for vindicating constitutional rights, but the victims of discrimination often lacked the financial means to maintain them, and in some parts of the South, threats of economic or physical reprisal were a powerful deterrent to resort to the courts. Also, a number of southern states had passed antibarratry statutes, making it even more difficult for the individual to sue.

It was proposed therefore in Part III that the attorney general be empowered to go into the federal courts on behalf of aggrieved parties to seek injunctive relief against violations of civil rights. Ample precedent existed for the use of this procedure. In antitrust cases and scores of other situations where the public interest cannot be adequately protected by individual lawsuits, the attorney general is authorized by statute to bring an action for preventive relief. (In the opinion of many, in fact, no statutory authority was necessary. Attorneys general had in the past brought injunctive proceedings to enforce established rights even in the absence of a specific authorizing statute.)

With the passage of the Civil Rights Act of 1957, the barrier was broken. But the gains were modest indeed, even in voting rights—the one area dealt with directly. The unfulfilled responsibility of Congress to enforce the Fourteenth Amendment as interpreted by the Supreme Court remained.

While civil rights legislation in the 86th Congress, including that offered by the Administration, by the Senate majority leader, and by civil rights advocates, was unable to make any progress in the Senate, this record of legislative inaction was in no sense paralleled by what had transpired in the legislatures of the several states. Foes of the Supreme Court's mandate against segregation in the public schools were making progress, unfortunately, while we in Congress were standing still. In the effort to frustrate and defeat public school desegregation and equal protection under the laws for minority groups, seven southern states have passed thirty laws, twenty-five of which involved the field of education—all designed to prevent or hamper desegregation of the public schools.

The approaches to substantive legislation in the 86th Congress were varied. The most comprehensive was the civil rights bill by Senator Douglas and myself and other senators. This bill was a broad-scale attempt to provide federal leadership in school desegregation by making technical and financial assistance available at the local level. It contained a strong endorsement of the Supreme Court's decision on the desegregation of public schools, "expressing the moral ideals of the Nation" and it declared the intent of Congress to protect the rights upheld in that decision. It authorized the secretary of health, education and welfare to render technical assistance and services, and make grants to states and localities in order to aid in the transition to a system of desegregated schools. Where conciliation and technical assistance failed, the bill authorized the secretary to develop plans for desegregation and ultimately to seek to enforce them in the federal courts.

The bill contained also an improved version of Part III of the 1957 bill authorizing the attorney general, acting on the signed complaint of a person unable to seek effective legal protection for himself, to bring a suit for injunctive relief against state officers or other persons acting in concert to deny equal protection of the laws to anyone because of his race, color, religion, or national origin. The attorney general was permitted under the bill to seek protection for local officials attempting to comply with court orders, and for persons and organizations who defended the civil rights of others.

The proposals first recommended by the Administration included a recognition of the Supreme Court's desegregation decree as the law of the land; limited technical assistance for communities prepared to desegregate; direct criminal sanctions against persons who obstruct court orders, such as the Little Rock rioters; and provision for the retention and production of voting records by state registrars (a measure designed to meet the tactics of Alabama registrars who sought to avoid Justice Department investigations of denials of the right to vote to Negroes, by destroying or disposing of records). In addition, Administration bills were introduced to extend the life of the Civil Rights Commission for another two years; to assure education to military dependents in areas where local public schools were closed to avoid desegregation; to put a statutory base under the President's Committee on Government Contracts, and to give the attorney general subpoena powers in voting-rights cases.

A different approach was embodied in a bill introduced by the majority leader, Senator Lyndon Johnson of Texas, who in 1959 placed his personal prestige behind civil rights legislation. Three sections of Senator Johnson's bill paralleled proposals made by the Administration, by me, and by several colleagues which would outlaw "hate" bombings of schools, churches, synagogues, homes, and business places; extend the life of the Civil Rights Commission; and give the attorney general subpoena power in investigations concerning the right to vote.

However, that section of his bill proposing the creation of a Community Relations Service—similar to the mediation and conciliation services to deal with labor-management disputes— has aroused the greatest interest. This proposal poses a serious problem. One had to be most careful that the subject of conciliation was not whether to obey the law or how far to obey it, but rather, how to obey it and how to avoid a crisis in community relationships. The recognition of the Supreme Court decree on public school desegregation contained in the Administration bill was not contained in the Johnson bill, a most significant omission when we consider the Community Relations Service it created. With appropriate amendments this proposal could have represented a meaningful contribution—but not alone, only in conjunction with other meaningful provisions.

There were other, less controversial proposals. In 1957 and 1958, a series of bombings of homes, schools, churches, and Jewish temples in various parts of the South shocked and outraged the nation. These were crude expressions of bigotry, attempts to intimidate those who sought to assert their constitutional rights and others who espoused the religious ideal of the equal dignity of man. Detection and prosecution of the miscreants who commit these offenses often pose formidable problems for local law-enforcement agencies. To meet this problem I introduced a group of seven bills, with Senator Keating, directed against the "hate bombers" and against "hate mail." Co-sponsors of the legislative package were Senators Gordon Allott of Colorado, J. Glenn Beall of Maryland, Wallace F. Bennett of Utah, John Sherman Cooper of Kentucky, Thomas H. Kuchel of California, and Thomas Martin of Iowa.

The first bill in the group outlawed the transportation of explosives across state lines for the purpose of damaging or destroying a religious, school, or business structure. An additional number of senators joined the others as co-sponsors of this measure. The problem of "hate mail" was dealt with by three proposals which would prevent using the mails to incite crimes of violence, including unlawful destruction of, or damage to, any building or to transmit threats directed at interfering with existing law or court orders. It was apparent that the problems of "hate bombers" and "hate mail" were closely interrelated and should be dealt with together.

My colleague Senator Keating and I took a trip into parts of the South, where hate bombings had occurred, toward the close of 1958 in order to see personally the situation surrounding the acts of violence and terror. These bombings demonstrated the urgent need for legislation both in our national interest and in the interests of our struggle for peace.

But needed civil rights legislation was not in the cards during 1959. Democrats, with their eyes on 1960, seemed content to defer a schismatic struggle within the party on civil rights until the pressures of a presidential year could be counted on to minimize the sectional split on this question. Republicans also seemed tacitly to accept 1960 as a better year in which to deal with this issue. Congress again had failed to meet its responsibility.

The record of Congress on civil rights cannot be viewed with pride. Some progress has, of course, been made. By objective standards, the fight against the filibuster in January, 1959 was practically a failure, but the strength of the opposition to it revealed by the fight seriously impaired the value of that device as an instrument for delay. Although Congress has still to pass substantial legislation dealing with racial segregation, by 1960, the question was no longer *whether* to legislate, but *how*. The obstacles were still formidable, yet the objective had assumed far greater importance as a domestic issue—and even as a burgeoning foreign policy issue.

In July, 1959, a Gallup public opinion survey showed that three out of every five Americans approved the Supreme Court's public school desegregation decision—an increase of 5 per cent over a poll taken five years earlier; it included about three out of every four persons interviewed in the North. These figures are probably a fair reflection of the shift in public opinion contributing to the progress of civil rights enforcement during the last decade.

Unfortunately, however, public opinion polls do not measure the depth of conviction of the persons interviewed. The Supreme Court had said in 1954 that public schools should be desegregated "with all deliberate speed." Time might be allowed a school board for the solution of certain administrative problems but not because the community was hostile to desegregation.

This was clearly a moderate opinion and one to which a great majority of the public could subscribe. In time, however, "moderation" seemed to take on quite a different meaning. For many people it became not a reasoned approach to the solution of a difficult problem but a mechanical formula. For them Governor Faubus and the South's Citizens' Councils stood at one pole and the NAACP at the other, and the "moderate" answer lay somewhere in between.

The difficulty with this brand of moderation is that it does not rest upon any solid foundation of law or upon the Constitution. As the words and deeds of some southern extremists became more violent, others found it easier to assume the stance of moderates. The southerner who opposed incitement to violence or barring the doors of schools could qualify himself as a moderate under this view even if he urged all means short of these force-measures to preserve school segregation.

This irresolution of public opinion has been successfully exploited by the segregationists. Although the Supreme Court's decision had been expected, the first reaction of southern officials was one of shock rather than outright defiance. There followed resolutions of interposition—the "right" of the state to insert its sovereign powers between those of the federal government and its own citizens—a "right" the Civil War was fought to end. These resolutions were accompanied by detailed plans for delaying actions based upon the construction of elaborate administrative obstacles for Negro children and the use of pupil placement and private tuition schemes. When, however, southern segregationist leaders believed that public opinion was not aroused to support the Supreme Court as anticipated, southern officials were emboldened to take more aggressive action. In such a situation citizens' organizations to marshal public opinion become an indispensable element in the process of government. We all know that government except by consent of the overwhelming majority of the governed becomes almost impossible over any measurable time in a free society.

Well over fifteen hundred national and community relations organizations conduct programs for the development of intergroup understanding and the achievement of equality of opportunity among all Americans. Charity organizations on the local and national levels were among the earliest groups to concern themselves with the problem. Concern for such community improvement was one of the activities of the early national labor organizations and of agencies developed by ethnic groups at the turn of the century. Most effective in achieving equality of opportunity for Negroes was the National Association for the Advancement of Colored People, founded in 1909. The National Urban League was founded the next year to improve the living and working conditions of Negroes, and the Julius Rosenwald Fund in 1917 with a similar goal. Jewish rights were early the concern of the B'nai B'rith, founded in 1813, whose Anti-Defamation League was organized in 1913 to continue this work. The American Jewish Committee, founded in 1906 to continue a charity function for immigrant Russian Jews, soon concerned itself with the civil rights of all Jews. Other organizations with similar programs are the American Jewish Congress, the Jewish

Labor Committee, the Jewish War Veterans, and the National Community Relations Advisory Council. Ethnic group organizations alert to the civil rights issue have included the Japanese-American Citizens League, the Mexican-American Movement, Italian, Polish, Slovakian, Greek, and Lebanese groups, and many more. Indeed, a listing of organizations concerned with civil rights and a brief description of their activities would easily fill a large volume. National church bodies have appointed special departments to deal with the problem. In the 1940's several hundred citizens' committees were established on a voluntary basis in large cities throughout the country to foster relations between people of all colors, races, creeds, and national origins in their communities.

The spectrum of support and co-operation is typified by the organizational memberships—political and social welfare groups, labor unions, national religious organizations, and veterans' groups—within the National Civil Liberties Clearing House and the Leadership Conference on Civil Rights. The internal problems of racial discrimination within many of these member organizations sap some of the vitality from the national movements against segregation. But the ways in which these internal problems have been met sometimes have provided a source of strength for progress in civil rights.

All the major national religious groups, for example, have taken strong public positions for desegregation of the public schools and obedience to the law of the land. In many cases, these pronouncements have been implemented locally in the words and deeds of the clergy. The ministers of Atlanta have exercised a positive and calming influence to seek to effect a peaceful transition to a desegregated school system in the midst of the tensions that surround them. But ministers, too, have been affected by the great pressures toward conformity in the South. Many were compelled to retreat in the face of crisis and remain silent—a few even joined the segregationists. In some areas it is possible to count the numbers in the clergy who have had the courage of their consciences simply by listing those who have been transferred or forced out of their pulpits by their congregations. A special study of the positions and actions taken by the ministry of Little Rock, made by Professors Thomas F. Pettigrew and Ernest Q. Campbell of Harvard University, demonstrates why the dilemma has been especially difficult for the Protestant clergy.

Organized labor has long been a source of strength in the struggle of the Negro for equality of opportunity—yet even here discrimination and segregation persist in some labor unions. With the progress of the labor-union movement, new avenues of advancement opened up for Negro workers. And leaders of national unions have generally lent support to the drive against discrimination on all fronts. But growing industrialization, particularly in the South, has brought with it tensions and disagreements. Hostile southern leaders have found in the issue of racial equality a handy stick with which to beat newly organized unions, and union officers too often have taken the path of least resistance. In many southern communities and in some northern industry, too, unions with segregated locals, which negotiate dual wage rates and promotion scales for whites and Negroes, constitute as great a barrier as management to equality of opportunity. Many leading national union officers have sought diligently to meet this problem. The long-standing friendship of labor and Negro leaders continues—but it is often strained, and even here law and the public opinion to back it up have a useful place.

These examples can be multiplied. The national struggle against discrimination is reflected in the institutions which form an integral part of our culture as well as in the federal government itself. While our declared national policy is against racial segregation and discrimination, practice does not always conform to profession. Efforts to deal with United States officials in the South who discriminate against Negroes seeking federal employment, farm credit, and other benefits have not always been successful.

Generally, however, the record of federal judges in implementing the decision of the Supreme Court on desegregation has been a creditable one. Many judges believed (and their feelings were reflected in decisions before the Supreme Court ruled) that racial segregation was an immutable part of the fabric of southern life. Once the Court had decided, however, only a very few judges disputed its decision. The United States district courts have been on the whole most conscientious, whatever might be the personal views of the judges, in striking down schemes which constituted outright evasion or defiance. In fact, the late Judge John Parker of the United States Circuit Court of Appeals in Louisville, Kentucky, anticipated the Supreme Court in opinions outlawing statutes requiring racial segregation in intrastate transportation.

Many judges are nevertheless convinced that the answer to the South's problems lies in the passage of years rather than in firm and present action. While not challenging the basic decision, they have often given wide scope to the "with all deliberate speed" provisions in the Supreme Court's decree permitting time for desegregation and, in effect, have countenanced the use of devices aimed at delay and the limiting of the numbers of Negro children to be admitted to desegregated schools. With the Supreme Court reluctant to act as final arbiter in desegregation cases which do not involve novel or fundamental issues, the influence of the lower federal courts has been considerable.

Defiance of the law and efforts to frustrate it in certain areas of the South; the lapses in government leadership, especially in the Congress; the lag in that public opinion which had so much to do with passing the 1957 Civil Rights Act; internal battles within economic, religious, political, and professional institutions facing the issue—all have combined and interacted to slow progress toward desegregation throughout the South, and especially in the states of the Deep South. Viewed in a historical perspective, these may be only symptoms of a society in the throes of transition. But in a world in chaos, we will not be permitted unlimited time. Hesitancy and indecision by some in public office will have to give way to conscientious leadership. And that "moderation" which is not based on the law but on winking at its defiance must yield to the considered judgment of Americans who do not merely sympathize with the strivings of minority groups for full citizenship, but believe their realization to be demanded by the integrity of the Republic and our Constitution.

Progress in civil rights on a number of fronts during the decade preceding 1954 foreshadowed and perhaps made inevitable the Supreme Court's decision on school segregation. In turn, the decree has fostered continuing progress in racial desegregation of housing, employment, public accommodations, recreation, and entertainment.

Nor should the contribution of the racial desegregation of the United States armed forces to over-all progress in this field be underestimated. In July, 1948, President Harry S Truman issued Executive Order 9981, forbidding discrimination in military service and establishing a Committee on Equal Treatment and Opportunity in the Armed Services to stimulate progress. President Eisenhower, with his status as commander in chief, carried on this policy with vigor as soon as he took office. By 1954, all the services reported that segregation had been completely eliminated.

These reports were optimistic. National guard units in a good many states remain segregated, and even in the regular armed forces, token desegregation and other discriminatory practices persist, though without official knowledge or sanction. The services have come a long way from the days in World War I when Negro combat troops were assigned to French units. Today, white and Negro draftees live and train together and share equally in the peacetime army. This experience cannot help but condition the stereotyped ideas of many draftees. In some cases the effects may be transitory, in others, lasting. This generation of Americans is less prejudiced than the last—and the broadening scope of military experience must surely be counted as an important contributing factor.

The activities of civil rights groups in the North, where discrimination is not sanctioned by law, differ, of course, from such activities in the South. At first, the mainstay of laws against discrimination in the North was the enactment of civil rights statutes by the states, and ordinances by municipalities. The earliest of these laws were designed to prohibit the exclusion or segregation of minority groups in places of public accommodation—hotels, restaurants, and so forth. At common law, places of public accommodation had been deemed to be "affected with a public interest," and thus were thought to be more amenable to legislation than other, more "private," enterprises. In the 1930's, some states took tentative steps toward prohibiting discrimination in employment opportunity, but these were limited mainly to employment in government, by public utilities, or on public works projects.

Shortly after World War II, however, spurred by the national wartime FEPC program, several states enacted laws establishing fair employment practice standards. In the late 1940's, also, states began to exhibit an increasing interest in discrimination in housing. (Housing, because of neighborhood patterns, becomes in effect almost exclusively either Negro or white; this is, after all, at the root of officially unsanctioned school segregation and limited opportunities in economic and social and educational advancement.) Litigation against housing authorities in a number of northern cities resulted in the institution of open-occupancy practices in public housing, and a number of states enacted laws prohibiting discrimination in houses built with government funds. In 1957, New York City took a bold pioneer step by enacting an ordinance, the Sharkey-Brown-Isaacs Fair Housing Practices Law, prohibiting discrimination in the sale or leasing of multiple dwelling units or units in a project development. Preliminary results were encouraging, and in 1959 several other states and localities followed suit.

Almost all state civil rights laws rely, at least in part, upon techniques of conciliation, persuasion, and community education and action. At the outset, however, "educational" and "legal" approaches conflicted. Most states created new agencies with powers to issue cease-and-desist orders and to enforce them by actions for injunctive relief in the courts. Others merely authorized existing agencies to investigate complaints and to conduct educational campaigns against discrimination.

Time has proved the comprehensive approach the more successful. Frequent resort to the courts has not been necessary, but the existence of legal sanctions has provided an inducement to co-operation and early settlement. It should also be noted that public accommodations laws providing for injunctive relief rather than criminal penalties have generally proved to be more effective.

As we shall see in succeeding chapters, the progress made in the past decade in making equality of opportunity a reality for minority-group Americans has been truly remarkable. And those responsible for making, executing, and interpreting the nation's laws cannot help but be impressed by the firsthand evidence of both the rewards and the challenges of a society in transition.

The idea that law is powerless to influence the attitudes and behavior of society is but a corollary of the nineteenth-century philosophy of Sumner and Herbert Spencer—that attempts by legislation to interfere with the natural law of "the survival of the fittest" are both ineffectual and undesirable. A half-century of social welfare legislation attacking poverty and disease, providing some security for the aged and disabled, establishing minimums of wages, hours, and conditions of labor, eliminating predatory competitive and monopolistic practices in the conduct of business affairs, have made this philosophy an anachronism.

Legislation and court decisions affecting racial discrimination are the most recent examples of the use of law as an instrument of social progress. They have shown clearly the interaction of law with education and with a developing public opinion to change the standards of conduct. The Montgomery, Alabama, bus boycott, led by Rev. Martin Luther King, is perhaps the most dramatic recent illustration of the effectiveness of non-violent community action to bring about basic social change. It should be noted, however, that the immediate goal sought—racial desegregation of that city's buses—resulted directly from a federal court decree.

In the five years following the school segregation decisions, the elimination of discrimination in many of our institutions was accelerated. Open-occupancy housing, increasing job opportunity for racial minorities, the ending of racial distinctions in the use of public facilities, changed the face of the largest cities in the North and in border areas. A relatively small belt of states in the Deep South has become increasingly isolated as an area stubbornly denying equality of opportunity—with a national and international impact, however, far exceeding its own narrow geographical limits.

On the horizon there is at least a faintly discernible outline of an era in which all but the archaic vestiges of prejudice and racial discrimination will have disappeared. This does not mean, as the segregationists would insist, that widespread intermarriage between Negroes and whites will result, nor are there analogous social implications. No law or community action can or should require any such thing. We will be, as we have been, always free to marry and make friends with whomever we wish. But, at least, we shall not deny to one-tenth of the population its chance to make a way in America equally with the rest of us. The whole thrust of the civil rights struggle is to prevent a denial of existing rights, not to afford new rights. The challenge is to achieve this objective without a useless and debilitating expenditure of our energies in conflict and bitterness. Law as an instrument for effecting orderly change has already proved its value. It will continue to help us meet the challenge.

Chapter Five

Discrimination in Employment

The use of the authority of law to restrain racial and religious discrimination in employment is not often recognized as one of the crop of war babies from World War II. In 1941, during a period of increasing labor shortage because of the war, there remained an untapped labor reservoir of Negro unemployed who were kept out of expanding defense industries because of long-established patterns of racial exclusion.[1] These patterns had been strengthened in the hard depression years of the early thirties when Negroes were squeezed out of their customary low-grade menial jobs as porters, waiters, and unskilled workers. In many instances, Negroes were also barred from unions. The hiring gates at many defense plants were closed to them.

Negroes were no longer willing to accept such a situation without protest. Those who had lived in the comparative freedom of northern cities had developed their own organizations. Indeed, a story was circulated in Washington, D.C., at the time, that the first FEPC Executive Order issued by President Franklin D. Roosevelt was the result of a threat by A. Philip Randolph to organize a Negro "March on Washington."[2] Randolph was president of the Brotherhood of Sleeping Car Porters, AFL, and vice president of the American Federation of Labor.

The ironic problem of the simultaneous existence of Negro unemployment and labor shortages was discussed by the cabinet. Mayor Fiorello H. La Guardia of New York, head of Civilian Defense, was authorized to prepare an Executive Order that would outlaw discrimination in defense industries. In a series of meetings with interested individuals, including Mr. Randolph, the draft order was expanded to cover employment in government.[3] On June 25, 1941, the historic Executive Order 8802 was issued forbidding racial or religious discrimination in employment by any company holding defense orders.

The Fair Employment Practices Committee was set up under this Order. It organized and held a number of public hearings which extended even into that stronghold of segregation, Birmingham, Alabama. The Committee, chaired by Mark Ethridge, publisher of the *Louisville Courier-Journal,* used these hearings to demonstrate that discrimination was a rigid barrier to employment in defense industries. Within a year, FEPC was made a part of the War Manpower Commission; it would have expired there silently had not the wartime labor scarcity driven home the object lesson of the economic loss deriving from racial and religious discrimination.[4]

In 1943, Attorney General Francis Biddle undertook to examine the problem. The substantial exclusion of Negroes from defense work had led to outbreaks of trouble in southern army camps, and race riots in New York, Detroit, and Los Angeles. Surveys showed that seven out of ten Negroes in the North believed that they were being discriminated against in war work; more than half of the Negroes in the South felt the same way. On the other hand, surveys of white attitudes in the South showed that only 7 per cent were willing to give Negroes equal opportunities for employment and only 12 per cent approved equal wages to Negroes for equal work. The figures in the North were somewhat better, where 19 per cent advocated giving Negroes an equal chance for jobs and 31 per cent favored giving them equal pay for equal work. Furthermore, 69 per cent of southern white workers said they might object to working with Negroes. In the North, 63 per cent of the white workers replied that they would not object.[5]

The government was faced with a difficult choice. Not to strengthen FEPC would further weaken Negro morale and would hamper the war effort by allowing needless labor shortages to continue. But to make FEPC strong would chance increasing widespread southern and scattered northern antagonism toward the agency. Nevertheless, the Administration on May 27, 1943, issued Executive Order 9346 requiring a clause in all government contracts forbidding employment discrimination. This Order also gave FEPC a full-time chairman and sufficient funds to maintain a small staff which could investigate complaints personally where they originated instead of trying to handle them by mail from Washington.

Monsignor Francis J. Haas, an expert at conciliation and a fighter for principle, was named chairman of the new committee. Other members came from industry, Negro groups, and labor unions: David Sarnoff, president of the Radio Corporation of America; Miss Sara Southall, supervisor of employment and service of the International Harvester Company; Samuel Zemurray, president of the United Fruit Company; and Charles L. Horn, president of the Federal Cartridge Company. Negro members were Earl B. Dickerson, alderman of the City of Chicago; Milton P. Webster, international vice president of the Brotherhood of Sleeping Car Porters; P. B. Young, publisher and editor of the *Norfolk Journal and Guide;* and Charles H. Houston, Washington attorney. While William Green of the American Federation of Labor and Philip Murray of the Congress of Industrial Organizations were named as members, their alternates were the ones really active in the FEPC—John Brophy for Mr. Murray, and Frank Fenton and later Boris Shishkin for Mr. Green.[6]

The results of the activities of this new, strengthened FEPC are best described in its printed report issued on January 1, 1945:

At critical points in the production program minority-group Americans have played an essential role. Every twelfth American in prime war industries is a Negro. In Federal government service every eighth worker is Negro. Mexican-American citizens by the scores of thousands have been keyed into the aircraft, shipbuilding and mining industries. Citizens of recent foreign extraction, under handicaps of different language and manners, have been accepted freely on our production lines.

The war morale of minority group Americans lacks nothing in comparison with that of their majority group fellow workers. It might have been otherwise; yet the Nazi and Fascist powers derived small comfort from their attempts to weaken American war production by driving the wedge of hate between groups.

The report also noted:

Resistance has not been a matter of the compass. Southern shipyards were persuaded to use Negro welders, aircraft plants to upgrade Mexican-Americans, white workers to cooperate with colored workers in the same production lines. Reluctant Eastern manufacturers of highly involved war mechanisms through experience discarded their belief that Negro workers could not acquire the requisite skills. Government agencies accepted in new positions qualified minority workers referred by Civil Service. Trade unions policed their own non-discrimination policy in the case of recalcitrant locals. Employers rearranged work schedules to permit Sabattarians and Orthodox Jews opportunity to observe religious customs.

These solutions have mostly been accomplished by informal negotiations without benefit of publicity.

Yet despite this record, FEPC had difficulty in obtaining appropriations from a Congress in which southern members carried on an unremitting warfare. They charged FEPC with being "the most dangerous force in existence in the United States today" and insisted that it would, if allowed to continue "unchecked," create "more trouble and do more damage to the supreme effort we are making to win this war than an army of saboteurs." [7] Southern leaders characterized FEPC as "a race irritant" which would "bring about conditions which will result in a disservice to all races." [8] By lengthy debate in the spring and summer of 1945 and threats to hold up the major war agency appropriations bill—of which the FEPC appropriation was a tiny part—southern congressional leaders succeeded in cutting FEPC's appropriation for 1945-46 by more than half, from $599,000 to $250,000.[9] And with the war's end, they quickly managed to put FEPC out of existence.

Some members of Congress tried to embody in federal law the lessons in democracy learned from the experience of the FEPC. A bill to establish a permanent FEPC, the Chavez-Norton bill, was introduced at the beginning of 1946.[10] It was met by a southern filibuster which easily succeeded in killing it. Since then, despite support from leaders of both parties, FEPC has become a perennial civil rights hopeful, introduced in nearly every Congress, but never so far with a real chance of success. It reached its high water mark with a diluted FEPC bill that passed the House of Representatives in the Republican controlled 81st Congress and failed in the Senate—again killed by filibuster.

The developments leading to FEPC had some parallels on the state level which resulted, in time, in the creation of a pattern of state legislation against discrimination in private employment. In March, 1941, the governor of the state of New York, acting on an accumulation of evidence that minority-group members had been denied equality of opportunity in seeking employment in defense industries, appointed a Committee on Discrimination in Employment as a subcommittee of the State Council of Defense. This subcommittee was authorized to study employment discrimination in defense industries and to seek to eliminate it by conciliation and persuasion.

During its life, the Committee on Discrimination in Employment handled over one thousand cases and succeeded in settling over 95 per cent of them satisfactorily. Its reports indicate that the Committee started many investigations on its own initiative, although a substantial proportion of its cases did stem from complaints by job applicants or dismissed workers.[11]

In March, 1944, the Committee, carrying out one phase of its mandate, drafted legislation for consideration by the New York State legislature. One of its proposals would have prohibited discrimination in private employment.[12] Governor Thomas E. Dewey, in a message to the legislature on the Committee's proposals, said that the subject needed more study, and suggested the creation of a special commission for this purpose. The legislature promptly set up a New York State Temporary Commission Against Discrimination consisting of eight members of the legislature (four Republicans and four Democrats) and fifteen members from the public.

The Temporary Commission held open hearings during November and December, 1944, in five of the largest cities of New York State: Albany, Buffalo, New York, Rochester, and Syracuse. These hearings served to publicize the existence of widespread discrimination in employment based on race, creed, color, and national origin. They also demonstrated the economic cost and adverse effect of such discrimination on the community.[13]

The Temporary Commission, which was chaired by then state Senator (later U.S. Senator) Irving M. Ives and had as its counsel, serving without remuneration, Charles E. Tuttle, filed its report in January, 1945. It made four findings. First, "discrimination on grounds of race, creed, color and national origin are too serious a menace to democracy to be safely neglected." Second, "whatever moves are made against them must seek to win a supporting public opinion." Third, "while wise legislation may assist progress, any attempt forthwith to abolish prejudice by law can do serious harm to the anti-discrimination movement." Fourth, "prejudice is the fruit of ignorance and is subject to the healing influences of education in the broadest sense of the term." [14]

The Temporary Commission's suggestions included a proposed bill directed against discrimination in employment. Known as the Ives-Quinn bill, this legislation was approved by the Assembly on February 28, by the Senate on March 5, and by Governor Dewey on March 12. By its terms it became effective on July 1, 1945. It was the first state law against discrimination in private employment, and like the (federal) FEPC, it was a war baby.[15]

The state of New York thus became a pioneer in the development of new machinery to ensure equality of employment opportunity for all and to help eliminate the gaps which exist between our democratic ideals and our actual practices. The New York State law served as the prototype for fifteen other state laws for combating discrimination in private employment. Therefore, it deserves full examination.

The law opens with a declaration that it shall be deemed an exercise of the state's police power for the protection of the public health, peace, and welfare, and in fulfillment of the civil rights provisions of the state constitution. It then contains a legislative finding "that practices of discrimination against any of its inhabitants because of race, creed, color, or national origin are a matter of state concern, that such discrimination threatens not only the rights and proper privileges of its inhabitants but menaces the institutions and foundation of a free democratic state." Finally, it announces the creation of a state agency with power to eliminate and prevent discrimination in employment because of race, creed, color or national origin.[16]

The next section of the statute declares that "the opportunity to obtain employment without discrimination because of race, creed, color, or national origin is hereby recognized and declared as a civil right." [17]

The third section of the statute contains definitions. This is noteworthy for several reasons. First, its definition of "employment agency" is very broad, covering every person undertaking to procure employees the opportunity to work. There is no requirement that they receive a fee or other remuneration for this service. Similarly, the term "labor organization" is defined very broadly to include "any organization which exists and is constituted for the purpose, in whole or in part, of collective bargaining or of dealing with employers concerning grievances, terms or conditions of employment, or of other mutual aid or protection in connection with employment." [18]

On the other hand, the term "employer" specifically excludes employers of fewer than six persons as well as social clubs and fraternal, charitable, educational, and religious associations and corporations.[19] The largest and most economically significant portion of the labor market was thus covered by the law. The state had no wish to interfere with existing personal relationships which might have developed between small employers and their staffs, nor did it wish to undertake the enormous task of policing their employment practices. The same reasoning led to the exclusion from the term "employee" of domestic servants and individuals employed by their parents, spouses, or children.[20]

The fourth section of the statute created a State Commission against Discrimination in the executive department. The Commission consisted of five members appointed for five years by the governor with the advice and consent of the Senate. In order to ensure continuity, the original terms were staggered so that each year saw the expiration of the term of only one member.[21] The present annual salary of commission members is $13,700.

The fifth section authorizes the Commission to formulate policies to effectuate the purposes of the statute and to make recommendations to state agencies and local governing bodies in aid of such policies and purposes.[22]

The sixth section spells out the general powers and duties of the Commission, including such technical matters as the employment of staff, the promulgation of rules and regulations, the opening of offices, the making of reports, the issuance of publications, and so forth.

In addition, the Commission is authorized to receive, investigate, and pass upon complaints, and to hold hearings. In connection with such hearings the Commission is empowered to subpoena witnesses, administer oaths, take testimony under oath, and require the production of books or papers relating to any matter under investigation by the Commission.

Finally, the Commission is empowered—in order to assist it in carrying out the educational aspects of the law—to create such advisory agencies and conciliation councils as in its judgment will aid in effectuating the purposes of the law.[23]

The seventh section of the law contains the meat of the Act. This section describes the acts outlawed by the statute by defining the term "unlawful employment practice." [24] Thus it becomes an unlawful employment practice for any employer covered by the Act to refuse to hire or employ or to bar or to discharge from employment any individual because of race, creed, color, or national origin; or to discriminate against such individual in compensation or in terms, conditions, or privileges of employment.

Recognizing the key role in employment opportunity played by some labor unions, the Act also makes it an unlawful employment practice for a labor organization to exclude or to expel from membership any individual because of race, creed, color, or national origin, or to discriminate in any way against any members or against any employer or any individual employed by an employer. A third paragraph makes it an unlawful employment practice for any employer or employment agency to print or circulate any statement, advertisement, or publication, or to use any employment application form, or to make any inquiry in connection with prospective employment which expresses, directly or indirectly, any limitation or discrimination as to race, creed, color, or national origin or any intent to make any such limitation or discrimination. There is, however, provision made for an exception in cases where the Commission finds any of these factors to be a bona fide occupational qualification.

Finally, this section provides that any employer, labor organization, or employment agency which discharges, expels, or otherwise discriminates against any person because he has opposed a practice forbidden by the law, or filed a complaint under it, or assisted in any proceeding under it, thereby commits an unlawful employment practice. Similarly, any person who aids, abets, incites, compels, or coerces the commission of an unlawful employment practice or attempts to do so, thereby engages in such a practice.

The eighth section spells out the procedure to be followed in connection with the handling of complaints.[25] It authorizes the filing of a complaint by "any person claiming to be aggrieved by an unlawful employment practice," or by his attorney. The complaint must be in writing and sworn to. The statute also authorizes the filing of complaints with the Commission by the state industrial commissioner and the attorney general (a provision which has largely lapsed into disuse), and by an employer whose employees refuse to co-operate with the provisions of the Act.

After a complaint is filed, the chairman of the Commission designates one commissioner to investigate the matter, and if, after investigation, the commissioner determines that probable cause exists to credit the allegations of the complaint, he is required to try to eliminate the unlawful employment practice by conference, conciliation, and persuasion. To encourage success and peaceful settlements in this process, and to give the Commission the freedom for effective negotiations, the statute specifically provides that neither the Commission nor its staff may disclose what has transpired in the course of such endeavors.

If the process of conference, conciliation, and persuasion proves fruitless, the investigating commissioner may then require the respondent employer, labor organization, or employment agency to appear at a hearing before three members of the Commission to answer the charges. Prior to the hearing, this respondent may file a written answer. He may be represented by counsel and may present testimony at the hearing in his own behalf. At the discretion of the Commission, the complainant may be allowed to appear, to testify and to be represented by counsel.

The Commission is not bound by the strict rules of evidence prevailing in the law courts. Testimony is taken down under oath and transcribed. If the Commission finds a respondent has engaged in an unlawful employment practice, it is empowered to state its findings of fact and to issue an order requiring the respondent to cease and desist from such unlawful employment practice and to take such affirmative action as, in the judgment of the Commission, will effectuate the purposes of the act.

The Act now specifies that the appropriate action includes, but is not limited to, hiring, reinstatement, or upgrading of employees, with or without back pay; restoration to membership in any respondent organization; or the extension of full, equal, and unsegregated accommodations, advantages, facilities, and privileges to all persons, as, in the judgment of the Commission, will effectuate the purposes of the law. The Commission's order is enforceable by the state courts upon application by the Commission. The Commission may dismiss the complaint if it finds that the respondent has not engaged in unlawful employment practice.

The last sentence of this section provides that any complaint alleging discrimination must be filed within ninety days after the act occurred.

The ninth section of the law established a procedure of judicial enforcement and review of orders by the Commission.[26] As has been noted above, the Commission may apply to the state Supreme Court for an order enforcing its own order, and a dissatisfied respondent or complainant may apply to that court for review and possible reversal of the Commission's order. The findings of fact of the Commission are, however, made conclusive if supported by sufficient evidence in the record considered as a whole.

The tenth section provides that any person who willfully resists, prevents, impedes, or interferes with the Commission or any of its members or representatives in the performance of their duties under the Act, or who willfully violates an order of the Commission, shall be guilty of a misdemeanor and punishable by imprisonment of not more than one year, or fine of $500, or both.[27]

An eleventh section specifically provides that the provisions of the Act shall be construed liberally for the accomplishment of its purposes.[28]

The importance of the New York State Law Against Discrimination is that, for the first time, a state undertook by statute to bar discrimination in private employment and, at the same time, set up a special administrative agency empowered to use the full authority of the state to safeguard equality of opportunity in employment. Furthermore, such power could be invoked by means of a court order enforceable by contempt-of-court proceedings instead of by the means which had hitherto been used, either civil suit for damages or a nominal penalty by the person discriminated against, or criminal prosecution by the district attorney.

The use of the cease-and-desist order enforceable by the courts is the ultimate weapon of the New York State Commission Against Discrimination (SCAD), a weapon which SCAD has found no need to invoke in employment cases. The mere existence of this weapon has greatly strengthened the effectiveness of the conciliation procedure and has made the hearing procedure a rarely invoked practice. For when the respondent engages in conciliation, he is much more likely to be amenable to suggestion when he knows that he may be subject to the compulsion of a court order if he fails to listen to reason, and insists on continuing the discrimination.

Another virtue of the New York law is that by creation of the administrative agency it shifts from the person who is discriminated against, most of the onus of defending his right to be free from discrimination. Of course, even under the New York law, he must take the time to complain to SCAD and to file a verified complaint. From that point on the responsibility of carrying the matter further rests with SCAD. Under previous antidiscrimination laws, the person discriminated against had to bring suit himself or complain to the local prosecutor and then try to persuade an often reluctant public official, busy with many other responsibilities, to initiate the necessary criminal prosecution.

Despite the obvious merits of the New York law, there were many who opposed it. At the legislative committee hearing on the bill in February, 1945, there were many business organizations which opposed the adoption of the bill. Among those speaking against it were the Bronx Board of Trade, the Brooklyn Chamber of Commerce, the Chamber of Commerce of the

Borough of Queens, the New York Board of Trade, the Real Estate Board of New York, the Associated Industries of New York State, and the New York State Laundry Owners Association.[29] They argued that the bill would drive industry out of the state and might cause race riots. Some also questioned the constitutionality of the law and its feasibility. These fears, of course, have proved groundless.

Even before the New York law could be tested, one other state and one city took action along similar lines. Across the Hudson River, New Jersey adopted a law against discrimination in employment.[30] It differed from New York only in naming its enforcing agency the Division Against Discrimination, familiarly called the DAD, and in placing it in the state Department of Education. The DAD is headed by an assistant commissioner of education appointed by the state commissioner of education, and he is authorized to act along the same lines as SCAD in New York.

In 1946, Massachusetts became the third state to pass a law against employment discrimination that was substantially similar to that of New York.[31] It became unlawful for an employer to make any record of the race, creed, color, national origin, or ancestry of an applicant for employment, but it extended the statutory period of limitation for complaints to six months instead of the ninety days in the New York law. Another change in the Massachusetts Act required every employer covered by the law, employment agency, and labor union to post in a conspicuous place on his premises a notice setting forth excerpts of the law and other relevant information.

In 1947, Connecticut became the fourth state to adopt such legislation.[32] It went two steps beyond its three predecessors by making its law applicable to employers of at least five instead of six or more persons, and included within the coverage of the law social clubs and fraternal, charitable, educational, or religious associations or organizations. The Connecticut law adopted the six-month statute of limitations and added an innovation by authorizing the Commission to initiate complaints on its own motion where it had reason to believe the law was being violated.

A different approach was tried by Wisconsin and Indiana. In 1945 and 1947, both states enacted laws dealing with discrimination in employment, but the opposition succeeded in preventing the inclusion in these two laws of vital enforcement provisions. Limited staffs were provided, but under both laws they could use only educational means to deal with discrimination.[33] It is most significant in our understanding of the problem that both these laws had little effect and that after ten years the Wisconsin legislature finally added enforcement powers to that state's law against discrimination in employment.[34]

By 1949, the next major legislative year, when forty-four state legislatures were in session, the number of enforceable state laws against employment discrimination had doubled. Rhode Island,[35] New Mexico,[36] Washington,[37] and Oregon [38] joined New York, New Jersey, Massachusetts and Connecticut. The Rhode Island and New Mexico laws extended their coverage by including employers of four or more persons. Oregon followed the New York pattern of six employees, and the Washington law affected only employers of eight or more.

All had substantially the same definition of unfair employment practices; Rhode Island said that employers may not establish a policy of denying or limiting, through a quota system, employment of any group because of race, creed, national origin, or ancestry of such group. The Rhode Island law prohibited an employer from trying to hire anyone from any employment agency, placement service, training school or center, labor organization, or any other employee-referring source known to discriminate on the basis of race, creed, color, national origin, or ancestry. It forbade inquiries by labor organizations, employers, and employment agencies about an applicant's race, creed, color, national origin, or ancestry, and the making of any record of such data by an organization. It specifically barred the use by a labor organization of a membership quota system based on race, creed, or national origin.

Another advance in the Rhode Island law was the provision making it unlawful for an employment agency to comply with an employer's request for referrals which in any way indicated discrimination. The law authorized the filing of complaints by an aggrieved individual, by the Commission enforcing the law, and also by any organization chartered for the purpose of combating discrimination or racism or for promoting full, free, or equal employment opportunities.

Rhode Island extended the time within which a complaint could be filed to one year after the alleged act of discrimination occurred. New Mexico and Oregon, however, went further in this respect. Neither of these states put any time limit on the filing of a complaint.

After 1949, progress was slow. In 1951, a bill adopted in Colorado barred discrimination in private and public employment but established enforcement provisions against discrimination in public employment only, limiting remedies in private employment to education and persuasion.[39] In 1953, Kansas passed a purely educational law without enforcement teeth.[40] But in 1955, the opposition to laws against discrimination in employment was overcome in three states. Minnesota [41] and the major industrial states of Pennsylvania [42] and Michigan [43] raised the total of states with enforceable laws to eleven.

To achieve these advances, supporters of the laws had to accept compromises. In Michigan and Minnesota the laws covered only employers with eight or more employees, and in Pennsylvania only those who hired twelve or more. At the same time, many of the more stringent provisions of the Rhode Island law, such as those specifically banning the use of any labor union quota system, were included in the Michigan and Pennsylvania laws. A singular variation was included in the laws of these two states by a provision making it unlawful for any individual seeking employment to publish a situation-wanted advertisement which specified his race, creed, color, national origin or ancestry, or a limitation or preference as to the race, creed, color, national origin or ancestry of any prospective employer.

For some years the Fair Employment Practices Division of the Wisconsin Industrial Commission had sought with modest success to establish through court decision that it had enforcement powers. Wisconsin's law, passed in 1945, appeared to provide only for education and mediation in countering employment discrimination. Colorado's law was very clear about the absence of any enforcement powers. In both states, efforts to strengthen these statutes had been defeated repeatedly. But in 1957, both the Wisconsin [44] and the Colorado [45] state legislatures converted their statutes into standard laws against employment discrimination, with enforcement provisions. Colorado set up a commission to enforce the law. The Wisconsin statute simply added enforcement powers. This left only Indiana and Kansas with statutes which called for education and voluntary compliance.

By 1959, the total of states with enforceable laws against discrimination in employment had risen to sixteen. In California [46] and Ohio,[47] such laws with enforcement provisions were finally adopted after repeated efforts. And when Alaska became the forty-ninth state, it brought into the Union a previously adopted enforceable employment discrimination law.[48] These three statutes differ in some details from their thirteen predecessors, but all sixteen are substantially similar.

Parallel to the passage of state laws, there developed, from

1945 on, a large number of local ordinances directed against employment discrimination. In that year, Chicago adopted an ordinance barring discrimination by the city, its departments, officials, agents and employees, by city contractors and sub-contractors, and by private employers.[49] Enforcement was left to the police, however, and violations were punishable by fines up to $200. In 1946, Cincinnati [50] and Milwaukee [51] also adopted ordinances against employment discrimination. In the next few years a total of forty-five cities adopted such ordinances.

By and large, however, these laws had little impact. In most cases either no specific agency was created to enforce the law or the agency so charged was left without budget or staff to do the job properly. Furthermore, because of the limited police powers usually given to cities by state legislatures, the enforcement agencies had no power to use the type of cease-and-desist order enforceable by court order available to state agencies, but generally had recourse only to criminal prosecution. Hence these city ordinances, with few exceptions, lapsed into disuse although they remained on the books as declarations of public policy against discrimination in employment.

There are a few outstanding exceptions. The Philadelphia FEP ordinance, adopted in 1948, is an example of a valuable and effective ordinance.[52] A local Fair Employment Practice Commission was set up under it with a proper staff and budget. It could receive and investigate complaints, conduct hearings if conciliation failed, and issue cease-and-desist orders. If its orders were not complied with, it could certify the case to the city solicitor for prosecution. Violations of the ordinance or failure to comply with a commission order could be punished by fines up to $100 or imprisonment up to thirty days in case of failure to pay the fine. Minneapolis,[53] Pittsburgh,[54] and Youngstown, Ohio,[55] are other cities which have effective ordinances in this field.

The forty-five city ordinances range in type from simple declarations barring only the municipality from discriminating in employment to bans on discrimination in all private as well as public employment in the city. Some set up no enforcement machinery. Others create elaborate machinery including a commission and a staff as in Philadelphia. Below is a list of the forty-five cities which have enacted ordinances on employment discrimination. Many of them are in states which have adopted state-wide laws. In some instances, the state laws provided for adjustment and co-operation with existing local enforcement agencies. In others, the state law simply superseded the city ordinance. In Phoenix, Arizona, the ordinance was repealed indirectly by omitting it from a recodification of the city code.

Ordinances against employment discrimination have been enacted in the following cities:

Akron, Ohio
Bakersfield, California
Baltimore, Maryland
Braddock, Pennsylvania
Campbell, Ohio
Canton, Ohio
Chicago, Illinois
Cincinnati, Ohio
Clairton, Pennsylvania
Cleveland, Ohio
Des Moines, Iowa
Duluth, Minnesota
Duquesne, Pennsylvania
East Chicago, Indiana
Ecorse, Michigan
Erie, Pennsylvania
Farrell, Pennsylvania
Gary, Indiana
Girard, Ohio
Hamtramck, Michigan
Hubbard, Ohio
Johnstown, Pennsylvania
Lorain, Ohio

Lowellville, Ohio
Miles, Ohio
Milwaukee, Wisconsin
Minneapolis, Minnesota
Monessen, Pennsylvania
Philadelphia, Pennsylvania
Phoenix, Arizona
Pittsburgh, Pennsylvania
Pontiac, Michigan
Richmond, California
River Rouge, Michigan
St. Louis, Missouri
St. Paul, Minnesota
San Francisco, California
Sharon, Pennsylvania
Sioux City, Iowa
Steubenville, Ohio
Struthers, Ohio
Toledo, Ohio
Warren, Ohio
Waterloo, Iowa
Youngstown, Ohio

What has been the actual effect of these statutes and ordinances on job discrimination? There is some disagreement among students of this question concerning the extent to which the laws and executive agencies enforcing them, contrasted with other factors such as labor shortages, shifts in labor supply, etc., have been responsible for the substantial increase in job opportunities for members of minority groups in the areas having such laws. But it seems clear that these laws have had a real impact.[56] Employment of members of formerly excluded minorities by large employers in public utilities, financial institutions, and department stores demonstrates this. The climate of public opinion which made these statutes and ordinances possible also ensured that the laws would have meaningful impact.

First, it should be noted that the sixteen states with enforceable FEPC laws contain 50 per cent of the nation's population and almost 25 per cent of its Negro population. These states also include a substantial proportion of the country's Mexican-Americans and a majority of its Jewish people.[57] Hence, it can safely be said that the state laws against employment discrimination thus far enacted have made available to many former victims of employment discrimination a piece of legal machinery which they can invoke to assure themselves of equality in employment opportunity.

Second, in most of these states vast educational programs have been developed to carry on and encourage an understanding of the fight against inequality of opportunity. Many commissions publish pamphlets and circulate their annual reports, newsletters, and bulletins to a widespread list of readers. Seminars, workshops, and training sessions provide personnel managers, employment agency staffs, and others concerned with employment with valuable interchange of ideas and discussion on ways to solve problems created by discrimination.[58] In this way the entire community may become involved in one or another of the activities directed at the elimination of prejudice and discrimination.

Third, the annual reports issued by the various state commissions indicate that they consider their efforts successful. The Wisconsin enforcing agency claims a high degree of effectiveness.[59] New Jersey [60] and Oregon [61] also are forthright in their claims of good success. Others, such as Rhode Island,[62] assert that they have been effective, while still others express the view that they have made a definite impact on employment discrimination.[63] The number of complaints received and successfully handled is nowhere regarded as a criterion of effectiveness, and in general has not been large. In twelve years, the New York SCAD, for example, handled only 4,213 complaints of employment discrimination; New Jersey's DAD, only 1,664.[64]

Despite the fact that fifteen years of experience with FEPC laws have shown the groundlessness of the fears which they engendered, in every state where proposals for such laws have been made, strong opposition has come from some business and other groups. In California and Ohio, for example, such a law was defeated in every legislative session from 1947 until it finally was approved in 1959. Every state which adopted such legislation within the past ten years has had a similar experience.

The opposition bases its public attitude on an "appeal to reason." It affirms its abhorrence of prejudice and discrimination, and supports equality of opportunity. But its leaders argue that legislation cannot prevent discrimination. They quote Henry Thomas Buckle, the English historian, as follows: "To seek to change opinions by law is worse than futile. It not only fails, but it causes a reaction which leaves the opinions stronger than ever. First, alter the opinion, and then you may alter the law."

Much as I admire Buckle as a historian and thinker, I believe this approach ignores the fact that law itself can teach. Scientists studying human behavior know now that the best way to restrain discrimination is to initiate a community pattern of nondiscriminatory behavior. People living in integrated housing, for example—no matter how prejudiced they may have been —frequently come to appreciate neighbors of different racial and religious background just by living near them. Laws against discrimination operate in the same way. The law opens people's minds to the problem and a solution because behavior in violation of the law may carry punishment with it; living with the law—and the overwhelming majority of our people is law-abiding—can and often does remove the prejudice. The entire history of the wartime federal FEPC and the many state laws against employment discrimination have proved this fact over and over again.

Chapter Six

Equality of Opportunity in Employment

The tremendous progress of the last three decades in increasing equality of opportunity in employment must be credited to the influence of the federal government, to FEPC legislation, to the labor unions, and to civic and community relations organizations. This is dramatically shown by the gains scored for the Negro worker, the chief victim of discrimination.

In the white-collar jobs, considerable success has met efforts to persuade large employers to abandon discriminatory hiring policies. A survey, in 1958, of the staffs of large insurance companies in New York, where exclusion of minority groups had once been the rule, showed striking changes in the period following adoption of the law establishing the State [New York] Commission Against Discrimination, SCAD.[1] One company doubled the number of its Negro employees in eight years. Another hired 50 Negro applicants among a group of 500 high school graduates who were accepted. One of the largest insurance companies, which once employed only one Negro in its entire staff, hired 400 Negro girls for clerical work.

In banking and finance, SCAD conducted six studies and handled a number of complaints of discrimination in hiring members of minority groups—most of them involving the employment of Negroes. Most of the institutions against whom the complaints were brought are now employing an increasing number of Negroes. One large bank had employed only 24 Negroes in 1947, most in menial positions; in 1956, this institution employed over 300 Negroes, and their jobs involved many functions of the operation, including branch management.

Major advances have also been scored in retailing. A spot check of department stores shows that there is a sizable number of Negro salespeople, a rare sight fifteen years ago. The Retail, Wholesale and Department Store Union has been a leader in this fight in New York City and has set up effective machinery to handle problems of discrimination. The local which covers the city has 30,000 members, of whom 8,000 are Negro or Spanish-speaking workers.

The hiring pattern of public utilities companies has also changed in many cities and states, and in the communications industry Negroes are being hired as teletype operators, installers, and managers. In one company 60 per cent of all Negro applicants for apprenticeship training in technical skills were admitted. It is worth noting by way of comparison that up to 1943 there was hardly a single Negro telephone operator in the entire Bell system.[2]

Action against airlines constituted a major break-through in New York. Of thirty-two verified complaints brought before SCAD, twenty-four alleged discrimination because of color, six were filed by Jews, and one was by a Catholic. Not until December, 1957, was the first Negro hostess hired by an airline, but two years later, when an applicant for a job as flight hostess complained that she had been rejected because she was a Negro, the accused airline publicly affirmed that it had no policy against hiring Negroes in any flight positions.[3]

The annual reports of the fair employment practices commissions in other states are replete with success stories. In New Mexico, a complaint against the Mountain States Telephone and Telegraph Company led to an agreement requiring the company to revise its policies to make full provisions for Negroes, Mexican-Americans, Indians, and other minority groups in hiring and promotion on the basis of qualifications and merit.

In Massachusetts, two Negro girls filed complaints of employment discrimination against a Boston manufacturing concern after they were refused employment for jobs advertised in a local paper. The complainants were among fifty white and colored girls who had applied, and they charged that the personnel manager had rejected all the Negro girls. Investigation confirmed the charges. The company claimed in its defense that it employed only experienced girls, but when this was found to be false, the investigating commissioner found probable cause. The company than insisted that the girls it had already employed could not work harmoniously with Negro or Jewish girls, but conciliation was successful, and the company agreed to change its employment policy.

In Seattle, Washington, a special survey was made in November, 1958, by the State Board Against Discrimination, of municipal practices in recruiting firemen. As a result, the first Negro fireman in the city's history was engaged two months later. An industry-wide study by the Board of employment practices by oil companies in the state resulted in a major oil company, which operated its own service stations, hiring Negro attendants in 1958, for the first time.[4]

Considerable influence on the situation can be brought to bear by the federal government, which has long followed an active program to eliminate discrimination among government contractors and provide equal employment opportunities. In August, 1953, President Eisenhower established the President's Committee on Government Contracts consisting of fifteen members under the chairmanship of Vice President Richard M. Nixon.[5] The Committee's basic responsibility was to enforce the standard nondiscrimination clause which has appeared in all federal government contracts since 1941. It reads as follows: "In connection with the performance of work under this contract, the contractor agrees not to discriminate against any employee or applicant for employment because of race, religion, color, or national origin." [6]

The Committee was established by Executive Order of the President, and enjoyed no statutory authority from the Congress; hence its work was entirely informal and it received no appropriations of its own nor could it subpoena witnesses in any investigation. It could only recommend investigation or contract cancellation to the federal government agency or department which made the contract—obviously a secondary not a primary remedy. The upshot of this matter was the inclusion by the President in the Administration's 1959 civil rights recommendations to the Congress one to create a Commission on Equal Job Opportunity under Government Contracts, and to give this proposed commission statutory authority in the Civil Rights Bill of 1960. This effort was defeated in the Senate in the course of the debate on that bill, and as part of a chapter so illustrative of the frustration and intense conflict in congressional consideration of civil rights legislation it deserves and will receive more extended treatment later in this book.

In view of the fact that the rate of procurement by the federal government is more than thirty billion dollars annually, the existence of a statutory Federal Commission on Equal Opportunity under Government Contracts would provide machinery to protect the rights of hundreds of thousands of workers who are in the employ of businesses and industries fulfilling federal contracts. It would also furnish undeniable evidence that the federal government actively promotes a national policy of nondiscrimination in employment, and is dedicated to the realization of equal opportunity for its citizens in every field irrespective of race, color, creed, or country of national origin.

By adopting a new, direct approach to the problem of discrimination in employment early in 1959, the President's Committee was able to report significant progress in a number of states throughout the country. It held a series of on-the-spot "educational" conferences with companies against whom complaints had been made, and was able to persuade them to comply with the nondiscrimination clause. Nine plants in the South and elsewhere holding government contracts were among those which were persuaded to hire Negroes for jobs previously open only to white applicants.[7]

The Committee was successful in Dover, Delaware—in a state where trouble was encountered with public school desegregation—in August, 1959, where a synthetic rubber products plant employing 1,700 persons was persuaded to hire seven Negroes for the first time, including skilled factory workers, a laboratory technician, and a personnel clerk. Management had insisted that white workers would refuse to work with the new employees, but its fears were proved groundless. The company agreed not only to accept qualified Negroes, but at the Committee's suggestion, to go out and recruit them as notice that the once-closed door was now open.

In Fort Worth, Texas, an aircraft manufacturer employing more than 20,000, but no Negroes above unskilled jobs, hired two Negro girls for clerical jobs after conferring with Committee officials. One girl was placed in the personnel office where she could be seen by anyone seeking a job. An "orientation" program was also put on for employees.

Even in extremely difficult cases, some progress can be achieved. A tobacco plant in North Carolina agreed after lengthy negotiation to hire two Negro office workers and a laboratory technician, and announced it would accept applications from Negroes for other work previously closed to them.[8]

Another firm which had never employed Negroes, an electrical equipment company in St. Louis, hired four from a group of applicants provided by the Urban League after the Committee had taken up the problem with company officers. In Southern California, two oil refineries hired Negro chemists after discussions initiated by the Committee. This step meant the Negroes would also move into the all-white towns where the refineries were located.[9]

One of the extremely complex areas which the President's Committee has tackled deals with discrimination against longshoremen because of their race and national origin. Acting on complaints from the NAACP and the Urban League, officials of the President's Committee investigated charges that Negro and Puerto Rican longshoremen were being excluded from regular and permanent employment at specific piers and terminals along the New York and New Jersey waterfronts, including the Brooklyn Army Base. Union leaders and officials of the bistate Waterfront Commission went to work with the President's Committee to eliminate this denial of employment opportunities, with every prospect of breaking this barrier, too.[10]

The President's Committee was able to take effective action in clearing up a situation uncovered in Chicago by the Bureau on Jewish Employment Problems. In April, 1959, following a lengthy investigation, the Bureau charged that nearly 1,500 Chicago firms still followed a policy of employment discrimination against Jews and Catholics.[11] Of this number, twenty-eight involved corporations working on federal contracts. The President's Committee promptly investigated these complaints, all of which charged that orders placed with employment agencies by these firms excluded specific religious and racial groups from consideration. Fifteen of the cases were closed after the contractors agreed to take steps to eliminate and prevent such discriminatory practices. In seven cases the Committee decided it had no jurisdiction, and six others are still under investigation and study.[12]

Under the President's Committee on Government Contracts, educational techniques, mediation, and conciliation have been used in investigating 837 complaints between 1953 and April, 1959, usually charging discrimination on the basis of race or color. In co-operation with federal government agencies, employers, and unions, 245 of these cases have been settled through action approved by the Committee, 359 were found not to be in its jurisdiction, and 209 were being processed as this was written.

The actual number of individuals and business organizations involved in these and other actions taken by the President's Committee is small, but it demonstrates, nevertheless, that progress can be made even in the most stubborn cases when persuasion and education are backed by law.

Another step to eliminate discrimination in employment— within federal government agencies themselves—was taken by the Administration in January, 1955, when President Eisenhower created the President's Committee on Government Employment Policy, for this purpose, consisting of five members.[13] In a report covering the period from January, 1958, to June 30, 1959, this Committee said it had received a total of 238 cases, of which sixty-three had been referred for further study and decision. The remainder were either satisfactorily settled without the necessity for hearings or rejected as unfounded. Most of the complaints, 85.7 per cent, were from Negroes; the next highest number, 5 per cent, came from Jews. Other complaints came from Italians, Mexican-Americans, Spanish-Americans, Indians, Poles, Germans, Catholics, and Hawaiians. Most of them alleged that they were never considered for promotion.[14]

A bill with which I am associated would recognize the right of employment without discrimination as a "civil right" of every American. It would make unlawful all discriminatory practices in employment, and it would create a commission of seven members, with power to obtain compliance.[15]

The extent of the problem created by the denial of equality in employment opportunities is illustrated by its persistence. In most areas of employment the problem today is racial rather than religious in character, the victims being Negroes, Mexicans, and Orientals. While a significant amount of discrimination against Jews—and to a lesser degree against Catholics—still exists, discrimination against Negroes takes the form of total exclusion; against Jews, however, it is more likely to follow a pattern of token employment, quotas, and segregation in specific departments.

Employment agencies form one of the major barriers to equal job opportunities. In New York, a three-year struggle was fought in the courts before the power of SCAD was affirmed to prohibit employment agencies from questioning applicants about their race, color, religion, and national origin. A survey of Manhattan employment agencies in 1949 showed that about two-thirds of the agencies were willing to accept and fill orders for "white Protestant" white-collar workers in spite of the fact that they would be violating the New York State law in doing so.[16] On October 17, 1950, SCAD issued its first cease-and-desist order against an employment agency, but its authority was promptly challenged by the Association of Private Office Personnel Agencies, representing sixty of the 250 agencies in New York City. SCAD's power to issue cease-and-desist orders against inquiries about an applicant's race, religion, color, and national origin was upheld by the state Supreme Court in 1951, and by its Appellate Division in July, 1953.[17]

In Chicago, a survey in 1956 showed that out of 5,600 applicants, employment agencies placed 20 out of every 100 Protestant applicants, 17 out of 100 Catholics, but only 9 out of every 100 Jews.[18] In the San Francisco Bay area the same year, 75 out of 340 business employers who were interviewed by the Institute of Industrial Relations of the University of California admitted that they either limited the employment of Jews by a quota system or rejected them altogether.

Employment agencies in California, through their Association, adopted a resolution calling for the removal of all potentially discriminatory questions from their employment forms. But a study of Los Angeles in 1957 found that more than two hundred business firms discriminated on racial and religious grounds in hiring clerical personnel. Twenty-seven of these firms were major national corporations, and Negroes, Mexican-Americans, Jews, Roman Catholics, and Orientals were among those denied jobs.

Employment agencies often use such codes as "53's" for Jews, "99's" for Negroes, and "o" and "SP" meaning that Orientals and Spanish-Americans were not wanted. In some states, employment agencies use such designations as "Not recommended by Redbook" to indicate Negro applicants; "Can't play the saxophone" for Jewish applicants; or numbers, 1, 2, 3, and 1-3 to designate white and colored Puerto Rican, and white Spanish, applicants.[19]

Newspaper advertisements specifying religious requirements have virtually disappeared, although they were prevalent before World War II. Many newspapers, however, still indicate racial discrimination in spite of community pressure against such color labels. Jewish organizations are particularly concerned by the exclusion of Jews from executive posts, and their segregation in certain departments of large companies. In many instances, they see a relationship between this discrimination and social discrimination. Insurance companies are serious offenders, a recent national survey indicating that the percentage of Jewish executive employees in the home offices of seven major firms was less than half the number in the sales branch offices. Of those in the home offices, two-thirds were employed as lawyers, doctors, actuaries, and accountants, and therefore could not be regarded as administrative front-office, or policy-making employees. The study covered more than six thousand executives earning more than $10,000 a year.[20]

Discrimination against Jews is also found in financial institutions, even where state FEPC laws exist. Several years ago in a city with a large Jewish population, a study was made of seventy-two banks employing more than 20,000 persons. Among the bank employees were 300 Jews, and most of them were working for banks which were owned by Jews. A Jewish vocational group which made 121 contacts with twenty-one banks over a nine-year period, offering highly qualified workers, was able to find jobs for only fourteen, and ten of them were hired by one Jewish-owned bank. Restrictions are even more severe in small communities.[21]

Many executives in insurance and banking claim that the relatively low salaries necessitated by regulatory laws limiting the budget for administration are not acceptable to Jewish men and women because they can earn more in other fields, and therefore they do not apply for employment. The argument may contain some truth, but in three insurance companies paying the same low salaries as the others but with a reputation for merit employment there were 400 Jews among 2,300 employees, a proportion eleven times that of twenty-three other companies.[22]

Yet another problem arises where there is a tendency toward self-segregation: in such cases Jews and members of other minority groups fail to apply for jobs in industries where discriminatory practices have been removed, and continue to concentrate on companies which either are Jewish owned or do not discriminate. This is economically wasteful, and should be overcome by adequate education, publicity, and recruitment.

Another difficulty to be overcome among minority groups is the understandable lack of incentive to seek professional training in fields where they have been subject to severe discrimination for many years. If all barriers, for example, against the employment of engineers because of race, religion, or national origin were suddenly wiped out, there would still be relatively few Negro applicants for jobs. They have been excluded from this field so completely that very few Negroes enter schools which would train them to be engineers.

Lack of opportunity for on-the-job training and advancement presents a problem that often is more difficult to solve than total exclusion. A recent study of employment practices in Philadelphia showed that Negro workers receive lower salaries, fewer opportunities for on-the-job training, and are promoted less frequently than white workers. The survey was conducted by the Applied Psychological Services and covered a sampling of 300 Negro and 100 white workers living in the same neighborhood. George Schermer, executive director of the Philadelphia Commission on Human Relations, who released the report, declared, "There is no doubt that color continues to be a major factor in determining where a person shall work and how he shall advance on the job in Philadelphia." [23]

In the South, where growing industrialization is providing increasing employment opportunities, violence sometimes accompanies attempts to drive Negroes from their jobs. In Montgomery, Alabama, for example, James B. Peek, Jr., 22, owner of a restaurant in the downtown section called "Jimmy's Bar-B-Que," replaced three white waitresses with Negro employees. In September, 1959, within a few days after this action, Peek received a letter signed by the Ku Klux Klan warning him to discharge his waitresses and remove the Confederate flags that decorated his establishment. Peek defied the Klan and told reporters: "If any group of Klansmen have guts enough to come in my place and remove the Confederate flags, they are welcome to try it."

The Klansmen came. Forty or fifty of them crowded into Peek's restaurant and occupied all the tables and stools. They ordered coffee, but did nothing and said nothing for about an hour, when they silently marched out. Peek promptly complained to the police, and armed himself with a shotgun.

The incident came to a violent end when Peek killed a reputed Klansman with a blast from the shotgun. The slain man was William C. Horton, 38, a supervisor of the Alabama Power Company and the father of two children. The two men had got into an argument over the Ku Klux Klan stickers plastered over Peek's restaurant windows, and later had met at a suburban shopping center, where the shooting took place. Peek was held on a murder charge, but pleaded self-defense.[24]

A similar incident took place in Pine Bluff, Arkansas, in October, 1959, but ended with less tragic results, when two Negro car-hops at a drive-in restaurant were taken off their jobs. A group of sixty to seventy white men had previously crowded the inside of the establishment and jammed the doorways with their cars while they lingered for hours over coffee and cheap drinks. The owner of the restaurant insisted that he had not dismissed his employees—they were students at Agricultural, Mechanical and Normal College for Negroes. "I'm just holding back until things kind of cool off," he said.[25]

A more familiar kind of employment discrimination, the denial of teaching positions to minority-group applicants, attracted widespread attention in the Washington, D.C., area at the end of the 1959 school year. A teacher of Japanese descent charged that Falls Church, Virginia, a town a few miles west of the nation's capital, had refused to hire her solely because of her race. The Japanese woman, a third generation American, held the degrees of bachelor of arts and master of education, and had taught for two years previously in Middletown, New York. School Board members of Falls Church were not critical of her qualifications, but voted against considering her application solely because she was not a "Caucasian." The teacher was subsequently engaged by a private school in the area.[26]

For every one of such dramatic incidents involving the denial of equality in employment opportunities which are publicized in the press, there are many more which involve realization of opportunity and which never come to public attention. This is true of the effective role of the trade-union movement—which has had its discrimination problem—in combating discrimination within its own ranks as well as in industry. Most international unions today not only outlaw discrimination by constitutional prohibition but also use every opportunity to take action against it. Thus, the Auto, Rubber, Steel, Electrical, Garment Workers, Oil, Chemical, and Atomic Workers Unions, and many other unions, have succeeded in organizing in the South where they have insisted on complete equality of opportunity and access to union facilities. The Oil Workers were among the first to hold integrated union meetings in the South, and successfully fought Jim Crow practices by the refineries. The United Steel Workers fought serious internal and external resistance to enforce its nondiscrimination policy to wipe out North-South wage differentials. Wildcat strikes and threats of large-scale rebellion delayed but could not block this achievement, which took place in 1954.

Another militant fighter against racial discrimination in the South was the International Union of Electrical, Radio, and Machine Workers (IUE) which has waged another battle at the same time against disruptive Communist agitation. Its most serious opposition has come from the White Citizens Councils, which it has fought in Mississippi, Tennessee, and Alabama.[27]

Not all of the unions have been so quick to root out racial discrimination. Substantial progress has been made among them, and there has even been penetration into the building trades, the traditional "lily-white" center of unionism. In two outstanding cases it became necessary for President George Meany to threaten to revoke union charters in order to halt discriminatory practices, and in one case to seek to supply Negro workers to break a racial segregation pattern in the Reinforced Rodmen's Union in Washington, D.C.[28] In Cleveland, Ohio, Local 38, International Brotherhood of Electrical Workers, one of the largest affiliated locals, had resisted admitting Negroes to membership for over fifty-four years. The local's practice of placing workers, putting together work gangs, and controlling the apprenticeship program had effectively excluded Negro mechanics from all major construction in the area.

The opportunity to put an end to this practice came when a Negro electrician filed a complaint with the Cleveland Community Relations Board. After a hearing, the local was ordered to consider the complainant's application for membership. When the local refused, the Board appealed to the AFL-CIO. Prolonged debate between the local and the Civil Rights Department of the AFL-CIO, climaxed by a threat of expulsion from the international president of IBEW, led the local to admit three qualified Negro electricians in July, 1957.

The struggle with Local 8 of the Bricklayers in Milwaukee was another dramatic step. Two Negroes who had been denied membership were sustained by the Wisconsin Industrial Commission, which administers the state's fair employment statute. Local 8 appealed this decision to the circuit court of Milwaukee County, which held on November 30, 1956, that the order was unenforceable because the FEP code of the state did not bestow enforcement powers on the Commission. The complaint was therefore dismissed because it had no legal basis.[29]

The decision was upheld on appeal by the Supreme Court of Wisconsin, with one of the seven judges dissenting. Justice Fairchild based his dissent on the argument that a labor union could not be considered merely another voluntary association, and therefore had no right to withhold membership from any applicant because of his race or religion. He said:

We are engaged in a struggle to make equality and freedom realities for all Americans. In addition to political equality, the full availability to everyone of education and full opportunity for employment to the extent of his capacity are generally considered the basic essentials in order to erase from America anything which could be termed "second class citizenship." [30]

Reaction to the majority decision in this case was so strong that the Wisconsin legislature subsequently amended its FEP law to give the Commission enforcement powers. The two Negro applicants became members of Local 8 after the AFL-CIO issued an order demanding their admission.

In the needle-trades unions, which were founded by immigrant workers, exclusionary practices have always been opposed. The constitutions of the Amalgamated Clothing Workers of America, and the International Ladies' Garment Workers' Union, have always outlawed racial and religious discrimination, and the unions have enforced them as strictly as possible. Nevertheless, in some cases, there are allegations that Negroes and Puerto Ricans are still being denied equal employment opportunities.

The United Automobile Workers has also on numerous occasions combated racial discrimination. Machinery to handle the complaints of members was set up in 1957 under an agreement between the union and the National Urban League. This agreement, covering about 200,000 Negro workers in all the plants working under UAW contracts, was hailed as a new voluntary FEP.

Despite the efforts of these unions thousands of Negro workers in other industries still are either restricted to membership in segregated locals or excluded altogether from union membership. Segregation appears most often in the craft unions where workers may be hired in crews for a short-run job. In other unions, discrimination may also appear in sponsored social or recreational programs, with resultant increase in tensions.

Railroad brotherhoods operating north of the Mason-Dixon line agreed at a conference in 1953 to drop racially discriminatory practices, and the railroads agreed to hire men in every job category without regard to race, color, creed, or national origin. But in the South, a different situation prevails. Discrimination against Negro firemen on southern railways by the Brotherhood of Locomotive Firemen and Enginemen has led to a series of decisions by the United States Supreme Court striking down unfair practices by which the union deprived Negro firemen of certain rights to which their years of service entitled them.[31]

In the days of the steam engine, there was always a white engineer and a Negro fireman. The latter was never promoted to engineer. With the coming of the diesel engine, a "promotional" agreement between the Brotherhood and the railroads threw many Negro firemen out of work. The seniority of those who were still employed in 1949 was saved by the Supreme Court decision mentioned above; it threw out the "promotional" agreement and ruled that newly hired Negro firemen would have to qualify for promotion to engineer.

In November, 1959, the Supreme Court was asked to review a decision of the Circuit Court of Appeals for the Fifth Circuit upholding the Brotherhood in an action by which it compelled the Central Railroad of Georgia to introduce a "swing man" on the run from Columbus, Georgia, to Birmingham, Alabama. Negro firemen have traditionally held this post for twenty years on the basis of seniority which they acquired as a consequence of the union discrimination that allowed white firemen to become engineers but denied this promotion to Negro firemen. Since no new Negro firemen have been hired over the last ten years, the older Negro firemen now hold top seniority, while behind them is an entire list of white firemen. The introduction of a "swing man" on the run from Columbia to Birmingham would give white firemen part of the job that Negro firemen have been holding heretofore. As a result of this new assignment system, Negro firemen would lose about $100 a month in pay. The Brotherhood's policy is qualified by the condition that such spreading of work shall be "without reduction in pay," but its contention that the new plan was in accordance with a national policy was accepted by the lower federal courts.

The internal problem that labor faces in its struggle to eliminate racial discrimination from its ranks was dramatically exposed to public view at the AFL-CIO convention in San Francisco in September, 1959. A. Philip Randolph, head of the Brotherhood of Sleeping Car Porters, and only Negro member of the AFL-CIO Executive Council, charged three international unions with maintaining racial discrimination. One of them was the International Longshoremen, and in this instance AFL-CIO President George Meany rebuked Randolph for airing his grievances before the convention rather than the Executive Council, where, as a member, he could normally have brought them. An ultimatum, he said, "would play into the hands of those people determined to keep the color bar." [32]

One of the resolutions introduced by Randolph warned the Brotherhood of Locomotive Firemen and Enginemen and the Brotherhood of Railroad Trainmen to stop their segregation practices within six months or face expulsion from the AFL-

CIO. The resolution was defeated because of opposition to the ultimatum. The accused unions, one of which claimed over one thousand Negro members, declared that it was impossible for them to change their constitutions until 1962, but pledged that they would take steps to eliminate racial discrimination.

Another international union, the Air Line Pilots Association, which also excludes Negroes, was not included in Randolph's resolution because it had voluntarily agreed to abolish its Jim Crow rule. At the convention, President Meany pointed out that since 1940, when he became secretary of the American Federation of Labor, twenty-six international unions had abolished Jim Crow provisions in their constitutions.

Except perhaps in certain parts of the social-order-conscious South, it seems to be generally agreed that the spirit of our Constitution assures every citizen, whatever may be his color or race, certain basic rights to equality of opportunity in respect to voting, jobs, housing, and education. None of these opportunities is to be confused with the social relationships. Neither the Constitution nor the cause of civil rights dictates whom one should invite to dinner or entertain in one's living room.

Yet even in respect to voting, jobs, housing, and education, we see from the documented story related in this book that we have a long way to go to redeem the promises of our Constitution and of our republic.

In respect to equal job opportunities it is especially clear that the sanction of law is indispensable to the work of government and private agencies, labor unions, church organizations, civic groups, and representative agencies of minority groups themselves. It is law which gives a structure in which the processes of education, mediation, and conciliation may go forward. The citizen is entitled to the help of law; the structure of government requires law; and the existence of law avoids extralegal action. Most significantly and notwithstanding the widespread fears expressed wherever fair employment practices legislation has been considered, whether on the local, state, or national level, the record confounds opponents that have expressed this fear by the relatively small number of complaints and remarkably few court actions and the general success of the program. One thing is clear: the law must be fair, and the enforcement authority must be implemented by a dynamic agency judiciously administered and backed by a sympathetic public climate. The record is already good where it has been tried, but its circumference is still much too limited.

Chapter Seven

Discrimination in Politics

When we look at the patterns of discrimination today in our American civic and political life, we must consider at least three broad areas in which some form of discrimination exists. The first is in voting, the freedom of a citizen to go to the polls to choose those he wants to manage the public business. The second is in the candidate himself, the way in which the elected representatives are chosen. The third is political life—ringing doorbells, making a campaign speech, working for a candidate freely and openly.

Let us try to examine each of these to see how we stand in the balance sheet of discrimination in politics. Let us look first at voting.

Voting seems like an elementary right. Most of us probably just take it for granted. We do not think much about it—some of us do not even bother to register and vote. But it was not always this way, and it is not this way now in some parts of America. Happily most of the old-time discriminations have been swept away from our exercise of the franchise. After years of work by such dedicated leaders as Susan B. Anthony, American women were given the right to vote, everywhere in the

United States, just after the First World War by adoption of the Nineteenth Amendment, which forbids discrimination in voting on grounds of sex. It is hard for many of us to remember back to the days of those women who fought so valiantly for "votes for women"; we just take it for granted now.

Even before the right to vote was made nationwide, other limitations on suffrage had been eliminated. Property and religious qualifications had been dropped from early election laws; and after the Civil War our Negro citizens won the right to vote. With the enactment of women's suffrage, the laws were clear and clean; the right to vote was in the law for all adult Americans—but was it there in fact? Not quite. For there is a major denial of the voting right to Negroes in southern states, particularly in the Deep South, and it is going on right now. The famous September, 1959, report of the Federal Commission on Civil Rights has now authoritatively documented this fact beyond dispute.

In Macon County, Alabama, where the famed Tuskegee Institute is located, the FBI found that no registration board existed, obviously in order to prevent Negroes at that institution from registering. When new board members were appointed on court order, they simply failed to appear on registration day, July 20, 1959.[1] When the white light of publicity threatened to get Negroes the vote, a state law was passed gerrymandering a whole area around the city and making it part of a voting area where its effect would be neutralized. Teachers and students at Tuskegee were excluded from effective voting by this unnatural and unfair way of splitting up the districts in the county.[2]

In the neighboring state of Mississippi, Governor James P. Coleman made no bones about his determination to deny Negroes the vote. On June 21, 1957, he is reported by the *State Times* of Jackson, Mississippi, to have said: "I do not think Negroes are ready to vote in Mississippi at this time."

The record is replete with other examples. They range from the systematic striking of some thousands of Negroes from the voting registry in Louisiana parishes (counties) in the 1956 national election, and the resultant refusal of the grand jury there to indict under the federal statutes, to a whole catalogue of subterfuges and stratagems employed to deprive Negroes of the right to vote in parts of Alabama, Mississippi, Georgia, South Carolina, Florida, and other southern states. Indeed, we have seen the development of the antibarratry statutes in Georgia, South Carolina, Mississippi, Virginia, Tennessee, and other states in a pattern designed to cut off an individual, whose civil rights are endangered, from suing on his own behalf by denying him the help—even to the extent of a $25 loan—of other persons or organizations in the litigation. In this way a vise can be clamped on the opportunity of many of the people denied their civil rights merely by the denial of the opportunity to enforce those rights.

The greatest concentration of denials of the civil right to vote exists in four states of the Deep South—Alabama, Georgia, Louisiana, and Mississippi. The Southern Regional Council reports that in Mississippi, only 20,000 Negroes registered for the 1956 elections out of a total of 497,350 who were eligible; in thirteen counties where Negroes constituted more than 50 per cent of the population, a total of 14 votes were cast by Negroes in the 1954 elections; in five counties not a single Negro was allowed to vote. Altogether in the 1954 elections only about 8,000 voted.

In Alabama, 53,336 Negroes registered out of 516,245 who were eligible; nine rural counties have no Negro registrants; even industrial and partly unionized Jefferson County (Birmingham) registered only 7,000 Negroes out of 121,510 eligible.

In Louisiana, 161,410 Negroes registered out of 510,090

who were eligible, a high percentage for a southern state; yet in four Louisiana parishes not a single Negro voted.

In Georgia, 163,380 Negroes registered out of 633,390 eligible; five rural counties permitted only a scattering of Negroes to register; several more kept out Negro voters altogether, and dragged down Atlanta's generally high Negro returns.

A survey of the registration of Negro voters in 1958, made by the Southern Regional Council, shows that in the eight states where reliable figures could be obtained, there was a drop of 45,845 since 1956. The total number of Negroes registered in Arkansas, Florida, Georgia, Louisiana, South Carolina, North Carolina, Virginia, and Texas in 1958 was 1,028,827; in 1956, the total was 1,074,672. According to the 1950 census, there were 3,651,748 Negroes of voting age in these states. (The Federal Commission on Civil Rights estimate for 1958 totaled 1,038,364 for these states.)

The Council, which is composed of white and Negro southerners seeking to improve race relations, attributes the drop to the school segregation controversy. Its report, published under the title, *The Negro and the Ballot in the South,* estimates that only 25 per cent of the eligible Negroes were registered in 1958 as compared with 60 per cent of the eligible white Southerners. Since 1956, two southern states, Virginia and Georgia, have tightened voting requirements; five retain the poll tax; and literacy tests, which may be used to disqualify Negro voters, but are not used to disqualify white voters who take them, remain the rule in seven states.[3]

These percentages are similar to the findings published by the Federal Commission on Civil Rights on the basis of 1950 population figures. Why do these situations exist? How is it that qualified Americans can be kept off the voter lists and kept from the polls? Is the dominant white population determined that Negroes shall not vote—at least, that they shall not vote in any substantial numbers, or is it due to the inertia of the South's "social order" of segregation of the races? The findings are that registration places are kept deliberately closed, or are opened at inconvenient times. Negro applicants are told to "come back later," and told so many times that they get discouraged and give up trying.

Some southern registrars ask for impossible answers to detailed questions of constitutional interpretation in order to trip up Negro applicants for registration or subject them to examinations lasting as long as one hour, while white applicants are passed through in one minute. Some questions, asked only of Negroes, would stump a law school dean. One sample question is: "What is due process of law?" No matter how an applicant might answer this involved query, the registrar could always say the applicant did not explain the point correctly.

One of the significant aspects of this report is that problems of denial of voting rights in Deep South states are far more frequent in rural than in urban communities. Since our rural areas are the traditional backbone of personal freedom and independence, it is certainly to be hoped that these findings of fact will not be lost upon them.

For violations of civil rights there are criminal statutes, and those statutes certainly apply to voting, but are they effective? As a matter of fact, they apply to voting most severely because the right to vote has been held to be a federal right for which, in a criminal case, there may be a proceeding not only against state officials acting under the cover of law but also against individuals who conspire to defeat that right.

The attorney general has a right to proceed under Sections 241 and 242 of Title 18 of the United States Code, and under the decisions of the Supreme Court, which have interpreted those sections. Here is an excerpt from an opinion by Associate

Justice Felix Frankfurter in the second Williams case, Title 341, United States Code, page 77: "The right of citizens to vote in Congressional elections, for instance, may obviously be protected by Congress from individual as well as from state interference."

In Louisiana, a federal grand jury was impaneled to inquire into civil rights violations on December 4, 1956. It stayed in session for three days, then resumed on January 29, 30, and 31, 1957, and on February 1, 6, and 12. Witnesses were subpoenaed and other evidence presented to the grand jury in connection with the cases arising in Caldwell, De Soto, and Grant Parishes. No indictments were returned in these cases.

On February 12, 1957, an attorney from the Department of Justice outlined to the grand jury the evidence relating to cases arising in Bienville, Jackson, and Ouachita Parishes. In the Ouachita Parish case the local White Citizens Council and the registrar joined in a conspiracy to strike from the registration rolls the overwhelming preponderance of Negroes in that particular district. The conspiracy was very successful. Some 3,200 names were stricken from the list, leaving only about 600 out of a possible 4,000 Negro registrants.[4]

This evidence, the Department of Justice believed, indicated the commission of offenses against the laws of the United States which merited presentation to a grand jury. But after deliberating in private, the grand jury announced through its foreman that it had found no possibility of returning indictments in the Bienville, Jackson, and Ouachita Parish cases. The grand jury went on record as opposed to hearing any testimony in connection with these latter cases.

The case of *Byrd* v. *Brice,* decided in 1952, involving the parish of Bossier, Louisiana, [5] showed that the 1950 census indicated approximately 26,000 whites and 14,000 nonwhites.

The court found that there were 9,000 registered voters, but not one was a Negro. It found two violations of constitutional right. First, the registrar made registration favorable and easy for white applicants without according even remotely similar treatment to Negroes. Second, the registering applicant was required to establish his identity.[6] If the registrar had good reason to believe that the applicant was not the person he claimed to be, the registrar might require the applicant to produce two creditable registered voters of his precinct to attest to his identity under oath.

This provision was always applied to Negroes; for thirty-one years the registrar of Bossier had been unable to establish the identity of a single Negro applicant. On the other hand, she has had no difficulty in nine out of ten times in establishing the identity of white persons!

The court stated that the registrar could easily identify thousands of white applicants without the requirement for the two witnesses, but, it continued:

We are yet to find one colored applicant who has been able to make proof of his identity. The unwavering, immediate, and persistent requirement has been that the colored applicant had to get two creditable registered voters of his precinct to appear and make oath, and so forth. The record fails to disclose—and that includes the testimony of all parties—of a single instance of a colored applicant ever getting even a blank in his hands to fill out, as is the custom.

Unhappily these quasi-legal methods of discrimination are not the only ones used. Intimidation—even violence—has kept Negro citizens from registering or from voting if they do manage to get registered. Economic pressure on farm tenants, withdrawals of credit, threats of dismissal to Negro teachers, have been widely reported. In 1955, in Belzoni, Mississippi, a Negro community leader who refused to remove his name from the list of voters was shot and seriously wounded by a gang of white hoodlums. Homes of Negroes have been fired upon and bombed, and crosses burned in front of the homes of others. The lesson to be learned is easy: in many parts of the South a "good" Negro just does not vote.[7]

It is indeed deplorable that many southerners in the states with the worst records on Negroes' voting do not have a sense of shame over this denial of the basic American right to vote. These states otherwise have fine records of democratic government—for white citizens. Fortunately, this does not apply throughout all of the South. Some areas have no discrimination against Negro registrants seeking the vote. In one county of South Carolina, even, 86 per cent of its Negro adults are registered voters. In many southern urban areas, discrimination against Negro voters is not as great as in many parts of the rural areas. In the French-Catholic parishes of Louisiana, discrimination is less than in non-Catholic areas of the state.

But it is not only racial discrimination that Negroes have to face in the right to vote. Some states still maintain the poll tax, a requirement that each citizen pay for the right to participate in his own government. It is true that this poll tax is not heavy; in fact, it is a matter of only a few dollars, but we ought to encourage, not discourage, voting. To those who apologize for the poll tax and say it is not much of a handicap to voting, I would say that the job of building a vital Republic requires the elimination of every anachronistic handicap to popular participation—such as a tax on property qualification. The income of Negroes in the South is, besides, on the average, 40 per cent of that of whites; a poll tax can be and is another practical barrier to Negro voting.

Every election time public-spirited Americans of all political faiths join to urge their fellow citizens to vote. "Vote as you please, but vote!" is a popular slogan on election day, and it is a good slogan. But in five states the poll tax stands in the way. Many representatives and senators favor a constitutional amendment forbidding any state from levying a poll tax on citizens who wish to vote for senators, congressmen, or presidential electors. Others hold that no constitutional amendment is needed, that a simple statute will suffice. Only action on the federal level, however, will destroy this outmoded barrier to full voting participation. The Senate has passed the anti-poll tax amendment but it cannot be submitted to the states until the House of Representatives concurs.

The Federal Commission on Civil Rights' 668-page Report issued in September, 1959 is a national call to action against discrimination in and denial of the voting right. It is a well-reasoned, middle-of-the-road document, proposing some solid, hardheaded recommendations drawn up by a bipartisan group representing all sections of the country—North and South—and dedicated to the securing of constitutional rights for all citizens. It is not radical or inflammatory—it is hardly even impatient. The Commission was established under the Civil Rights Act of 1957, and its two-year term was extended for another two years by the Congress in September, 1959.

The Report contained the Commission's findings and recommendations in three major areas of discrimination: voting, housing, and education. It regarded the right to vote as the "cornerstone of the Republic, and the key to all other civil rights." The strongest emphasis of the Report, therefore, is on this area. To discover just what were the facts, the Commission and its staff did two years of research into all the aspects of voter discrimination. Many public hearings were held; some parts were aired on television. Whoever saw or read about them was impressed with the thoroughness with which the Commission went about its work.

One of the Commission's most important recommendations proposed that federal registrars be appointed to register voters for federal elections. These appointments would be made where there was clear evidence of discrimination; and federal registrars would serve until local authorities were prepared to assure honest registration for all qualified citizens. Federal registrars, of course, could have no authority in voting for state and local —only federal offices.

There is still an unsolved problem. Under the recommendations of the Commission, all that the federal registrar could do was to certify the names of qualified voters not on the state list of electors. In theory, men and women with these certificates could then vote. But since there might be many a slip between certification and actual voting, full federal administration of federal elections in areas practicing registration or voting discrimination might well have become a necessity.

To meet this objection United States Attorney General William Rogers unveiled a proposal for court-appointed voting referees to enforce the voting rights of qualified citizens. On January 26, 1960, he outlined a plan under which the Department of Justice would file civil suits against discriminatory officials after receiving complaints of voting discrimination, and would sue to restore the plaintiffs to the voting rolls. If the court found that a "pattern or practice" of discrimination existed, it would then appoint "voting referees" to receive complaints of deprivation of the right to vote. These complaints, including others in the area besides the original complainants, would be heard, and the referees would list those qualified to vote. If the court approved this list, it would then become part of a court order, and anyone who thereafter attempted to prevent a person on the qualified list from voting would be liable to a charge of contempt of court without a trial. The referees, who would have subpoena power, would enforce the court order on registration and voting. It is this plan which was in substance incorporated in the Civil Rights Act of 1960.[8]

Other kinds of discrimination in voting affect others of our citizens—they include the denial of the right to vote for residents of the District of Columbia and special weighting of rural-area representation in Congress and in state legislatures. But this kind of discrimination can be changed by law, while the discrimination against Negroes voting is extra-legal and requires new law to change it. Many Washingtonians vote by absentee ballot in their own original home states, but this is no answer for the citizen who has no legal residence outside Washington. And I would guess that it is no answer even for the absentee voter himself. I know many a Washingtonian who would be happy to vote in District elections if there were any, but who keeps an outside local residence to be sure he can exercise his rights as a voter.

This is not just for the people of our national capital, and it is not just for Americans outside Washington, D.C. To deny the vote to any American is to deny a part of democracy to us all. For the Negro in the South, and for the residents of Washington, D.C., their loss is the loss of each of us. The real discrimination is the discrimination against democracy itself.

Then there are discriminations in the weight of representation given to the votes of varying groups of citizens. If you live in South Dakota *west* of the Missouri River you have three times as much political weight as if you lived in the same state *east* of the Missouri. The reason? The last census showed 494,000 people lived east and had one congressman. But one congressman also represented the 159,000 people who lived west of the river. This does not mean that those living west of the river are any wiser, or that they somehow deserve more representation than the people living east of the Missouri.

There is representational discrimination also in many state legislatures. If congressional districts vary a good deal in size, at least they can be changed, and the variations, while unfortunate, are not catastrophic. But many state legislatures have not changed their apportionment for a generation or more. While some states see the need to readjust their internal representation, many ignore the whole matter. I wish to make it clear that a bicameral legislature like the United States Congress may properly make one house representative of geographic areas like counties, but every effort should be made to give representation by population in at least one house. Americans are concentrated in greater numbers than ever in larger and larger metropolitan areas, and I suggest that this problem will grow, not diminish, in the years to come.

What about discrimination in political life itself? Here the record is good. Aside from anti-Negro discrimination in the South, there is little discrimination in active politics in America today. Even in the South there is evidence of a change.

There are now four Negro congressmen sitting in the House of Representatives, and that number will most likely increase. No one can say there is no prejudice against a Negro candidate, but that is a very different thing from actual discrimination. Indeed, in at least one instance the reverse is true. The leading official of New York county, the president of the borough of Manhattan, Hulan Jack, a Negro, was overwhelmingly elected although the Negro population of Manhattan is less than a quarter of that borough's total. Mr. Jack ran into difficulties while in office, but this does not detract from the significant fact of his election.

Members of minorities suffer little discrimination in active political life. Judge D. S. Saund, a congressman from Southern California, is a good example. I do not know how many natives of India there are in Congressman Saund's district, but there certainly are not very many. But Congressman Saund, born in Amritsar, India, was elected by his non-Indian district in 1956 and re-elected in 1958. Or take the case of Congressman Steven Derounian, who was born in Bulgaria. The Bulgarian-born voters of his New York district in suburban Nassau County cannot be very numerous; it is to the votes and support of all kinds of Americans that he owes his election and re-election to Congress.

What is true of these men is true also of Catholics, Jews, and other Americans of a great variety of national and racial origins. In the Senate last year I welcomed as my colleague Hawaiian Senator Hiram Fong, of Chinese descent; on the same day, the House of Representatives greeted its new member from Hawaii, Congressman Daniel K. Inouye, of Japanese origin. Expressing his gratification over the election of these men, President Eisenhower said: "I think this is a very fine example for democracy at work, in operation, and I believe it's a good example for the whole world; and I am, for that reason, highly gratified with the results." [9]

In the Senate and House today you will find Americans with a score of different racial, religious, and national backgrounds. Happily this has been true for many years in our country. Irish and German and Scandinavian names came into the lists of senators and governors and congressmen early in our history, then Italian, Polish, and a host of other names.

A few years ago a study was done on foreign-born congressmen.[10] Perhaps the list is not the best evidence of our freedom from discrimination, but it is useful in showing how even those citizens born outside our own national borders could succeed politically in the free atmosphere of American politics. Here is the list of foreign-born members from the earliest days of the Republic up through the 1948 elections:

COUNTRY OF ORIGIN	TOTAL
Austria	3
Canada	49
Czechoslovakia	3
Denmark	6
England	55
Finland	1
France	8
Germany	41
Greece	1
Hungary	3
Ireland	122
Italy	3
Luxembourg	1
Mexico	1
Netherlands	2
Norway	10
Poland	6
Portugal	1
Russia	3
Scotland	40
Sweden	5
Switzerland	1
Wales	9
Total	374

It is interesting to know, too, that these congressmen were nearly evenly divided in their politics, and that they represented every state save four.

As we move toward greater unity in American life, I am convinced that distinctions of race, religion, and national origin will become less and less important in our political life. Campaign speeches and leaflets addressed to this or that special minority seem to me to be diminishing over the years.

How can we sum up our record on discrimination?

Outside the South, there is not much discrimination in voting or in political life. There is some prejudice, certainly, but little discrimination. In the South, there remain areas of discrimination against the Negro voter and against the Negro in politics, as the Federal Commission on Civil Rights and other groups have reported. Some elements in the South, however, are moving to extend the right of Negro citizens to a full franchise. In Memphis, for example, where "Boss" Crump once reigned supreme, five Negroes were among the forty-four candidates who ran for fourteen posts in the city elections of August, 1959. One was given a good chance in pre-election estimates of election to the five-member City Commission if Negroes voted for him in a bloc. About 30 per cent of the registered voters in Memphis are Negroes. The threat was enough to persuade some of the white candidates to drop out of the race and throw votes to support other white candidates. None of the Negro candidates on the Volunteer ticket won, but in several cases they came in second. Moreover, the votes of Negroes probably were enough to oust the incumbent city commissioner of finances who had sworn on a television show to maintain segregation. The Negroes showed that even if they did not run a candidate of their own race, they could hold the balance of power in a close election.[11]

Nationwide discrimination in politics today is largely the discrimination of voter representation. To some extent in Congress, but far more in our state legislatures, our farm and small-town population is overrepresented. Our cities, and especially our rapidly growing suburban communities, are as yet underrepresented.

For candidates, the American record is good—outside the peculiar circumstances of the South. Our democracy has in this respect worked well. Over the many decades of modern politics, discrimination has been a minor force in America. The ballot has been the final arbiter, and the ballot has defeated any effort to discriminate against this race or that, this religion or that, this national group or that.

Prejudice there is, because none of us is perfect, and the tensions of our times are great. But prejudice is quantitative; discrimination is qualitative and disabling. When Al Smith ran for the presidency back in 1928, anti-Catholic prejudice worked against him. He could, however, become a candidate because there was no discrimination. Now that Senator John F. Kennedy of Massachusetts, another Catholic, has been nominated for the presidency by the Democrats, I am sure, and all observers agree, that although prejudice may still be a factor, it would be much less than it was a generation ago, and, most importantly, will not be a decisive factor in the 1960 campaign.

Our democracy is a living, changing force; its form today is not what it was a generation ago. In another forty years it will have still different characteristics. We have our imperfections; that we all recognize. As we carry on our democratic way of life against the assaults upon it by extremes of right and left, we must reduce these imperfections.

Chapter Eight

Minorities and Housing

In few areas of civil rights in the United States is the gulf between what we say and what we do more apparent than in housing. One-sixth of our population—twenty-seven million Americans—face restrictions in their choice of a home solely because of the color of their skin or because of the way they worship God.[1]

This situation is a sharp contradiction of our heritage and our professions of freedom and equality. Responsibility rests heavily on many shoulders. Federal and local governments, the housing industry, local improvement associations, customs and codes, have all played their role. The large and small islands of minority concentrations spread across the map of our country are a constant reminder to the world of our failure to ensure first-class citizenship for all Americans.

Organized residential segregation, as a national pattern, is a relatively recent phenomenon on the American scene. It is true that voluntary concentrations of minorities, particularly of immigrants of one nationality or faith, have been commonplace. It is understandable that immigrants from the same country or same home town, insecure in their new environment, would be

135

drawn together by common ties of language, custom, or religion. But, until recent years, such homogeneous neighborhoods grew by choice and not by necessity. With the next generation, or with growing financial security, the new American was free to move out into the mainstream of American life if he chose. No "ghetto" hemmed him in. This freedom of movement has been traditional in the American social structure. This is no longer an easy matter.

Today's ghetto is no voluntary affair. It is a racial concentration from which the only escape is often into another racial concentration. Its residents are generally American in background, language, and custom. They include the wealthy and the poor, the uneducated and the intellectuals. They are the college president, the ditchdigger, the banker, the street sweeper, the society matron, the laundress—and 95 per cent of them are Negro Americans.

Equal right to shelter has been recognized as an inherent civil right in the United States since 1866. Yet, almost a century later, most minority persons seeking a home are unable to enter the open market because of their race—nationality or religious belief are sometimes handicaps here also. Integrity, intellectual distinction, or wealth will often not ensure that a member of a racial minority can bargain freely for the home of his choice.

Granted the means, he may buy any automobile, any furniture, any clothing, any food, any article of luxury wherever they are offered for sale. Indeed, his patronage is avidly sought. But in one area, our free enterprise system breaks down: a home for his family is the one commodity a minority person cannot purchase freely on the American market.

The result of this practice of exclusion has been the increasing growth of residential segregation especially for racial minorities; today it is an established institution in every section of our nation.

Segregation and discrimination are inseparable companions. A restricted housing market is automatically an inequitable housing market. Forced to find housing in circumscribed districts, the minority home-hunter is subjected to economic disadvantages and personal injustice. But the damage does not stop there.

All of society pays a high price for discrimination in housing. Every facet of American life is affected by residential patterns. Segregated housing means *de facto* segregated churches, schools, hospitals, places of public accommodation, recreation facilities, and welfare and civic activities. Evidence of the moral, social, economic, and psychological cost of this inequality of opportunity mounts daily.

In a study in 1952, more than six hundred social scientists were asked: "Does enforced segregation have detrimental effects upon those segregated and/or upon those who do the segregating?" More than 90 per cent of the answers were "yes" with respect to those who are excluded, and 83 per cent were "yes" with respect to those who do the excluding.[2]

In 1959, the New York State Psychological Association declared that "discriminatory practices in the rental and sale of housing facilities . . . have direct and indirect detrimental influences upon the formation and functioning of personalities among individuals subjected to such practices." For the first time in its history, this distinguished group of scientists voted in support of social legislation. It called for enactment of a state law to bar discrimination in private housing, asserting that "prohibition of such practices will contribute not only to the welfare of individuals subjected to them, but also to the general good of all residents of our state." [3]

In 1942, the first comprehensive study of the Negro in America was completed. This monumental work, *An American Dilemma,* was under the direction of Dr. Gunnar Myrdal, who was joined by a working staff which included some of the foremost scholars of our time. The study, financed by the Carnegie Corporation, graphically described the burgeoning Negro ghettos which were developing in our cities, pointed out the role of federal and local governments in perpetuating segregation, and understood the inevitable psychological and economic consequences.

Dr. Myrdal forecast the building boom which was to follow the war years and warned that community planning, taking into consideration segregation and the abominable housing conditions for Negroes, should begin immediately.

"Gross inequality in this field [housing] is not only a matter for democratic American conscience, but it is also expensive in the end," he declared.[4]

Yet, sixteen years later, a major research report disclosed that "segregation barriers in most cities were tighter in 1950 than ten years earlier," and that in general the trend has been toward increasing residential segregation.

In November, 1958, the Commission on Race and Housing released the main findings of its three-year, $400,000 study in a summary report entitled *Where Shall We Live?*

The Commission itself was an independent group of New York citizens, chaired by Earl B. Schwulst, president of the Bowery Savings Bank. Serving with him were sixteen prominent business and professional leaders, whom Mr. Schwulst described as "men who are generally regarded as conservative." [5]

The scope of this study, the irrefutable documentation of the facts, the prestige of the Commission membership, and the forthrightness of the Commission's unanimous conclusions and recommendations all point to the increasing awareness of the basic civil rights problem of discrimination and segregation in housing, and its mounting gravity.

Although not comparable to racial discrimination in pervasiveness or severity, restrictions in housing based on religion also affect several million Americans. Isolated areas remain where residence by Roman Catholics is resisted. However, it is principally Americans of the Jewish faith who are denied free access to the housing market.

In 1957, the Jewish population of the United States was estimated to be 5,255,000.[6] Although adequate housing on an open market is available in most of the nation, anti-Jewish barriers are to be found throughout the United States. The Federal Commission on Civil Rights held its first hearing on housing discrimination in New York City in February, 1959. At that time, the Anti-Defamation League of B'nai B'rith presented testimony based on reports from its twenty-seven offices. Here are some of its facts:

Lying within suburban Westchester County, New York, is the Incorporated Village of Bronxville. This community, referred to in the testimony as "The Holy Square Mile," has the reputation of admitting only persons who profess to be Christians. According to the ADL report, no known Jewish families are home owners in this town of 6,500. But Bronxville is surrounded by villages and towns where Christians and Jews live in normal, healthy community relationships.

Approximately 50 per cent of the Jews in the United States reside in New York City. Yet the survey conducted by the ADL found that approximately one-third of the luxury co-operative apartment houses in Manhattan, managed by thirteen of the city's leading real estate firms, had no Jewish tenants.

In the Chicago metropolitan district, residential communities such as Kenilworth, Lake Forest, Barrington, and Palatine are for practical purposes almost completely closed to Jews, while large areas in numerous other North Shore communities practice similar discrimination. In Chicago proper, the evidence indicated that more than half of some five thousand co-operative apartments accept only gentiles. The report holds that in almost every major American city and suburb, restrictive devices are used to exclude persons of the Jewish faith.

According to official estimates, in 1957 the nonwhite population of the United States numbered approximately 18,700,000 persons. And it is on this group, 95 per cent of whom are Negroes, that residential discrimination falls most heavily. Sharing the acute disadvantages of nonwhites are Puerto Rican migrants to the mainland and Mexican-Americans in the Southwest.

Many of us may not realize that Negro Americans were not always hemmed into rigidly segregated areas—either in the North or in the South. In the early 1900's, the majority of Negroes in northern and midwestern cities lived in clusters in racially mixed neighborhoods.[7] In 1910, Negroes lived in practically every section of Chicago, and a third of them were living in areas with less than 10 per cent Negro residents.[8] In Minneapolis and in Columbus, Ohio, Negro residents were scattered throughout the city.

Social discrimination was hardly noticeable in New England where a small, stable Negro population lived in numerous towns and cities. Integration was customary in church, school, and community activities.

In 1934 only 5 per cent of the Negroes in Charleston, South Carolina, lived in blocks that were 100 per cent Negro, and 7 per cent lived in blocks that were more than 90 per cent white. While the majority, more than 55 per cent, were in blocks that ranged from half nonwhite to all nonwhite, close to 40 per cent lived in blocks that were more than half white.[9]

This pattern was not untypical of many cities in the South, where most of the dwellings occupied by Negroes were servants' quarters near residences occupied by whites, or were substandard dwellings on streets where low-income whites also lived.

In many of these mixed areas, the attitudes of white residents toward Negroes were similar to those they held toward other whites. There were the usual gossiping, exchange of services, and visiting among whites and Negroes.[10] Even today, it is not exceptional in the South to find Negroes living on one side of a street and whites on the other.

In 1910, 90 per cent of the nation's 9,800,000 Negroes lived in the South, with the vast majority in rural areas. In 1950, less than 70 per cent of the more than 15,000,000 American Negroes lived in the South. More Negroes lived in the North in 1950 (almost 5,000,000) than there had been in all of the Confederate states at the time of the Civil War.[11]

Moreover, in 1950—and increasingly in 1959—Negroes lived predominantly in urban areas, both North and South.

Beginning around 1915, the Negro, like the former European immigrant, began to move in search of more abundant opportunities for himself and his family. Not only did he move from the farms of the South to the industrial centers of the North and West, but within the South itself he began to concentrate in urban areas.

Some 95,000,000 people, representing more than half of the population of the United States, now live in what the Bureau of the Census has described as standard metropolitan areas. These are cities of 50,000 or more, plus the rings of satellite communities which surround them. Population experts estimate that 70 per cent of the nation's population will live in such areas by 1975.[12]

Further complicating this over-all redistribution in the decade between 1940 and 1950, the increase in the Negro population in the fourteen largest metropolitan areas was four times greater than the white increase.

In historic perspective, the advancement of the Negro American in the last century is an epic of achievement. He is American to the core, his language is English, and his religion generally is Christian. Yet no group migrating here from a foreign country has faced such severe barriers.

As Robert Weaver points out in *The Negro Ghetto:* "The most striking difference between the experience of white and colored immigrants is that while the [white] immigrant who improves himself economically and culturally has a chance to move out into another section of the city and generally be accepted as an individual, the Negro has no such escape." [13]

By 1920, patterns of residential segregation began to crystallize. As wave after wave of migrants arrived from the Deep South, already established Negro neighborhoods filled and overflowed. More often than not, these were the sections with rundown housing which more affluent whites had abandoned.

As a rule, the newcomers had little money and were illiterate and unskilled. Previous experience had not prepared them for urban living. Accustomed to social isolation from white people in the South, and insecure in their new environment, they sought out areas of Negro concentration. Often the "Old Settlers" and upper-class Negroes were as unenthusiastic over the "invasion" as were the whites.

An elderly upper-class Negro woman who had lived all her life in the North is quoted by Myrdal as saying:

The Negro invasion began about 1915. Until that time we had been accepted as equals but as soon as the Southern Negroes began coming in we were relegated to their class. Our white friends shunned us and we were really without social life until our own group was better organized. . . . We really do not mingle with the Southern Negro and they do not come near us as they know that we are Northerners.[14]

This woman was president of a local society composed of Negroes who had lived in the North for at least thirty-five years.

It was in this same period after World War I that the development of the residential subdivision on the outlying areas of the city began. The well-to-do led the exodus. Few Negroes could afford this new housing, and those who could found the areas closed to them as developers and financial institutions attached increased importance to homogeneity of neighborhood.

Measures to restrain the Negro's movement were many and varied. Racial zoning and the racial restrictive covenant appeared on the scene. The majority power structure and vested interests in the "Black Belts" joined in this new approach. Everywhere, racial segregation was on the increase.

This trend continued and became intensified during the period from World War II up to the present time. Currently, this pattern of population movement—farm to city, South to North and West—coupled with an inadequate housing supply and a racially restricted market is leading rapidly to a nation whose central cities are predominantly occupied by minority families and low-income whites, living in overcrowded, constantly worsening slums, ringed around by all-white suburbs. The moral, social, and economic fabric of our entire society is seriously concerned by this situation.

The American Council to Improve Our Neighborhood (ACTION) has set down the major remedies which are essential if the critical housing problems facing urban communities are to be solved. Since 1956, ACTION has been engaged in an exhaustive analysis of the basic facts related to housing conditions over the country. This highly specialized agency, headed up by Andrew Heiskell, chairman of the board of *Time* magazine, is composed of leaders from business, industry, labor, city planning, and civic life.

ACTION's series on housing and community development has been prepared by some of the best informed and most competent urban specialists in the country. They say: "What is needed is a whole range of measures to make central cities more attractive to upper-and middle-class whites and to allow nonwhites to live where they can afford to live and want to live. Such measures can be achieved only through a major effort of all levels of government and must include large-scale financing, public education, nondiscrimination laws, and experimentation with new programs of urban renewal and relocation housing."[15]

Since the depression years of the thirties, the federal government has become a major factor in the location, character, design, financing, and cost of every American's home.

The National Housing Act of 1934 established the Federal Housing Administration for the specific purpose of bolstering up the sick construction industry. In the twenty-five years of its existence, FHA has developed from a depression-inspired emergency agency into the most important single factor in the real estate market. It may fairly be said that no other agency, government or private, has had as great an effect in shaping the character and appearance of American communities.

FHA insures private mortgages for financing of new and existing homes, and for home repairs and improvements. It has set standards for the whole home-building industry and has substantially changed lending practices; it has determined where housing shall be built, for whom, at what price, the character of construction, and the methods of financing. Its influence has been so pervasive that conventionally financed building inevitably has been affected by its practices. FHA standards have become the norm for the real estate market.

FHA has not ignored the question of race and racial housing patterns. The *FHA Underwriting Manual* contains the criteria used in judging eligibility for FHA benefits. It is designed for the guidance of both FHA staff and those who would benefit from FHA assistance. From 1935 until publication of the 1949 edition, this manual insisted on social and racial "homogeneity" in projects receiving its benefits. It said: "If a neighborhood is to retain stability, it is necessary that properties shall continue to be occupied by the same social and racial classes." [16] It also warned against "adverse influences" such as "inharmonious racial groups." And the manual offered a model racial restrictive covenant.[17] New FHA-insured developments (approximately 30 per cent of all new housing) [18] were blanketed with covenants barring Negroes, Chinese, Mexicans, American Indians, and other minorities. It was only after the United States Supreme Court on May 3, 1948, held that racial restrictive covenants were unenforceable [19] that FHA omitted the "homogeneity" from its *Underwriting Manual,* and it announced that it would not insure loans on property which had a racial covenant recorded after February 15, 1950.[20]

Despite this announced change of policy, FHA continued to insure mortgages while the builders and developers were excluding racial or religious minorities. Whole new cities were made possible where state laws did not at the time forbid segregation in governmentally assisted housing—such as the Levittowns of Long Island and Pennsylvania (New York has since enacted a law; Pennsylvania a partial law; and in New Jersey where a Levittown is under construction, the courts have ruled against segregation); Lakewood, near Los Angeles; Park Forest, near Chicago; and many other all-white suburbs which often surround our cities and towns. As a heritage of this period it is estimated that less than 2 per cent of all FHA-insured housing has been available to minorities.[21]

On the plus side of the ledger, FHA has in recent years stated a policy of encouraging open occupancy, and the agency has concluded formal co-operation agreements with those states which have passed legislation prohibiting discrimination in FHA-insured housing. But not enough states have passed such laws, and the problem is slow to yield. In July, 1959, the Michigan Advisory Committee to the Federal Commission on Civil Rights, headed by former Secretary of Defense Charles E. Wilson, reported that discrimination in housing was its "toughest problem." On the practices of federal agencies, the Committee said:

It is evident that in general the programs of the Public Housing Administration, the Federal Housing Administration and the Urban Renewal Administration have relieved the national housing shortage but are contributing to the spread and intensification of housing segregation.

Discrimination in government-assisted housing has not been the sole problem of the FHA. Urban renewal is today the keystone of all federal housing programs, but examination of its own official reports reveals its nationwide impact on minority families. The urban renewal program is vital to keep our big cities from near fatal deterioration, but a need for greater balance and for greater solicitude for relocation of families has hindered it. There is much improvement but still much difficulty. Approximately 55 per cent of all displaced families are nonwhite. The program to date has resulted in a net decrease of the housing supply by some 75,502 homes.[22] A substantial portion of new housing provided by urban renewal has been high-rent luxury units. Negro neighborhoods have been cleared to make room for housing which was often too costly for the former residents of the area, or for such facilities as municipal parking lots and public buildings.

Federal public housing has provided practically the mainstay of the new standard housing available to Negroes, outside of areas where states and municipalities have themselves undertaken public housing projects. But even this program has not been an unmixed blessing. In the principal southern region in which 1,019 public housing projects are located, there is a prevailing policy of designating project sites in areas already racially segregated, thus making the achievement of integrated housing a remoter possibility. As it is, only two such projects are completely integrated, while 958 are completely segregated. Almost all of the rest of the projects are segregated building by building.[23]

New projects which are segregated in effect continue to be planned, approved and constructed. Although no deliberate policy of inducing segregation through locating projects in areas with predetermined racial characteristics is followed in most of the New York, Washington, Chicago, and San Francisco regions, which have 1,007 public housing projects, we still find that only 441 (44 per cent) are completely integrated. The New York region is the only one where more than half of the projects (69.4 per cent) are completely integrated.

The solution to the critical lack of middle- and low-income housing in American cities demands that Congress commit funds for a sustained new drive in urban renewal, redevelopment, and slum clearance, with more initiative and greater balance in planning by state and municipal officials. An indispensable element to the success of such a program is the insistence by government officials at every level that race, creed, or color of applicants be no bar to their admission and that middle- and low-income housing be in adequate proportion.

Despite our near-decade of effort—often massive effort— since the passage of the National Housing Act in 1949, our rate of progress is even yet inadequate in wiping out the existing backlog in middle- and low-income housing or cutting the swift rate of housing deterioration and decay in large areas of our big cities. Congress should profit by the experience of the last few years and adopt a national urban housing program, to be spearheaded by the federal government. It should include:

1. Authorization of $5 billion to be spent over a fifteen-year period in an all-out attack on slums and urban decay through urban renewal programs; funds should be appropriated at the rate of $300 million annually (many feel it should be $600

million), with an additional $500 million available for expenditure at all times not in excess of $150 million in any one year, to be released at the discretion of the president as required by the demand for new or improved housing.

2. Creation of a $3 billion Federal Limited Profit Mortgage Corporation, similar to the Limited Profit middle-income housing program operating successfully at present in New York State, for the purpose of lending money to qualified rental and co-operative housing groups to build for the average middle-income family—the vast group too frequently ineligible for public housing although unable to afford private housing or the near-luxury rents obtaining on a good deal of urban-renewal construction.

3. Establishing as a minimum goal the construction of 35,000 units annually under the Public Housing Program in recognition of the federal responsibility to assist city and state authorities to provide decent housing for their low-income families; such a minimal publicly assisted housing program is essential to the success of urban renewal programs, particularly since so much of our urban renewal takes place on high-priced sites.

4. The long-overdue vesting of control of all legal as well as policy-making responsibility in the office of the administrator of the Housing and Home Finance Agency—and eventually the head of a Department of Urban Affairs, if one is created, as I believe it should be. We must put an end to the discouraging time lags which now occur because three or four housing commissioners are often required by law to approve several phases of the same project using federal funds.

5. Intelligent over-all, long-range planning by regional housing officials to integrate federal, state, and municipal programs so that they will replace rather than relocate slums in their areas; and the retention of a degree of flexibility in their low-rent levels so that desirable tenant families in public housing whose income rises will not find themselves suddenly classified as ineligible and forced to move out into substandard units.

To date, the City of New York has received more urban renewal funds than any other urban center, or any other state; yet, it is estimated that one out of every eight New Yorkers lives in substandard if not down-and-out slum housing. Our relocation problems are painfully familiar to those in other cities where minority groups are an increasingly large part of the population. In the borough of Manhattan today 42 per cent of the population is of Negro or of Puerto Rican descent. When an urban renewal project on the upper West or East Side displaces some hundreds of families, a new strain is put on other often deteriorated facilities. And when many of these families cannot be relocated on the site often because of the nature and public purpose the project needs to serve, the slum eradication may have succeeded but at a cost of added pressures on other slum or potential slum areas. The New York City Housing Authority states in a report published November 1, 1958, that although it houses about 100,000 families, it still cannot begin to meet the demand for public housing; it is faced with a backlog of over 60,000 approved applications.

Those facts, illustrative of experiences common to many city officials here today, certainly should encourage other changes to minimize disruption of family life, and speed up construction and renewal in slum areas. Such changes would include:

1. Encouraging the construction of public housing on urban renewal sites located in predominantly slum areas; allowing communities to count the cost of public housing as part of their local contribution under urban renewal, as in the case of any other public structure they build there, to the extent that it is not paid for out of federal monies or earnings.

2. Readjusting maximum relocation allowances to individuals and families from a $200 to a $500 maximum, and to commercial occupants from a $2,500 to a $5,000 maximum on urban renewal sites.

3. Attracting potential sponsors of urban renewal projects by

speeding up the various federal steps tied to acquisition, relocation, and construction by assigning responsibility for each project site to a single federal official; and by making each project sponsor eligible to apply for FHA mortgaging as part of his urban renewal approval.

Certain elements of the real estate industry, with their practices of discrimination, must accept a share of the responsibility for the growth of segregated housing in the United States. I hasten to add that there are an increasing number of real estate agents, builders, and lenders who scrupulously do not discriminate because of race or creed, but the climate in the industry still tends to operation under restrictive policies.

Until about ten years ago, the National Association of Real Estate Boards actually carried a provision in its *Code of Ethics* which said: "A realtor should never be instrumental in introducing into a neighborhood a character of property or occupancy, members of any race or nationality, or any individual whose presence will clearly be detrimental to property values in the neighborhood." [24] In 1950, the Board revised this canon and removed the references to race or nationality, but there are not a few indications that changes in actual practice are too slow, considering the social climate of our time.

So, too, is the norm within the realtors' own house: in only a few cities are a token number of nonwhite real estate operators admitted to membership in the real estate board. Moreover, organized opposition to legislation designed to ensure equal opportunity in the housing market is often spearheaded by the organized real estate business.

A whole sad mythology has developed around the subject of minority occupancy and property values. The contention that values will depreciate with the entry of a minority into a neighborhood is so widespread and well established that it amounts to an article of faith. Yet there is a wealth of scientific evidence to refute that conclusion.

During the course of the three-year study by the Commission on Race and Housing, an investigation of the effects of non-white entry on property values was conducted in seven cities on both coasts and in mid-continent.[25] The Commission found that the entry of nonwhites had either a favorable effect or no effect at all on property values in the majority of cases.

If white residents panic, and a mass exodus ensues, the expectation of a fall in property values becomes a "self-fulfilling prophecy," the Commission reported. In this case, it is the mass exodus rather than the entrance of a minority that gluts the market and depresses values. It is comparable to a bank run engendered by fears. On the other hand, if the white residents do not yield to the "myths" but behave in normal fashion, the pressure for nonwhite housing may bid prices up. It has been clearly demonstrated that in the many integrated neighborhoods where the concern is for good neighbors, regardless of race or creed, values remain stable.

There is an old cliché that nothing is sure but death and taxes. The wise man would head the list of certainties with the word "change." The face of American neighborhoods has been changing from the day the Pilgrims landed. Harry Golden, author of *Only in America* and *For 2¢ Plain,* gives one of the best modern and classic descriptions of the inexorable change in neighborhood composition in a "nation on the move." He tells of a visit to the cold-water tenement which was his childhood home on the lower East Side of New York City. It had been forty years since his last visit to the neighborhood, but he found the building still standing and still full of tenants. Golden writes:

I examined the names on the mailboxes, and where once they had been Rabinowitz and Cohen, they were now Perez and Amici. And as I stood in that hallway where I had spent my first fifteen years, the Negro and Puerto Rican kids looked at me as if I had just dropped down from the planet Mars.

You can write a social history of our country by just walking through these neighborhoods. First there were the Germans, then the Irish, followed by the Jews, then the Italians, and now the Negroes and Puerto Ricans. . . . What manner of children, of what nationality and history, will be staring at the "stranger" when the Puerto Rican novelist or Negro Vice President of the United States comes back fifty years from now? . . . I am certain that "This scene [will] be acted over . . . and in accents yet unborn." [26]

The term "changing neighborhood"—meaning a neighborhood in racial transition—has come to be synonymous with "problem neighborhood" in the minds of too many people. Whether or not it is indeed a problem area is squarely up to its residents and to the city officials charged with the proper administration of building codes. In the normal course of events, new neighbors of like income and cultural background move into a given area. Granted, of course, that landlords are not permitted to put ten families into living quarters which were designed for one!

Change as such is nothing to be feared. What must be countered is panic and flight and the likely result in overcrowding of the new-comers and property deterioration. The state of Maryland, in such a case, suspended the licenses of two Baltimore real estate operators for three months after the Real Estate Commission found that they had "engaged in a continued and flagrant course of misrepresentation" and in "misleading and untruthful advertising." It was charged that these men had deliberately engaged in activities calculated to incite panic selling in a racially changing neighborhood.[27]

"Not for Sale—We Believe in Democracy." With these words on signs placed on their houses, white residents of Springfield Gardens in Queens, New York, are well on the way to stabilizing their "changing neighborhood." Springfield Gardens is a community of well-kept one- and two-family homes. Negroes have lived in the area for many years, comprising about 10 per cent of its residents.

During the last few years, whenever a house was sold to a nonwhite person, the block would suddenly be inundated by real estate operators trying to create panic selling among the white residents. Rumors were spread by telephone calls, circulars, and personal visits to the effect that other white residents were allegedly selling out and that the street would soon be all-Negro. To combat an outburst of this kind in September, 1958, a community organization appealed for help to New York City's Commission on Intergroup Relations. A Neighborhood Relations Committee was organized; block meetings were set up; the facts were spread on the record; and a down-to-earth job of community relations got under way.

Springfield Gardens is one of hundreds of neighborhoods over the country where groups of citizens are banding together to save the community from those influences which would destroy it through prejudice and unfounded fear. But the ultimate answer to the very real problems of the "changing neighborhood" is an open housing market, where supply and demand come freely into play. When the criteria for purchasing shelter are the same across the country as those for purchasing any other commodity, the segregated neighborhood will be doomed.

While religious and racial discrimination in housing is clearly one of the basic civil rights problems facing the nation today, American conscience and common sense are stirring. This is reflected in the joint declaration of the Methodist agencies meeting in Dallas, Texas, on September 5, 1959, which states:

> Restrictive housing on the basis of race violates Christian principles. The freedom to choose a home and a neighborhood should not be limited because of a person's race. The right to rent or purchase, however, is not enough. Community acceptance which creates a sense of belonging is in the spirit of Christ.

An increased public awareness of the moral, social, and economic issues involved, plus the rising status of minority groups, have stimulated the growing movement for equal opportunity in housing. Many approaches are being brought into play: judicial decision, legislation, governmental administrative action, private developments in open-occupancy housing, and constructive educational and community programs.

In 1917, the Supreme Court nullified decades-old laws and city ordinances requiring Negroes to live in certain city blocks.[28] (News of civil rights decisions travels slowly in the South— Birmingham was still enforcing such an ordinance in 1950.) [29] With the invalidation of racial zoning ordinances, there was resort to the covenant restricting the right to sell property to white buyers for white occupancy. In 1915, Louisiana led off with a decision that enforcement of these restrictive agreements did not constitute a denial of equal protection under the law.[30] By the time the Supreme Court in 1948 struck down the racial restrictive covenants, nineteen states and the District of Columbia had rendered decisions upholding these agreements.[31] Most of these states lay in the North and West. The practical result of their decisions was to lay the foundation for Black Belts, large and small, that sprawl across the hearts of our cities and towns.

Early public housing was built on a segregated basis, and this was upheld by a federal court in Philadelphia in 1941.[32] But in 1953, a number of courts held that racial separation in public housing violated the Fourteenth Amendment.[33] As the matter stands today, no political subdivision can require residential segregation by law or ordinance, and no court can compel it through enforcing racial restrictive covenants.

Another important step came in 1957, when Judge James H. Oakley of the Superior Court in Sacramento, California, ruled that discrimination in the sale of housing financed with FHA or VA guaranteed-mortgage financing is unconstitutional. He held that the fundamental law requires that government benefits be conferred on an equal basis, and that private builders who avail themselves of federal assistance must follow the same principle of nondiscrimination required of federal agencies.[34] In the same year, the New York State Supreme Court upheld the constitutionality of the 1955 Metcalf-Baker Law, which similarly prohibits discrimination in all publicly assisted housing.[35] There is now a Negro family living in the development in question. On this case, the *New York Times* said:

This will give a boost to the more effective enforcement of the law throughout this state, it will buttress with precedent similar laws in four other states which have them now, and will speed passage of such legislation now being considered in half a dozen more. This is real progress.

In April, 1959, the Supreme Court of Florida ruled that the United States Supreme Court's 1948 decision holding racial restrictive covenants unenforceable is equally applicable to agreements containing religious exclusions. In New Jersey, the State Supreme Court upheld a similar New Jersey statute on February 9, 1960. Only in the state of Washington has any court failed to uphold one of these state statutes. In this instance, the Seattle Real Estate Board financed a suit challenging the law. The Superior Court on July 13, 1959, held that particular law unconstitutional.[36] The state has announced it will appeal the decision.

Proponents of equality of opportunity are relying increasingly on legislation, both to ensure individual rights and as a potent force for changing social habits. Dr. Donald J. Hager, head of the Department of Sociology and Anthropology of Los Angeles State College, has called the dramatic use of law, legislation, and litigation "a revolution in the tactics and strategy of civil rights efforts." [37]

The Preamble to New York City's Sharkey-Brown-Isaacs Fair Housing Practices Law in 1957 recognized that segregation in housing was against public policy and said:

Such segregation in housing also necessarily results in other forms of segregation and discrimination which are against the policy of the State of New York. It results in racial segregation in public schools and other public facilities, which is condemned by the constitutions of our state and nation. In order to guard against these evils, it is necessary to assure to all inhabitants of the city equal opportunity to obtain living quarters, regardless of race, color, religion, national origin or ancestry.

Law can be much more than an instrument of punishment or coercion. It can and should also be an affirmation of our noblest ideals—a standard to which the whole community may repair. Law cannot require a prejudiced person to change but it can deter him from translating prejudice into action violating the rights of others.

During the last decade, many states and cities have turned to the law to guarantee the equal right to shelter. As of June 30, 1959, fourteen states and thirty-two cities had passed laws or resolutions relating to discrimination in housing.[38] The state of New York actually set the pattern for this nationwide drive for "open occupancy by statute." In about 1945, the Metropolitan Life Insurance Company disclosed that its mammoth New York City apartment development, Stuyvesant Town, would be limited to white tenancy. The owner and builder of this huge city within a city, housing thousands of people, had been granted major tax concessions and other benefits by both city and state. Here was a basis for representatives of churches, unions, business, civil rights, and civic agencies to join in protesting this use of government benefits for racially restricted housing.

In the course of the ensuing long-drawn-out battle, a case was taken to court. The civil rights forces lost their case, but gained an idea for a new approach. In his decision, the judge said in effect that the issue was a matter for legislative rather than judicial decision. A short time afterward, representatives of thirty-nine religious, labor, minority-group, and civic organizations formed the New York State Committee on Discrimination in Housing to fix attention on remedial legislation. In one decade, seven city and state laws, barring discrimination in an ever-widening segment of the housing market, were enacted. Starting in 1950, during the administration of Gov. Thomas E. Dewey, New York was the first state to pass, with bipartisan support, a comprehensive antibias housing law, specifically defining housing segregation as a form of discrimination and covering urban renewal. In a step-by-step program, the coverage of these open-occupancy laws and ordinances was extended in New York State to include all publicly assisted housing, including housing subject to FHA- and VA-insured mortgages.

Then in 1957, the nation's first law barring discrimination in private housing came into being when New York City adopted the pioneering bipartisan Sharkey-Brown-Isaacs Fair Housing Practices Law. This ordinance bars religious and racial discrimination in the rental or sale of all apartment houses and developments of ten or more dwellings in the city's five boroughs. As originally drawn, the ordinance provided that violations be punished by fines up to $500, but this aroused considerable protest and was dropped. I had urged and advocated that instead of criminal punishment we should rely upon the processes of mediation, conciliation, and technical assistance, backed up by the injunction power of the courts. What I sought to do was to substitute for a more drastic remedy—criminal prosecution, which is less likely to be effective because it is much less likely to be strictly enforced—a remedy that is less drastic and therefore more likely to be enforced—the civil injunction. This is now in the New York City law.

In 1958, Pittsburgh enacted an ordinance with even more extensive coverage than the New York City law, and in 1959 four states in the nation passed the first antibias laws covering private housing not governmentally assisted; the states were Colorado, Massachusetts, Connecticut, and Oregon.

In addition to these six laws covering housing, California, New Jersey, New York, and Washington prohibit discrimination in all publicly aided housing, including that with FHA- and VA-insured mortgages; Minnesota, Pennsylvania, and Wisconsin prohibit discrimination in public housing and in some that is publicly assisted; Indiana covers urban redevelopment housing; and Michigan and Rhode Island, public housing.

Skeptics would find it worth their while to examine the effects of any of these laws. New York City is a good example: its ordinance dealing with private housing has been in effect since April, 1958. None of the dire predictions of increased tensions, depreciation in property values, inundation of neighborhoods, has come to pass. On the contrary, the evidence shows that slow but steady progress in carrying out the purpose of the law is being made.

After the New York City law had been in operation for one year, the Institute for Motivational Research conducted a scientific study of the attitudes of real estate owners and managers toward the Fair Housing Practices Law. It found the law gaining acceptance in real estate circles.[39] The IMR is now studying the attitudes of tenants toward integrated housing.

From a representative sample of those who manage and operate 125,000 housing units in the city, the investigation showed that many real estate people are co-operating with the law; that the majority of them believe an open housing market is inevitable; and that there is a decided trend among younger leaders in the housing industry to regard restricted policies as "passé and unsophisticated."

Interesting, too, are the complaints that have been filed during the first year. The New York City Commission on Intergroup Relations (COIR), charged with administering the FHP law, has received complaints from persons of the Roman Catholic, Greek Orthodox, and Jewish faiths; from Chinese, Puerto Ricans, and Italians; and from Negro Americans. Sixty-seven per cent of the complainants were in the middle- and upper-income groups; 40 per cent were professional or business executives; and 61 per cent attended college at least one year. Dr. Frank S. Horne, executive director of the Commission on Intergroup Relations (COIR), reports that complainants have sought apartments in various sections of the city at rentals ranging up to the highest level. One of the complainants was listed in *Who's Who in America,* and some could be described as independently wealthy.

Complaints had been filed at the year's end against some two hundred real estate operators, and only one challenged the principle of the law. In this case, the owner of an apartment house in the Greenwich Village section of Manhattan filed a suit in the state Supreme Court asking a declaratory judgment to invalidate the law.[40] He lost an earlier plea before the court, requesting that a subpoena summoning him to a hearing before the COIR be vacated. COIR has jurisdiction over 70 per cent of the city's housing. In New York State, where present antibias laws cover only about 7 per cent of the total housing supply (but where Gov. Rockefeller supports a state law similar to the New York City ordinance), the State Commission Against Discrimination estimates that more than three thousand nonwhite families have obtained apartments in new government-aided developments alone since the law took effect in 1956.

Genuinely interracial developments are not as rare over the United States as many people seem to believe. About fifty projects, designed to be integrated, were privately built in the decade following World War II.[41] Madison, Wisconsin; Yellow Springs, Ohio; Minneapolis, Minnesota; Village Creek, Connecticut; Palo Alto, California; and Chicago, Illinois, are among the cities and towns where planned open-occupancy developments have been successfully built. One of the largest of these is Sunnyhills, a subdivision of some 1,500 homes sponsored by the United Auto Workers in Milpitas, California. Nonwhite families are scattered throughout the development, and represent about 10 per cent of Sunnyhills' residents. The houses range in price from $10,700 to $16,000 for a three-bedroom, one-and-one-half-bath dwelling.

Tenancy in Prairie Shores, Chicago's newest private open-occupancy community, has stabilized at about 77 per cent white with no imposition of quotas on tenant selection despite its location on the edge of a Negro ghetto, according to Ford Kramer of the mortgage and management firm of Draper & Kramer, Inc. The first of five nineteen-story buildings planned for the development is now fully occupied. Each contains 342 units. Renters run the economic gamut from Mr. Kramer himself, who sold his large North Shore residence to move into the new building, to a radio-TV repairman. Units rent for an average of $33 per room, although comparable housing in the Chicago area rents for $45 to $65.

"Nobody is trying to make a sociological point," says Mr. Kramer. "These people just recognized a hell of a good buy when they saw it." Most of the families, he said, came from areas where they had had little previous contact with nonwhites.

New York City's Stuyvesant Town is now an integrated community, and its spokesman before the Federal Commission on Civil Rights hearing in New York, Frank C. Lowe, vice president in charge of the Metropolitan Life Insurance Company's apartment developments, told the commissioners that no tenant problems have resulted from his company's policy of nondiscrimination.[42] "Many races, creeds, colors, and nationalities are living in our housing developments," Mr. Lowe reported.

Glenclift, a rental development of 316 units in San Diego, California, is a story of integration in reverse! In March, 1955, only one-third of this development was occupied, and all of its residents except two were Negro families. By the end of 1956, it was totally occupied, with the ratio one-third Negro and two-thirds white. This is a case where sound management and planning have paid off in profits—both economic and social.

A southern reverse to the problem was provided by Augusta, Georgia, where a group of 108 Negro property owners brought suit in July, 1959, to halt a $1.5 million urban renewal program because it would compel them to integrate with white persons. The suit denied that the area was blighted and contended that Negro residents "deserve to keep the area in which they live unintegrated and to retain their properties for members of the colored race who now own them and who have owned them from the time this area was developed as a residential area." The suit flatly declared: "Your petitioners do not desire to be integrated with members of the white race or to live among them."

In New York City, long before enactment of the Fair Housing Practices Law covering such buildings, two luxury apartment buildings had been operated on an open-occupancy basis for several years. Mrs. Deborah Miller took over management of a large Fifth Avenue apartment house about six years ago. From the beginning, Mrs. Miller made apartments available to qualified Negro families. Today the racial ratio is about one-third Negro, two-thirds white. No exodus of white families occurred, and turnover is small. The length of the waiting list of applicants—more white than Negro—for apartments speaks for itself. Mrs. Miller operates a similar luxury building on the West Side of Manhattan.

Many co-operative apartment houses in New York City have had an open-occupancy policy since they were built: ten-year-old Queensview, an award-winning development of about 1,000 units in which about 10 per cent of the residents are nonwhite; Kingsview in Brooklyn, with about 300 units and 10 per cent nonwhite occupancy; Morningside Gardens in the Columbia University area in Manhattan, a mammoth community surrounded by expanses of lawns and trees, with about 80 per cent white and 20 per cent nonwhite residents; the International Ladies' Garment Workers' East River Houses, with about fifty Negro families in its 1,670 units; Amalgamated Houses in the Bronx, sponsored by the Amalgamated Clothing Workers, where all applicants were asked: "Would you mind living next to a Negro family?" (The few who said Yes were rejected!); Electchester, a 2,226-apartment development of the International Brotherhood of Electrical Workers, with about fifty Japanese, Puerto Rican, Negro, and Chinese families; and scores of similar thoroughly integrated developments.

James H. Scheuer, chairman of the executive committee of City and Suburban Homes, Inc., one of the country's major development companies, is an example of the growing number of businessmen who follow an open-occupancy policy. "Discrimination is bad business," Mr. Scheuer told the Federal Commission on Civil Rights. "While I also happen to believe that it is morally wrong, I shall leave the moral argument to others. My argument rests on the dollars and cents impact of discrimination upon the cities and business community of America." [43]

This private-enterprise builder—with extensive operations in New York and residential developments under way or scheduled for Washington, D.C.; Cleveland, Ohio; St. Louis, Missouri; Sacramento and San Francisco, California; and San Juan, Puerto Rico—told the commissioners that his own experience with integration of thousands of units of housing has proved to be good business. Furthermore, he declared, without an open housing market, efforts to revitalize and restore the nation's cities will fail.

Across the continent, Eichler Homes, Inc., the largest housing developer on the West Coast, has been selling an open-occupancy basis since 1954. "We have a very simple philosophy about this," the company's vice president, Edward C. Eichler, told an audience in Des Moines, Iowa, "We simply sell houses to any person whom we feel will make a good neighbor—and this is without regard to race, color, or religion." Eichler Homes are in the $19,000 to $25,000 range. There has been no property devaluation, no social problems, no white exodus, and no nonwhite inundation.[44]

There is an interesting sidelight about the Eichler company. In 1958, the executive vice president of the Associated Home Builders of San Francisco told the press that it is "natural that a builder would protect himself and his investment" by discouraging nonwhites from buying in all-white neighborhoods. "It is a generally accepted theory that minority races depreciate property values," he declared. "There may be no statistics to prove it, but as the representative of home builders, it is the theory under which I operate."

At once, Joseph L. Eichler, president of Eichler Homes, and largest builder-member of the association, publicly resigned from the home builders organization. He was flooded with congratulatory letters and wires; he received none of condemnation. "The quality of your social approach to this problem reflects the straight-forward and clean engineering approach which your homes so eloquently display," wrote a San Francisco doctor.[45]

Another widely known builder of integrated housing developments, and one who builds and promotes them exclusively, is Morris Milgram of Philadelphia. The name "Concord Park" has become synonymous with good planning, good economics, and good human relations. This highly successful development of 139 units, located on a fifty-acre site on the outskirts of Philadelphia, is a thoroughly integrated community with a controlled occupancy pattern of 55 per cent white, and 45 per cent nonwhite. Following its completion, the same company built Greenbelt Knoll—nineteen contemporary homes of outstanding design situated on a handsome wooded site, selling from $19,000 to $25,000. This small community is occupied by one-third nonwhites, two-thirds whites. There followed the fifteen-house Glen Acres and the twenty-five-house Maplecrest near Princeton, New Jersey, with approximately the same racial pattern as Greenbelt Knoll.

Modern Community Developers, Inc., was a natural outgrowth of Mr. Milgram's philosophy, activities, and success in the interracial housing field. This unique corporation is the nation's first lending agency devoted exclusively to servicing builders of open-occupancy housing. In addition to lending money to qualified borrowers for that purpose, MCD will also provide the technical "know-how" under managerial contracts. With its program well under way, Modern Community Developers is not only making possible the establishment of integrated communities in New York, New Jersey, Connecticut, Pennsylvania, Iowa, Delaware, and Washington, it expects to make a profit for its stockholders as well.[46]

A host of religious, civic, labor, and civil rights organizations have gone on record in support of equal opportunity in housing.[47] Hundreds of community and neighborhood groups have formed voluntary associations to work in this field: stopping "block-busting" real estate operators; building good will when nonwhite residents move in; setting up listing services for seller and buyer in an effort to open up areas previously closed to nonwhites. Committees against discrimination in housing are organized in a score of states, counties, and towns. Generally these groups are widely representative and carry on vigorous programs of community education and support for fair housing laws. Standing at the center of these many and varied activities to democratize the nation's housing market is the National Committee Against Discrimination in Housing, which serves as the clearing house for information, assistance, and guidance. This single-purpose civil rights agency is composed of thirty national organizations dedicated to support open, competitive housing markets as a basic civil right. Organized in 1950, it has had a profound impact on the nation's common sense as well as its conscience.[48]

Although residential segregation in the United States is greater now than at any time in our history, the pressures against the barrier of race and creed are becoming increasingly irresistible. Nonwhites are not prepared to be the principal support of the secondhand housing market; nor will citizens long tolerate being hemmed into what are too often rat-infested slums. The growing number of middle-class Negro Americans will not accept denial of entry into desirable middle-income housing— city or suburb; no longer will the Jewish scholar be closed out of a suburb; no longer will the Puerto Rican lawyer accept the fate of raising his family in El Barrio. Neither will the Mexican-American businessman endure the dirt-floor shack by the railroad, nor the Oriental-American acquiesce in being assigned to a home in Chinatown. And no longer can our system of free enterprise sustain the injustice and the economic and social hazards of a restricted housing market.

Nowhere has the urgency for change been more highlighted than in the unanimous conclusions and recommendations of the

Commission on Race and Housing, as presented in *Where Shall We Live?*

Here are some of the things these leading business and professional men had to say:

The opportunity to compete for housing of one's choice is crucial to both equality and freedom. . . . Compulsory residential segregation is the basic inequality that underlies or stimulates other forms of discrimination. . . . Only government and law can be directly effective on a large scale in reducing or eliminating discriminatory practices. . . . Non-white entry into residential areas does not necessarily depress real estate market values.

The Commission's number one recommendation was that the president of the United States "establish a committee on the elimination of discrimination in federal housing and urban renewal programs." It goes on to recommend that state legislatures "follow the example of the several states which have enacted legislation prohibiting discrimination in housing." The Commission calls on builders, mortgage lenders, and real estate brokers to conform to the principle of a free housing market. And then it calls on the responsible citizens of our country, working through organizations dedicated to equal opportunity in housing, to continue and expand their programs.

"It is universal experience," declares the Commission, "that governmental bodies seldom move on controversial issues without strong sustained pressure from organized citizen groups who play the roles of advocate, goad, and watchdog."

Morality in housing is essential for the future of our nation—it is a good investment, too.

Chapter Nine

School Barriers

An increasing number of instances of racial and religious discrimination in education—especially college and graduate school education—developed in the period after World War I. In the 1920's and 1930's, college and professional school facilities were taxed to the limit by the number of applicants for admission. Many—though still very much a minority—were the sons and daughters of immigrant parents of moderate means; they came from the large metropolitan centers and generally differed sharply from the traditional college student stereotype of the turn of the century. Young people of Jewish, Italian, and Irish extraction particularly were attracted by the so-called "free" professions of law, medicine, and dentistry.

Soon such applicants became aware of subtle but widespread discriminatory practices secretly employed by educational institutions to keep them out. Quotas were set up privately to limit enrollment of Catholics and Jews, and even in northern states also to permit no more than a token admission of Negroes. Application blanks contained queries on religion, church affiliation, color, national origin, parents' country of birth, and mother's

167

maiden name. Psychological tests and oral personality interviews were among other devices used to limit such enrollment.[1]

Although no educators admitted publicly the use of a quota system, they attempted to justify it on a number of grounds including an alleged need to ensure a representative and diversified student body. In practice, this meant discrimination against students from New York, Chicago, Philadelphia, and other cities with large immigrant populations. Graduates from institutions like the College of the City of New York met with increasing difficulty in entering professional schools despite their high grades and level of competence.

Surveys of college discrimination consistently showed that Protestant applicants formed the highest percentage of those admitted, with Catholics and Jews following in that order.[2] In many instances, Jewish students were compelled to go abroad to complete their training in the professions. Within the colleges, the student body often reflected the discriminatory practices of their elders in student activities, social life, and fraternities.

In recent years all of these practices have diminished for a variety of reasons. Newspaper exposure of discriminatory practices, protest by civic, educational, and social welfare organizations, revealing studies by federal, state, local, and voluntary agencies—all have contributed to the change. In some schools, particularly state universities, fraternities have been abolished; in others, fraternity members themselves eliminated discrimination, often in direct opposition to the national policy of their fraternities.[3]

Hundreds of colleges throughout the United States have removed questions on race, creed, and color from their application forms. A series of judicial decisions, which are discussed later in this chapter, began to turn the tide beginning in 1936, but it took statutory law to really change the whole course of events.

A decisive impact was made by the states which created administrative agencies with power to receive and investigate complaints and settle them by conciliation wherever possible or by cease-and-desist orders where necessary. This again was the back-up of law to the processes of conciliation, mediation, and agitation, which has been the modern key to significant advance in equality of opportunity. New York passed the first Fair Education Practices Act, in 1948, with jurisdiction over business and trade schools as well as all college and professional schools. New Jersey and Massachusetts in 1949 and Washington in 1957 adopted similar legislation. In Idaho, Illinois, and Oregon, the laws against discrimination by educational institutions were limited to the prohibition of questions on, or refusal of admission by virtue of, race, color, and creed.[4] There is recurring concern, however, over the possible return of discriminatory practices when the anticipated avalanche of applications—expected to double enrollments in two decades, and far exceeding existing facilities—begins to hit the colleges in the decade of the sixties.

The increasing opportunity for Negro students in colleges and graduate schools has been significant in several respects. It has meant not merely better educational training for Negroes with the potentialities for leadership, but growing communication between whites and Negroes who are the future educators, professional men, and political leaders; and with it a community of interest and a better understanding of racial problems. It has meant, too, that inroads were being made in the solid front of the Deep South. Indeed, soon after the 1954 school segregation decisions, discussed below, the University of North Carolina admitted Negro students, and the University of Florida gave up its long battle to bar its graduate schools to Negroes. Today, only a hard core of four states—Alabama, Georgia, Mississippi, and South Carolina—can still accommodate entirely segregated graduate and professional schools.

The most telling blow against discrimination in education on all levels, however, was struck by the historic United States Supreme Court decision of May 1, 1954, in the *School Segregation Cases* relating to public elementary and secondary school education. Although the Negro in the South was the immediate beneficiary of this decision, its effects have been and will be felt on all levels of education everywhere.

Those who most violently oppose the Supreme Court's decision in the school segregation cases call for the Court to reverse itself and return to the "separate but equal" doctrine. They overlook or refuse to recognize the fact that the South as a whole would be worse off in its fight to prevent Negroes from attending formerly all-white schools under a strictly applied "separate but equal" doctrine than it is now under the Supreme Court's decision in the segregation cases. For the truth of the matter is that though the "separate" part of the formula was rigidly enforced, the "equal" was never adhered to, even under the limited concept of equality enunciated in *Plessy* v. *Ferguson*.[5]

Although this case had nothing to do with education, the principle of "separate but equal" was applied to the schools as well as to transportation, hotels and restaurants, and other services. The case concerned Homer Plessy, a colored man, who was arrested in Louisiana for refusing to ride in a "colored" railroad coach, as required by Louisiana law. He brought suit against Judge Ferguson, who was to preside at his trial, to have the law declared unconstitutional. The Supreme Court heard the case on appeal and upheld the Louisiana law on the ground that the requirement of separate coaches for whites and Negroes was a reasonable regulation by the state. This was the decision subsequently applied to other cases of racial discrimination.

Any analysis made of the segments going into the full educational picture, such as physical plants, per capita expenditure of funds, teacher qualifications, library facilities, textbooks, etc., shows that in total and in each of the components, the Negro student in the South was shortchanged generally—with some exceptions—from the very beginning of the public school system to the time of the 1954 decision of the Supreme Court.

Two recent studies give some idea of the wide discrepancies existing between the educational opportunities afforded white and colored public school students at widely different times before the school segregation decision. The first is a study of conditions in the southern states, particularly Virginia, North Carolina, South Carolina, and Georgia in the period 1901-15.[6] The second is concerned with the South in general in a more recent period, 1939-52.[7]

The studies show that some progress has been made. Improvement has not always followed a path of steady growth; it has depended on economic and other variable factors. In South Carolina, for example, in 1900 the expenditure for the education of a Negro child was one-sixth of the amount spent for a white child. By 1915, the colored child's share had shrunk to one-twelfth.[8]

Statistics for North Carolina in 1915 emphasize the denial of equal opportunity in education. Negro students attended school on an average of 67 days per year; white students, 133 days. The average annual salary of Negro teachers was $112.31; of white teachers, $383.39. Yearly expenditure per Negro pupil was $2.91; per white pupil, $23.76. Pupil load per teacher for Negroes was sixty-four; for whites, thirty-six. Value of school property per child in the grammar and secondary schools was $2.57 for Negroes, $32.11 for whites.[9]

Similar conditions prevailed in the other states surveyed. The general picture did not improve; as a matter of fact, it declined until the 1930 rise turned the trend.

In 1900, the expenditure for each Negro pupil in the southern states was about 50 per cent of that for the white child. This expenditure declined until 1930 when a gradual rise began. In 1931-32, the percentage stood at 29.6; in 1937-38, at 34.6; in 1945-46, at 55.8. In 1951-52, the expenditure per Negro student was estimated at three-fourths of that per white student.[10]

On the threshold of the Supreme Court's ruling, a colored student was receiving at best only 75 per cent of his "equal" share of school expenditures. And this had been given primarily as a result of lawsuits fought and won under the "separate but equal" doctrine, and under threat of suits attacking the doctrine itself.

Even had the southern states actually reached a 100 per cent parity in the expenditure of educational funds, they would not have been able, by the expenditure of such funds, to remedy almost a century of neglect of the Negro student, nor to replace the educational heritage of which the child and his forebears had been deprived.

Against this background of denial of equal educational opportunity Negro students and their parents began a series of court cases to make "separate but equal" a reality. But as the cases progressed, the plaintiffs came to realize that the task they had undertaken was impossible. They shifted their attack to the doctrine itself, recognizing long before the Supreme Court spoke that separation was in effect inequality.

In light of the recent decisions of the Supreme Court and other federal courts in the educational field, it is interesting to note that the first inroads on the *Plessy* v. *Ferguson* case were made by a state court, the Court of Appeals of Maryland, in the case of *Pearson* v. *Murray* in 1936.[11] The plaintiff, Donald Murray, a Negro, sought to enter the law school of the University of Maryland. He was refused admission because of the laws requiring racial segregation, but was offered a tuition scholarship to study law outside the state. The Maryland high court held that the scholarship program was inadequate to meet the requirement of equality under the Fourteenth Amendment and ordered the university to admit Murray. Thus he became the first Negro to be admitted to a publicly supported "white" school on the basis of a court order in a state with laws requiring racial segregation in public education. Subsequent developments make it significant to point out that Murray was represented by a young Baltimore lawyer named Thurgood Marshall, the man who led the fight before the Supreme Court in the 1950's against school segregation.

Two years later the Supreme Court, in *Missouri* ex rel. *Gaines* v. *Canada,* reached a conclusion similar to that of the Maryland court.[12] It ordered a Negro applicant named Lloyd Gaines to be admitted to the law school at the state university, holding that the out-of-state scholarship offered him did not meet the test of "equality." In this case, the Supreme Court began considering for the first time the intangible factors affecting a student's education, such as the peculiar nature of the curriculum, the prestige of the school, and so forth.

Twelve years after the Gaines case, in 1950, the Supreme Court had two other cases which materially affected the "separate but equal" doctrine in education. On one day it decided a case from Oklahoma and one from Texas, which were to further define and expand the concept of educational equality.

In the Oklahoma case, the Court held that once admitted to the state university system, a student could not be segregated within the school. The graduate school of the University of Oklahoma had admitted G. W. McLaurin on the basis of a previous *per curiam* decision of the Supreme Court ordering the admission of a Negro student to the state university where the state did not provide the required education elsewhere.[13] The school authorities had, however, attempted to completely segregate McLaurin from other students by assigning him to a special seat in the classroom, a special desk in the library, and a special table in the cafeteria. Once again the Supreme Court considered the "intangibles" in striking down these practices as unconstitutional because "such restrictions impair and inhibit his ability to study, to engage in discussion and exchange views with other students, and in general, to learn his profession." [14]

The other case was *Sweatt* v. *Painter,* in which the Court ordered the University of Texas to admit a Negro applicant to its law school, notwithstanding the establishment of a separate law school for Negroes by the state.[15] In arriving at its decision that the "separate" school was not the equivalent of the state university, the Court considered library facilities, size and quality of the faculty, accreditation, courses and related activities available to the students, and "those qualities which are incapable of objective measurement but which make for greatness in law schools." [16]

This line of decision by the Supreme Court, and its decisions affecting discrimination in areas other than education as well as recognition of the tremendous inequalities still existing after a half century of "equality" with separation under the *Plessy* v. *Ferguson* rule, prompted the men who were finally responsible for the strategy of the legal attack on the Plessy rule itself. This decision was said to have been made at a 1945 meeting of one hundred NAACP leaders, mostly lawyers.[17]

On May 16, 1950, in the federal court in Charleston, South Carolina, a suit was filed on behalf of sixty-seven Negro children and parents of Clarendon County, asking that the children be admitted to the public school system of the county without regard to race. The trial judge decided that this was a case attacking the constitutionality of state laws requiring segregation and referred it to a three-judge federal court. Thus began the direct constitutional attack on public school segregation.

On June 21, 1951, the court, in a 2 to 1 decision, upheld the "separate but equal" doctrine, but required school officials to report to the court after six months on progress toward equalization of the dual school systems. The plaintiffs, through Thurgood Marshall and other NAACP lawyers representing them, appealed to the United States Supreme Court. The Supreme Court sent the case back to the lower court for further proceedings. Once again the three-judge court refused to rule on the integration issue and based its decision on the "separate but equal" doctrine. Again, on May 10, 1952, the NAACP attorneys appealed to the Supreme Court.

In the meantime, four other cases based on the theory of the Clarendon County case were filed at widely scattered spots. In Washington, D.C., Topeka, Kansas, Wilmington, Delaware, and Prince Edward County, Virginia, Negro children and their parents filed suit to require admission of Negro applicants to "white" schools. They took the joint name before the Supreme Court from the suit brought by Oliver Brown of Topeka, Kansas, against the local Board of Education to require it to admit his eight-year-old daughter to the public school nearest his home instead of the much more distant "colored" school. It was the first of the four cases to reach the docket of the Supreme Court, hence the name for all: *Brown* v. *Board of Education*. The Washington, D.C., case was the only one not handled by NAACP lawyers. It differed in that the remedy sought was asked under the "due process" clause of the Fifth Amendment rather than the "equal protection" clause of the Fourteenth because segregation in the District of Columbia was under federal control.

All four cases were considered by the Supreme Court at the same time, and on June 8, 1953, the Court proposed five specific questions relating to the constitutionality of school segregation under the Fourteenth Amendment and the method of eliminating it if it were unconstitutional. The United States Department of Justice, which had filed a brief *amicus curiae* on the side of the students, was asked to participate in the arguments. The reargument took place exactly one year after the original argument, on December 8 and 9, 1953.

On May 17, 1954, the Supreme Court rendered its decision in the school segregation cases, *Brown* v. *Board of Education*.[18] In it the Court held

that in the field of public education the doctrine of "separate but equal" has no place. Separate educational facilities are inherently unequal. Therefore, we hold that the plaintiffs and others similarly situated . . . are, by reason of the segregation complained of, deprived of the equal protection of the laws guaranteed by the Fourteenth Amendment.

The decision was unanimous. This fact is itself a potent answer to the alarums later raised against the decision in some quarters in the South.

In the companion case from the District of Columbia, the Court ruled that racial segregation in the schools of the District violated the due process clause of the Fifth Amendment.[19] And a year later, on May 31, 1955, the Court filed its historic opinion instructing federal district courts

to take such proceedings and enter such orders and decrees consistent with this opinion as are necessary and proper to admit to public schools on a racially nondiscriminatory basis with all deliberate speed the parties to these cases.[20]

It is this phrase—this formula—"with all deliberate speed" which is the most portentous in the whole history of segregation following the Civil War.

At the time of the school segregation decision seventeen states and the District of Columbia required racially segregated public education, and four other states permitted it. The former were Alabama, Arkansas, Delaware, Florida, Georgia, Kentucky, Louisiana, Maryland, Mississippi, Missouri, North Carolina,

Oklahoma, South Carolina, Tennessee, Texas, Virginia, and West Virginia. The latter were Arizona, Kansas, New Mexico, and Wyoming. In the seventeen states requiring segregation, the Supreme Court's decision affected approximately ten million white, and two and a half million colored children attending public schools.

The District of Columbia and most of the "border" states at once took action to integrate their schools without even awaiting the Supreme Court's final decree. For Arizona, Kansas, and New Mexico, compliance with the decision also was not long delayed because integration in varying degrees had existed in those states for a number of years. Moreover, in the year between the Supreme Court decisions of May 17, 1954, and May 31, 1955, desegregation was begun in five states for the first time—Delaware, Maryland, West Virginia, Missouri, and Arkansas.

In thirteen communities of Delaware, including Dover, the capital, and Wilmington, the largest city, the schools were integrated without incident. The fourteenth community, Milford, was forced by pressure from segregation forces to reverse its decision to commence desegregation.

Baltimore, Maryland, with a school population of over 140,-000, integrated its entire system with the opening of the 1954-55 school year. Only one incident occurred, and it was quickly suppressed. The Baltimore situation is unique because it permits a student to transfer to any school in the city if it is not crowded. This affords students ample opportunity to attend any school they choose without facing racial restrictions.

With the opening of the September school term in 1954, out of fifty-five counties in West Virginia twelve completely desegregated, and seventeen did so on a partial basis. Eleven other counties had no colored students.

St. Louis, Missouri, at midyear following the 1954 decision, desegregated nine high schools, merged two teacher-training institutes, and integrated all of its school personnel in these institutions. Twenty-nine other communities in Missouri also acted promptly and integrated eighty-nine high schools and forty-one elementary schools without incident within the first year.

Arkansas became the first Deep South state to integrate any school. As early as September, 1954, the high schools in Fayetteville and Charleston, Arkansas, accepted Negro students. At the end of the first year, nearly 250,000 colored and white children were attending some five hundred public elementary and high schools together, for the first time.

The principal lesson of the first year was that desegregation was best accomplished where the authorities took a firm position on the side of law, made that position clear, and used all available legal means to support their position. Thus, in Washington, D.C., and Baltimore, authorities quickly squelched the opposition spearheaded by the National Association for the Advancement of White People, a racist organization headed by Bryant Bowles, an agitator who was later convicted of murder. But Bowles was successful in attempts to upset school desegregation in Milford, Delaware, where local authorities vacillated and reversed their decision to comply with the Supreme Court's order. Similar vacillation marked the experience of White Sulphur Springs, West Virginia. After several days of integrated operation, its School Board, threatened by violence and a student strike, rescinded its action and reinstituted segregation in its schools. It took a year and a half, and a court order, to reverse the Board once again. This time the desegregated schools operated peaceably.

In another West Virginia town, resistance was met in an entirely different manner. Parents picketed an integrated school in Four States, resulting in teachers leaving the school. School authorities sought an injunction to end the interference with the desegregation program, and in issuing such an injunction, Marion County Judge J. Harper Meredith commented: "It cannot continue and I won't permit it to continue. If necessary, I'll fill the jail until their feet are sticking out of the windows." [21]

Desegregation proceeded smoothly thereafter. Because of its importance as the capital of the nation and of the free world and because it was involved in one of the cases brought to the Supreme Court, Washington, D.C., and its desegregation program are discussed in a separate chapter.

In contrast to this striking progress, the first year of desegregation also saw the beginning of organized opposition. Two closely related factors contributed to its development. One was the White Citizens Councils and similar white supremacy groups. The other was the decision of the majority of southern politicians to cast their lot with the segregation forces to the bitter end. The first White Citizens Council was organized at Indianola, Mississippi, on July 11, 1954; others were rapidly organized throughout the South. By November, 1956, membership in the Councils and other pro-segregation organizations was reported by the Southern Regional Council to be in excess of 315,000.

The purpose of the Councils was to exert pressure, social, political and most of all, economic, against all citizens, colored or white, who supported the principle of equality of opportunity as interpreted by the Supreme Court. While publicly eschewing violence, the Councils created an atmosphere in which violence was comprehensible. Pulitzer Prize-winner Hodding Carter, editor of the Greenville, Mississippi, *Delta Democrat-Times,* in viewing the activities of the Councils, wrote an article entitled, "A Wave of Terror Threatens the South," published in *Look,* March 22, 1955. His fears have been unhappily verified by subsequent events.

The first reaction among most public officials in the South to the Supreme Court's decision was one of dutiful, if reluctant, acceptance. There were, of course, exceptions. However, as the voices of the White Citizens Councils and other forces of opposition grew louder, the attitude of most public officials shifted —shifted all the way from disapproval to defiance. The most authoritative defiance came from 100 senators and representatives who signed a document urging resistance to the Supreme Court decision, but by "any lawful means," and filed it in the Congress of the United States. This "Southern Manifesto," introduced by the dean of southerners in the Congress, the late Senator Walter George of Georgia, on March 12, 1956, declared in part:

The unwarranted decision of the Supreme Court in the public school cases is now bearing the fruit always produced when men substitute naked power for established law. . . . We regard the decision of the Supreme Court as a clear abuse of judicial power. . . . We decry the Supreme Court's encroachments on rights reserved to the states and to the people. . . . We commend the motives of those states which have declared the intention to resist forced integration by any lawful means. . . .

The signers of the Manifesto, like the spokesmen of the White Citizens Councils, denied that they sought to encourage violence, but the reaction of the extreme segregationists was to resist integration by every means, not just "lawful means." This reaction is explained by a statement of a young lawyer of Clinton, Tennessee, commenting on the riots occurring in that community: "What the hell do you expect these people to do when they have 90-some-odd Congressmen from the South signing a piece of paper that says you're a Southern hero if you defy the Supreme Court?" [22]

Two forces were in motion—the orderly processes of law seeking to apply the Supreme Court's decision and the organized resistance to it. These forces clashed in every state affected by the decision, and the results have largely determined the progress of desegregation—or lack of progress. The results emphasize the need for congressional recognition of the Supreme Court decision and the implementing back-up of statutes enacted by the Congress to make the decision a reality. Briefly, here is what happened in each state:

Alabama is one of the four states that have resisted integration on all levels of public education, with the exception only of the temporary attendance of Miss Autherine Lucy at the University of Alabama in February, 1956. The Lucy case is a good example of the mythology of "outside interference" so often heard in the struggle against segregation. According to this mythology, Miss Lucy was hired by the NAACP to apply for admission to the state university even though she had no interest in a college career; and it was further suggested that she had been chosen for this purpose to embarrass the late Senator Walter George, Senate spokesman for "the South," whose wife was affectionately referred to as "Miss Lucy."

As a matter of fact, it was reported that the NAACP knew nothing of Miss Lucy's application for admission; that she had applied by mail and the university had enrolled her as a matter of routine. When she appeared for classes, she was told her admission was a mistake, as the university did not accept Negroes. She went to the NAACP for legal assistance and a federal court order admitted her to the university in February, 1956. Some university students and persons—allegedly pro-segregationist advocates—from the adjoining area rioted for three days, with the result that university officials again excluded her. Subsequently, she was expelled for statements made in a legal document submitted to a federal court on her behalf, and though litigation followed, she was never readmitted.

Several cases are now pending in the federal courts seeking

admission of colored students to Alabama schools, but none of the children has so far gained entrance. One of the difficulties is presented by a state pupil-placement law which has been found constitutional on its face by the federal courts. It will be necessary to prove by experience that the law is discriminatory in its application and is administered to block public school desegregation.

The second factor slowing down the desegregation process in Alabama is the exclusion of the NAACP from the state since June, 1956, by a court order. The Association was enjoined from operating, and fined $100,000 for refusing to produce its membership records. Although the Supreme Court has twice reviewed the action of the state court and held the Association justified in refusing to disclose its members, neither the fine nor the injunction have yet been set aside by the state court. As a consequence, many persons who would normally look to the NAACP for legal assistance have not been able to institute legal proceedings to secure school desegregation plans.

Arkansas for a while appeared to be the state that would show the Deep South the way out of the darkness of segregation in public education. Arkansas boasted quietly and justifiably that it was the only state in the Deep South to admit colored students to the state university without a lawsuit and the only one to begin desegregation voluntarily, following the 1954 Brown case decision.

In the little town of Hoxie, the state could point to the most significant victory in the whole desegregation story, not only in terms of law enforcement but in terms of "changing the hearts and minds of men." So far, no community that has desegregated its schools has overcome the obstacles faced by Hoxie. Located in a section of the state known as "Little Dixie," with a community climate described as being more Mississippian than

Arkansan, Hoxie nevertheless decided through its school officials to proceed voluntarily with desegregation. This decision was based, at least partially, on the belief of School Board members that it was the moral thing to do. One long-time resident of the state who participated in the legal proceedings made necessary by the School Board's decision said: "If integration can work in Hoxie, it can work anywhere in the South."

Work it did, though not without difficulties. Chief of these was a protest movement organized by a group called White America, Inc., assisted by White Citizens Councils from neighboring Mississippi. The disturbances caused as a result of activities of these groups forced the schools to close for three weeks early in August, 1955. (Some Arkansas schools have terms based on the harvesting season.) This challenge was met by the School Board's application to the federal courts for an injunction against those interfering with operation of the schools. The injunction was granted and upheld after a long course of litigation in which the United States Department of Justice intervened to support the School Board. Hoxie has since continued operating its schools on a desegregated basis without any further serious interference. This again emphasizes that if public officials, determined to enforce law, are given adequate legal tools to do the job, they can overcome overt manifestations of racial prejudice even in a public atmosphere normally hostile to desegregation.

A few other school districts slowly followed the example of Hoxie, Fayetteville, and Charleston, and by September, 1957, eight had desegregated. Then came Little Rock.

The Little Rock School Board had drafted a seven-year plan of desegregation which would begin at the high school level in September, 1957. The plan had been announced two years previously and had been upheld in the federal courts in a suit brought by colored parents who considered it too gradual. The plan had been locally initiated, without any proceedings in the federal courts as there had been in other communities.

Several attempts were made to block integration by court actions in which Governor Orval E. Faubus participated, but they were unsuccessful. Then, the evening before the school desegregation plan was to go into effect, Governor Faubus ordered out the National Guard under the allegation of threatened disorders. Impartial observers, however, as well as the mayor and chief of police of Little Rock, denied that such threats existed. On September 4, with the whole world looking on, the National Guard turned back the nine colored children who had been enrolled at Little Rock's Central High School.

The attorney general of the United States, at the invitation of Federal Judge Ronald M. Davies, entered the case, which by this time had attracted international attention. The world's spotlight turned on Washington, D.C., where President Eisenhower had summoned Governor Faubus on September 14 in an attempt to solve the crisis, which proved unsuccessful. Six days later, Judge Davies issued an injunction restraining Governor Faubus from using the National Guard to prevent the colored children from attending Central High.

Violence and organized opposition then developed in Little Rock, where it had not previously existed. The National Guard was abruptly withdrawn, and for all practical purposes the mob was allowed to take over.

Local authorities appealed to President Eisenhower, and the President ordered federal troops into the city to prevent obstruction of the court's orders. For the rest of the year, colored students attended Central High under the protection of these troops, and later, of the National Guard, which was by then inducted into federal service.

During the school's summer recess of 1958, the Little Rock School Board received a two-and-a-half-year delay in integration from Federal Judge Harry Lemley. His decision was appealed, and its reversal by the Circuit Court was upheld by the Supreme Court, meeting in a rare special summer session. After this decision, the four Little Rock public high schools were closed pursuant to a newly enacted Arkansas law, and remained shut during the entire term 1957-58. Some students were provided with makeshift courses at hastily organized "private" schools; others went to other communities; schooling for the remainder was not provided at all. This law was held unconstitutional in June, 1958, by a federal court.

By this time Little Rock was beginning to react sharply to the experience of closed public schools. Citizens' groups were organized to save the school system and to prevent a threatened "purge" of teachers. A few ministers working quietly and without publicity lest they find themselves displaced from their pulpits—as at least nine were—found ways to support the forces of law and order.[23] Businessmen, feeling the pinch caused by the reluctance of industry to settle or expand in a troubled area, were increasingly reconciled to the necessity for school desegregation. As a result, a plan supported by Governor Faubus to continue segregation backfired.

An election to replace six School Board members was conducted in Little Rock in May, 1959, and three pro-Faubus members were recalled, but three anti-Faubus members were kept in office. The action of the Governor's School Board in firing teachers accused of accepting desegregation had roused the community to action, and it defeated for election the die-hard segregationists on the Board. The newly constituted School Board, while also not favorable to desegregation, was willing to abide by court decrees rather than close the schools. This election paved the way for the reopening of Little Rock's high schools in August, 1959, with colored students attending two of the schools on a desegregated basis.

An interesting footnote was the failure of the T. J. Raney High School to reopen because of financial difficulties. This was perhaps the most widely publicized of the South's "private" schools organized to replace the public school system. With its failure probably died any hope that this type of school could attract mass enrollment to avoid integration in the public school system.

In *Delaware* progress has been slow. At the end of the 1958-59 school year, seventeen school districts were recorded as having desegregated schools, a gain of only four since 1954. Some districts have, however, increased the degree of desegregation within their own systems. Moreover, a series of lawsuits was instituted to speed up desegregation, and as a result the State Board of Education has assumed responsibility for submitting a state-wide school plan. In accordance with a federal court order, the State Board instituted a "grade-a-year" plan in the state's thirty-nine districts, beginning with the fall term of 1959 and extending over twelve years. Colored parents are likely to appeal the decision approving this plan because they believe it fails to conform with the Supreme Court's requirement of "deliberate speed."

In *Florida,* Virgil Hawkins won a nine-year legal fight in June, 1958, when a federal district court ordered the state to admit qualified Negroes to its graduate schools. Mr. Hawkins had been seeking admission to the law school of the Florida State University. He became the first Negro to be admitted on a desegregated basis to any level of education in Florida. In September, 1959, however, the Dade County School Board began an experiment in desegregation in a Miami school, but it was short-lived.

Georgia is another of the four states that still resist all attempts to desegregate their public schools. It appears, however, that a break-through may occur in Atlanta, where a federal court order has been issued instructing the city to present a desegregation plan within a "reasonable" time. Mayor William B. Hartsfield and other public officials have shown willingness to accept desegregation as required by the courts, but they still have to overcome the obstacle of state legislation requiring schools to close if ordered to admit students of different races.

In *Kentucky,* the course of desegregation has been marked by a steady increase in the number of colored students attending former "white" schools. The story can perhaps best be told by the statistics. A lone Negro student was admitted to a summer-school class in Lexington in June, 1955, and since then the number of colored students in "integrated situations" has increased, term by term, until 31,768 out of 41,793 colored students were attending desegregated public schools at the close of the 1958-59 school term.

(The term "integrated situation" is used by *Southern School News* to describe Negro student attendance at a school where there is some degree of integration. When applied to a school district it indicates that an official program of school desegregation has been instituted. The *Southern School News* is a monthly publication established by newspaper editors and educators to report objectively on educational developments in the South. It is considered the most authoritative source for such information. The statistics used here are generally from *Southern School News*.)

Ten Kentucky counties and four large cities emulated Lexington and instituted limited desegregation in the fall of 1955. This involved twenty-four of the state's 224 school districts. With the opening of the 1956-57 term, Louisville, the state's largest city, and all but fifteen of the state's 120 counties began some degree of desegregation. This process continued until 80 per cent of the state's Negro school population were in desegregated school districts by the end of the 1958-59 term.

Desegregation in Louisville affected some 40,000 white and 12,000 colored students in the elementary grades. Louisville school authorities have been highly commended for their preparations and the smoothness of the operation. Once again the completeness of the program was undoubtedly a factor in its success. This progress was speeded up by the insistence of Negro parents and children that their rights be granted, through lawsuits if necessary. At least seven court orders were issued requiring Kentucky school boards to initiate or accelerate desegregation.

Progress made was not without interruptions caused by protests and disturbances. It is to the credit of Kentucky's educational and governmental leaders that these incidents caused no more than temporary interruptions in the carrying out of their school programs.

In the towns of Sturgis and Clay, riots occurred in September, 1956, because of school desegregation, and it was necessary to call out the National Guard to protect the children attending school. In September, 1956, in Henderson County, two attempted boycotts of desegregated schools failed shortly after their initiation. In the midst of the disturbances, the colored children were returned to segregated schools on the basis of a ruling by the state attorney general that their enrollment had been technically illegal.

The following September, colored children returned to the Sturgis schools pursuant to a federal court order. Minor disturbances occurred but ended shortly, and the children continued their schooling without further interruption.

Louisiana has not as yet admitted any colored students to

public schools below the college level on a desegregated basis. Orleans Parish (New Orleans) was ordered by a federal court to submit a school desegregation plan by March 1, 1960. When no satisfactory plan was submitted, the court ordered that desegregation begin in the first grade in September, 1960. One of the unfortunate aspects of the resistance to the Supreme Court's decision in Louisiana was that the state attempted to reverse its policy of admitting colored students to its state-supported colleges. Louisiana State University and other state schools of higher learning had admitted colored students since 1950, in accordance with court decrees obtained by colored students seeking admission.

In 1956, the state adopted legislation requiring any applicant to a state-supported college to have a certificate of scholastic eligibility from his high school principal and school district superintendent. Another statute adopted at the same time provided for the dismissal of any school official who contributed to integration. These laws were ruled unconstitutional the following year by a federal court. In the meantime, however, they caused a sharp decline in the number of Negroes registered for college courses.

Maryland is another state which has moved steadily toward compliance with the Supreme Court's school decision. After the total desegregation of the Baltimore school system, counties throughout the state began their programs of desegregation. By the end of the 1956-57 school term, a total of thirteen of the state's twenty-two counties with colored students had some mixed classes. With the opening of the 1959-60 term, every county in the state was operating its schools under a desegregation program.

Mississippi has been by far the most stubborn in all ways in its resistance to any type of school desegregation. As a result, it is the only state which has not begun desegregation and which does not have any of its school districts under a court order to do so.

Missouri moved rapidly to complete the job of complying with the Supreme Court's decision after an auspicious beginning in February, 1955. With the opening of the term in September, St. Louis and Kansas City, the two largest cities, desegregated their schools in all grades. At the same time, the State Commissioner of Education announced that 52,800 of the state's 66,000 colored students would be in schools in which segregation had ended.[24] By June, 1959, all of the state's schools had been substantially desegregated except some in one or two counties in the southeast section of the state.

North Carolina has theoretically accepted the decision of the Supreme Court, but has avoided any large degree of compliance by a program of "token integration." Using a pupil-placement plan which the federal courts have held valid on its face, school desegregation has been at a minimum.

In the fall of 1957, twelve colored students were accepted in the cities of Greensboro, Charlotte, and Winston-Salem, in previously all-white schools. By the end of the 1958-59 school year only four of the state's 174 school districts had begun to desegregate. Colored parents, with the assistance of the NAACP, have filed several lawsuits to speed up the school desegregation process in North Carolina.

Oklahoma's official policy has been one of compliance with the Supreme Court's decision. Oklahoma was the first state in the South to take positive action to speed up the process of desegregation of its schools. It did this by adopting a fiscal policy that penalized school districts maintaining segregated schools.

As a consequence of the state's position, rapid progress has been made. In the first year of compliance, 1955-56, Oklahoma City, Tulsa, and eighty-six other districts desegregated. In the following year, 182 districts reported mixed classes, and by the end of the 1958-59 term, 238 districts were reported as desegregated. (Reduction of school districts by consolidation reduced this number to 186 out of 250 bi-racial districts.)

No serious disorders have resulted from the state's policy.

South Carolina is the last of the four states maintaining a policy of total segregation. On April 16, 1959, Rev. I. DeQuincy Newman, a Negro leader of this state, testified before the Senate Subcommittee on Constitutional Rights that it was impossible for a colored person to secure a medical education in South Carolina. Many had, therefore, left the state and qualified elsewhere.

More than twenty years after the Gaines decision requiring the admission of colored applicants to professional schools within their state of residence, South Carolina still refuses to comply. This weakens the argument of those who say that the South will work out its desegregation problem if it is not "hurried."

Tennessee is moving painfully and slowly to comply with the Court's decision.

Oak Ridge, then under the federal government's control, was the first community to institute mixed classes in its schools, which it did in September, 1955. It took a federal court order in Anderson County, however, to compel the School Board to enroll twelve Negro students in the high school at Clinton a year later. There followed a period of rioting with John Kasper, leader of a White Citizens Council group, prominently on the scene. In order to continue operation of the schools, it was necessary to call out the state police and the National Guard. Subsequently, in October, 1958, Clinton High School was partially demolished by a dynamite explosion.

In the fall of 1957, Nashville began a "stair step" class-a-year program of desegregation with its first grade. This plan is under attack in the courts as being too gradual. Nashville also was shaken by a school dynamiting when one of the newly integrated schools was severely damaged. No other school districts have desegregated or given any indication of doing so.

The Tennessee experiences indicate that when only a few schools comply with the Supreme Court's decision they become symbols and attract the wrath of the racial hate groups. They thus become vulnerable to the type of violence that has been visited on the schools of Clinton and Nashville. It appears significant that the only school district to escape this violence has been the one under control of the federal government.

In *Texas* desegregation began with the fall term of 1955, when about sixty school districts in the south and west of the state desegregated classes on various levels of the elementary-secondary school system. This was reported as affecting some 1,650 Negro students. The next year the number of districts increased to over one hundred, but slowed considerably in succeeding years. Thus for the 1959-60 school year only 125 of the state's 720 bi-racial districts had any degree of desegregation. Progress was slowed primarily by legislation aimed at blocking desegregation, especially a statute requiring voter approval before a school district could initiate desegregation. This is under court attack, but no final ruling on it has been made despite its apparent lack of constitutional justification.

The larger cities in the state have shown a strong reluctance to begin desegregation. Houston (which operates the largest segregated school system in the nation) and Dallas have yet to admit a colored student in compliance with court orders to proceed to a desegregation plan "with all deliberate speed." The orders were issued to the Houston School Board in October, 1957, and to Dallas in January, 1958.

A most notorious case of continued segregation notwithstanding court orders occurred in Mansfield in September, 1956.

Colored students, who had been ordered by a federal court to be admitted to a high school in that city, were prevented from enrolling by a mob of several hundred. Governor Allan Shivers called out the state rangers and reportedly refused to let Negroes enter; then school authorities were caused to transfer the colored students to another school district, thereby in effect nullifying the court order.

Virginia gave early indications of a "moderate" approach to the Supreme Court's ruling in the Brown case. A commission appointed by the governor, the so-called "Gray Commission," made recommendations that would allow communities within the state to proceed on a "local option" basis. Cities like Norfolk, Arlington, and Alexandria were said to be prepared to comply with the Supreme Court's decision. But this moderate approach was reversed as Virginia assumed the role of "leadership" in the fight against desegregation and devised a program of "massive resistance," based on the abandonment of public education, which was slated to become a model for the South. The resources and powers of the state were to be mobilized to support a program of resistance. The program included laws providing for pupil placement and tuition grants in "private" schools, and repeal of the commonwealth's compulsory school attendance law. Children shut off from the public school system attended makeshift classes in church basements, stores, and office buildings, transferred to other communities, or went without education. In northern Virginia over two hundred students under sixteen years of age dropped out of school altogether.

The Virginia legislators had no illusions about the constitutionality of the laws they passed to seek to prevent school desegregation. But, under state court decisions, many statutes stayed in effect long enough to achieve, at least in part, their desired effect.

State and federal courts began to condemn the school-closing laws early in 1959, and Virginia's "massive resistance" program disintegrated. The slogan then became "token integration" as state officials retreated to a prepared second line of defense; pupil-placement schemes, it was thought, could prolong even the transition to "token desegregation" over periods of twelve years or more.

Certainly, the abandonment of massive resistance was significant. Virginians had decided, after painful experience, that the cessation of public education was too high a price to pay for retaining segregation, and this decision helped to clear the air. In February, 1959, seven schools opened on a desegregated basis, and others followed soon after. However, Prince Edward County announced that it was abandoning its public school system rather than begin desegregation as ordered by a federal court in September, 1959. The struggle was far from over.

In most Virginia communities, the school closings had a profound effect on preparing the climate for public acceptance of desegregation. Therefore, when the schools reopened, the communities were ready to comply with court orders.

One exception was Front Royal, where the beautiful new high school finished out the year with only 21 colored boys and girls as the entire student body, while over 1,000 white students crowded into a school conducted in a union hall and financed by a local textile union. After long negotiation, however, a plan was worked out to permit the opening of this school on a regular, desegregated basis in September, 1959. Enrollment totaled 20 colored and 417 white students, with about the same number of white students still attending the private school.

How much damage was done in Virginia by the year-long closing will never be fully estimated. Many of those who dropped out of school altogether may never return to complete their education. Others who would have been high school seniors have probably discovered how great are the difficulties in gaining admission to college. Some had to take additional courses at considerable expense in order to make up what they had lost. The school system itself lost many valuable teachers.

The changed public attitude had its political effects also. Governor J. Lindsay Almond, Jr., who had sponsored "massive resistance," now proposed a "moderate" program to the legislature. This was adopted by a one-vote margin, and among other provisions offered a local-option plan to take effect in March, 1960. Shortly thereafter a new legislature was elected in which the "moderates" retained control. Governor Almond is now satisfied that the South must allow "some integration," and informed a news conference to this effect in October, 1959, after being elected chairman of the Southern Governors' Conference.

After some initial difficulties, *West Virginia* moved rapidly to operate its schools in conformance with the Brown decision, so that by June, 1958, every county in the state was operating under a desegregation program.

Minority groups other than the Negro have also been subjected to discrimination and segregation in education because of their race. Mississippi, which limited attendance at "white" schools to persons of the Caucasian race, compelled Orientals and other students to attend "colored" schools. Georgia's definition of colored included those of "African, West Indian, Asiatic Indian and mestizo" descent. On the other hand, Oklahoma required students of African descent to attend "colored" schools, but classified all others as "white" for school purposes. The rest of the states requiring segregation provided for "white" and "colored" schools without further defining the terms. Apparently more specific definitions were left to administrative discretion.

Three states at the time of the Brown decision provided a tri-racial school system. Delaware, Mississippi, and North Carolina established separate schools for Indians in addition to those for white and colored pupils. In California, the last of the legal discriminations in education against Orientals was removed in 1947 when the law was repealed requiring separate schools for Chinese, Japanese, and Mongolians. Indians were also affected. California, Texas, and Arizona also required or permitted separate schools for children of Spanish-American descent. New Mexico, however, constitutionally prohibited school segregation of children of Spanish descent.[25]

The legal basis for segregation was destroyed by court decisions in California in 1947 and in Texas in 1948. Arizona schools practicing segregation voluntarily abandoned it by 1949. School segregation for Mexican-Americans now results rather from residential patterns, school district gerrymandering, and assignment to special schools because of language difficulties. The problem of segregation in effect resulting from residential patterns is familiar in northern and midwestern big cities too, but it is not, as in the South, a product of governmental creation but rather the result of personal bias and social custom which law and informed public opinion are seeking to correct.

In the whole area most directly affected by the Brown decision (the seventeen southern and border states), there are about 2,900 school districts with both white and colored students. At the end of the first school year following the final Brown case decision in 1955, 540 of these districts had begun to desegregate. By June, 1957, the number had risen to 684, and a year later, to 770. At the close of the 1958-59 school term, the number stood at 742. The decrease resulted from the consolidation of school districts and the migration of Negro students from desegregated districts. The total number of districts desegregated at one time or another in this period was 819. The job was but one quarter done.

What do these figures mean? For one thing, they show that after five years of school operation following the Brown decision, three-quarters of the school districts had not yet begun to comply. Even in the 25 per cent that have, the number of colored students integrated has generally been small. Moreover, the initiation of a desegregation program in no way guarantees all Negro students the right to attend desegregated schools. The gradual plans adopted by some communities (such as Delaware's one-class-a-year program), the segregated housing pattern, gerrymandering of school districts, and the reluctance of colored citizens to demand equal educational opportunity because of local pressures are all factors contributing to the small number of students actually attending classes with white students.

More significant than the total figure is the decreasing number of new desegregated school districts annually. Each year since the Supreme Court's decision, a smaller number of new districts has been operating schools on a desegregated basis. The reasons for this condition are many. Chief among them is the fact that seldom, if ever, in the history of this nation have so many pressures been put on one group of people—the colored citizens of the South—to deny their constitutional rights. These pressures have been of all kinds: legal, political, economic, social, and physical.

The chief tactic of delay has been simply to do nothing. In this way, four states have been able to maintain intact their racially segregated school systems. This puts the burden on each individual parent to enforce his child's constitutional rights by litigation. In order to do this, he must be prepared to take his case all the way to the Supreme Court, several times if necessary.

Litigation costs are high and estimates difficult because of the number of variables involved. The average cost to the plaintiff of a case fought from the District Court through the Court of Appeals to the Supreme Court, once, is estimated at $18,000 exclusive of counsel's fees. This estimate assumes that attorneys for the National Defense and Educational Fund of the NAACP, who are employed on an annual salary basis, would appear as counsel.

Any estimate of the cost of such litigation should also include a recognition that costs to the defending School Board will, in all probability, run to almost twice as much, or about double the average annual expenditure of $128.85 for educating the child in the entire twelve years of elementary and secondary school.[26]

By pleading difficult conditions, by enacting new legislation, and by other means, states have been able to avoid following the Brown decision for many years. An aggravated example is Clarendon County, South Carolina, which is not scheduled to begin its desegregation program until 1965 although it was one of the original defendants before the Supreme Court. The decision of the federal District Court which set this date may be reversed on appeal, but the appeal procedure itself may take a year or two. Since most of the children segregated in the South's schools come from families of very modest financial status, the task of engaging in long, drawn-out, and very expensive litigation is generally far beyond their means. Also, a number of southern states have enacted antibarratry and related statutes to make it more difficult for these parents to get any outside help to litigate. These are Arkansas, Georgia, Mississippi, South Carolina, Tennessee, and Virginia.

Another delaying tactic has been the adoption of legislation by the several states designed to avoid the effect of the Supreme Court desegregation decisions. When Senator Paul Douglas of Illinois introduced in the 85th Congress a civil rights bill, of which I was a co-sponsor, he submitted a memorandum listing over one hundred laws adopted in the South designed to avoid following Supreme Court decisions in school desegregation cases.[27] I also submitted to Congress a list of laws passed in the 1959 sessions of the legislatures of seven southern states, designed to withhold equal opportunity to colored citizens; twenty-five of them deal with public education.[28]

Although many of these laws have been declared unconstitutional, they nonetheless frustrate those who seek their constitutional rights for the time necessary to have the laws struck down; in some cases, it is years. It is becoming increasingly obvious that many southern lawmakers realize the inevitability of school desegregation, but are fighting a delaying action.

Typical of these unconstitutional laws were the school-closing laws of Virginia and Arkansas, both struck down by the courts. But while they were in operation they caused 16,300 students in the two states to lose 1,890,000 pupil-days of education, according to the figures of the United States commissioner of education.

Despite this tragic experience, other southern states are ready to enforce laws requiring a total or partial closing of their public education systems. Some states have made it a criminal offense to obey the mandate of the Constitution as found in the Brown case. Georgia, for instance, has made it a felony, punishable by two years' imprisonment, for any school official to spend tax money for desegregated public schools. Mississippi has made it a criminal offense for white students to attend school with colored students in tax-supported schools. Other laws have been enacted to prevent communities within a state from adopting plans for desegregation. Georgia has charged its state police with the duty of entering any county or municipality to prevent school integration. This is obviously aimed at the city of Atlanta, whose public officials have indicated a willingness to conduct their schools in accordance with the dictates of the federal Constitution.

Besides making it more difficult, by restrictive legislation, for colored citizens to obtain their rights, some states have sought further to limit them by attacking the NAACP because it has been one of the chief aids to desegregation suits brought by Negro parents. Legislation was enacted in six states designed to prevent the NAACP from rendering legal or financial assistance in desegregation cases, and in some states, from functioning at all. Even expressions of opinion favorable to desegregation have been inhibited in some southern states by legislative investigations, registration statutes, loyalty oaths, and sanctions against teachers and other state employees.

Two states, South Carolina and Arkansas, passed laws prohibiting members of the NAACP from holding public employment. When it became obvious that the Supreme Court would rule such legislation unconstitutional, South Carolina repealed its law. It passed another statute, however, to obtain the same results by requiring all persons publicly employed to reveal all the organizations they have joined over a period of five years. Arkansas' anti-NAACP law was also declared unconstitutional, and, like South Carolina, it passed another statute requiring school teachers to list their organizational affiliations.

In Alabama, the NAACP has been prohibited by a court injunction from operating since June, 1956. In this case, the Association was fined $100,000 for refusing to reveal its membership list. The Supreme Court has twice ruled that the NAACP does not have to produce this list, but the case had still to be heard in the state court, and the injunction thus remained in effect. In Texas and Louisiana, the NAACP resumed operations after having been enjoined.

Other methods have also been resorted to, even criminal acts, to keep citizens from asserting their rights in desegregating the schools. One of the chief weapons has been the application of the boycott and other economic pressures.

An example of how such a campaign works was given by

Billie S. Fleming, president of the Clarendon County Improvement Association, when he testified before the Senate Subcommittee on Constitutional Rights on April 16, 1959. This is the county which brought one of the original school desegregation cases before the Supreme Court, and according to Mr. Fleming's testimony, the following has occurred since the 1954 decision:

Those who were litigants in the case have been unable to obtain employment. Harry Briggs, whose name appeared as a plaintiff in one of the school cases, lost his job and was forced to leave the county. Farmers who were members of the NAACP found it impossible to rent harvesting machinery to gather their crops. As a result, they were compelled to let their crops rot in the fields.

In one area of Clarendon County, the White Citizens Council supplied a list of all school petitioners and known members of the NAACP to cotton gin operators. Any Negro farmer whose name appeared on the list could not get his cotton ginned. Negro businessmen discovered that wholesalers in the county would no longer sell them the merchandise they needed to operate their businesses. They were compelled to go to other parts of the state to secure sources of supply at increased expense. The White Citizens Council also received the co-operation of every lending institution in the county in cutting off credit from those advocating desegregation. As a result, no loans were made to any person whose name appeared on the "blacklist." It became necessary for such a person to seek credit elsewhere.

Similar means are being employed in Fayette County, Tennessee, where a White Citizens Council is openly using the boycott weapon against Negroes. The aim is to force at least one thousand Negroes to leave the county in order to change the present white voting minority into a majority at the ballot box by November, 1960.

Such economic pressure tactics were allegedly widespread,

particularly in South Carolina and Mississippi. When these methods failed, then in some places threats and violence were resorted to. Riots took place in Mansfield and Clinton, Tennessee; Clay and Sturgis, Kentucky; Tuscaloosa, Alabama; Milford, Delaware; and other places. In Clinton and Nashville, Tennessee, schools were blown up by dynamite.

Individual leaders of the desegregation fight, and parents of children in the school cases, have been the particular objects of violence and intimidation. Mr. Fleming reported that his home had been hit and damaged by buckshot. On another occasion, he alleged his home was threatened by a caravan of Ku Klux Klansmen, escorted by the county sheriff in his official automobile. Mrs. L. C. Bates of Little Rock, Arkansas, leader of the NAACP and sponsor of the colored children who were admitted to Central High School, has been compelled to maintain a guard at her home at all times. Her house has been the target of several bombings and constant rock throwings.

The home of Rev. F. L. Shuttlesworth in Birmingham, Alabama, was heavily damaged by dynamite on Christmas night in 1956. His church was later saved from destruction when a dynamite bomb was found and removed from the premises. Rev. Mr. Shuttlesworth is a leader in the desegregation movement, and he attempted to enroll four colored children in a segregated Birmingham high school. In connection with this incident he was beaten and threatened with death by a mob.

In Sorrento, Florida, an attempt was made to burn the home of a man whose children were held judicially eligible to attend a white school.

In Old Fort, North Carolina, Mr. Albert Joyner, who had attempted to enroll Negro children in a local school, was physically attacked.

The restaurant of the father of one of the colored students who had attended Clinton (Tennessee) High School was damaged by explosives, as were the homes of thirty Negro residents of Clinton.

These and similar incidents have made it extremely dangerous to be involved in civil rights litigation in some sections. A study published by the American Friends Service Committee, the Department of Racial and Cultural Relations of the National Council of the Churches of Christ in the U.S.A., and the Southern Regional Council lists 225 acts attributable to racial violence in the South since May 17, 1954, including six killings, twenty-nine woundings by gunfire, and thirty home bombings. Many of these were directly associated with the school desegregation problem.

In view of these circumstances, a Negro parent seeking to assert his child's constitutional rights to attend a desegregated school in some sections of the South must have unlimited courage, resources, time, and energy to carry on the fight. He must be prepared to litigate with the state, and defend himself against organized resistance groups and, sometimes, unknown terrorists. Because so few parents, either white or colored, can meet these qualifications, the pace of desegregation has slowed almost to a halt in important parts of the South. Only the federal government has the strength and the resources to meet this critical law-enforcement crisis.

I believe it essential to strengthen the hand of moderates in the South, who will find it very hard to make measurable civil rights progress unless the authority and majesty of the United States government backs the Supreme Court's decision. This does not imply drastic action, criminal penalties, force, or the use of troops, as civil rights opponents like to argue, but it implies a persistent determination to get the needed laws passed by the Congress, with heavy reliance on our judicial processes to back up the use of mediation, conciliation, and technical assistance to see that measurable civil rights progress is made.

Measures are needed to range Congress and the Executive alongside the Supreme Court in declaring and accepting responsibility to carry out the guarantee of equal protection of the laws in education under the Fourteenth Amendment. Also necessary are federal technical and financial assistance, federal leadership for states and local communities whose schools are still segregated, and federal legal assistance, through injunction suits, where private persons are unable to vindicate their own constitutional rights.

Technical assistance should be made available to state and local governmental units in collecting and disseminating information leading to public understanding and support of public school desegregation. The secretary of health, education and welfare should be authorized to make grants to school districts and local governments to defray additional costs incurred in the process of eliminating segregation, including expenses for educational specialists, hiring additional teachers, and enlarging existing school facilities. The secretary should have the power also to prepare or assist in the preparation of local desegregation plans, and to expedite their adoption. He should be backed by the attorney general with power to bring suit in representative cases against any community or district which refuses to comply with the Supreme Court's decision, and on behalf of any individual or group of persons financially unable to bear the cost of litigation.

I am devoted to the bipartisan support of civil rights legislation and, in that spirit, have given steadfast support to the measures proposed by my Democratic colleagues, like Senator Paul Douglas of Illinois. In this spirit I have ardently supported my own Republican Party leaders—President Eisenhower in his affirmative stand on civil rights, former Senator William Knowland of California when he took the lead in getting a civil rights bill before the Senate in 1957, and Senator Everett

Dirksen, his successor as Senate minority leader, when he supported the Eisenhower administration's civil rights package in 1960. I see nothing inconsistent between bi-partisanship on this issue and working within my own party for leadership in the civil rights fight. The Republican Party, in the tradition of Lincoln, must muster maximum strength for such leadership, indispensable to the achievement of Congressional civil rights bills. While the Democrats have their strong and influential southern wing, Republicans have the advantage of freedom from sectional divisions on civil rights. My party must demonstrate the determination to place the majesty and authority of the United States government behind the assurance of civil rights, including not only voting rights but the opportunity for an unsegregated education in the public schools, and the enjoyment of public facilities, wherever located, equally by all. Even in my own party there is still a great deal to do. But bi-partisan action continues to be the basis for civil rights progress in the Congress.

Chapter Ten

Decade of Change in Washington, D.C.

Washington, D.C., is our capital city, the symbol of the entire nation. An incident of racial discrimination there is a national—and sometimes an international—incident, for Washington is more than a capital city. It is the "window through which the world looks into our house." Embassies, legations, and representatives of foreign nations abound in Washington. They often judge the United States on the basis of what they see and experience in the capital city. In a world where the majority of people are nonwhite, racial discrimination in Washington is potent propaganda in the hands of those unfriendly to us; it affects adversely our relations with those who are or should be our allies. The significance of such incidents has been heightened by our leadership of the free world in the struggle between democracy and Communism.

One would suppose that the cosmopolitan capital of a nation whose interests range the earth would have had little truck with racism; that only an occasional "wool-hat" who got on the wrong train would indulge in racial discrimination. But Washington is a southern city geographically and in spirit, and until very recently racial discrimination was widespread. Almost every aspect of the city's business, social, educational, and recreational life reflected the pattern of racial segregation.

Some years ago, in the famous report issued in 1947, the President's Committee on Civil Rights described the situation in the District of Columbia as a "graphic illustration of a failure of democracy." It summarized the situation as follows:

> For Negro Americans, Washington is not just the nation's capital. It is the point at which all public transportation into the South becomes "Jim Crow". If he stops in Washington, a Negro may dine like other men in the Union Station, but as soon as he steps out into the capital, he leaves such democratic practices behind. With very few exceptions, he is refused service at downtown restaurants, he may not attend a downtown movie or play, and he has to go into the poorer section of the city to find a night's lodging. The Negro who decided to settle in the District must often find a home in an overcrowded substandard area. He must often take a job below the level of his ability. He must send his children to the inferior public schools set aside for Negroes and entrust his family's health to medical agencies which give inferior service. In addition, he must endure the countless daily humiliations that the system of segregation imposes upon the one-third of Washington that is Negro.[1]

The Committee concluded that the "situation that exists in the District of Columbia . . . is intolerable." Nor was the Committee alone in this judgment. In December, 1948, an impressive documentary report issued by the National Committee on Segregation in the Nation's Capital described the racial practices in Washington as a "blot on our nation."

Located below the Mason-Dixon line, on the border between Maryland and Virginia which both officially endorsed segregation, the District of Columbia in its racial practices was indeed a "Southern town with a northern exposure."

The Washington of today is completely different. The change which has taken place in its racial patterns during the past ten years is phenomenal. Although racial discrimination still exists, its more blatant forms have sharply declined. Significantly, this change has been accomplished peacefully and without the community tensions which marked efforts to eliminate segregation in Alabama, Arkansas, Georgia, Louisiana, South Carolina, Mississippi, and other southern areas. That is why the progress of desegregation in Washington, D.C., is so instructive. Backed by law, it was effected by men.

Within the space of one year, from June, 1953, to June, 1954, segregation vanished from the District's restaurants, theaters, and playgrounds. In the public school system, which was rigidly segregated prior to the Supreme Court's decision in 1954, white and colored pupils now sit side by side in the classrooms, compete with each other in athletics, and participate in all school activities. In other areas of daily life, the change has been slower, but steady and progressive.

Some of these changes were preceded and accompanied by considerable public clamor. But the great strides made in dropping racial bars have resulted in bettering the relations between white and colored people. The District of Columbia has become a model for the whole South. It has proved that effective and peaceful desegregation can be accomplished rapidly even where large numbers of people are affected and the proportion of Negroes is substantial. A study of the techniques used is vital to any study on the subject.[2]

This shift in racial attitudes and practices started before the school segregation decisions by the Supreme Court. For several years, the tempo of change in segregated Washington had been proceeding at an ever-increasing rate. The vigorous stand taken in 1948 by the United States Department of the Interior for nonsegregated operation of all governmental recreation facilities in the District of Columbia was one of the first actions which sparked a vast change throughout the city. Several legal and community efforts were launched against segregation. The voice of government, the court suits and legal briefs filed by hardworking lawyers, the plea of the reformer, the exhortation of the minister, priest, and rabbi, the stirring of the public conscience against the patent injustices of the rules of segregation—all combined to stimulate re-examination and revision of the status quo.

One after another, various places of public accommodation, sometimes because of such pressures and sometimes voluntarily, opened their doors to all, regardless of race. Racial bars were lowered in parochial schools, restaurants, colleges and universities, nursery schools, hotels, playgrounds, swimming pools, housing projects, professional organizations, churches, athletic events, some areas of employment, theaters, places of public assembly, and many other aspects of community life. A revolution in community behavior was effected.

Both major political parties had promised during the 1952 election campaign to end racial segregation in the District of Columbia, and the Eisenhower Administration, which had prevailed, worked to achieve that goal. Indeed, almost immediately after his inauguration, President Eisenhower announced in his first State of the Union message to Congress: "I propose to use whatever authority exists in the office of the President to end segregation in the District of Columbia, including the Federal government." An order to establish a nondiscrimination policy for all District government agencies under the jurisdiction of the District Commissioners was issued, with some modifications, as the Non-Discrimination Policy Order of the District Commissioners, in November, 1953.

In the *Thompson Restaurant Case,* the Department of Justice supported efforts to end racial discrimination in the public eating places in Washington. The decisive step in community desegregation came in June, 1953, when the Supreme Court unanimously upheld in that case the validity of an old civil rights ordinance, forbidding discrimination in restaurants, which had been enacted in 1873 by the former Legislative Assembly of the District of Columbia. This law had lain unused and virtually forgotten ever since the Legislative Assembly had been abolished in 1874 and replaced by the present Commissioners form of government under which the residents of the District have—unhappily—no right to vote on local affairs.

Public interest in this ordinance was aroused when the National Committee on Segregation in the Nation's Capital dramatically disclosed its existence on December 10, 1948, and commented on how it had "mysteriously disappeared" from the compiled statutes of the District of Columbia. In May, 1949, a committee of lawyers, including such distinguished members of the District bar as the late Charles H. Houston and the late Judge James A. Cobb, presented to the District Commissioners a memorandum opinion holding that the ordinances of 1872 and 1873 were still in effect, and requesting that the District Commissioners issue a public announcement that they would be enforced.

In September, a Co-ordinating Committee for the Enforcement of the District of Columbia Anti-Discrimination Laws was established to co-ordinate the efforts of numerous organizations and individuals who had become interested in enforcing the ordinances, and to initiate a test case.

In February, 1950, the District Commissioners announced that "exhaustive search of the acts of Congress and the regulations of the various Boards of Commissioners since 1874 fails to disclose any express repeal of these acts" and that "the Board of Commissioners has instructed the Corporation Counsel to prosecute the next complaint of violation of these acts." A test prosecution was instituted in the Municipal Court in March, 1950, against the John R. Thompson Company, the operator of a restaurant which had refused service to four "well-behaved and respectable persons," including three Negroes.

In July, 1950, Judge Myers quashed the information, holding that the ordinances of 1872 and 1873 had been repealed "by implication." A related case involving a refusal by the Thompson company to admit another group, consisting of two Negroes and a white person, was appealed to the Municipal Court of Appeals, which held by a vote of 2 to 1 that the 1873 ordinance was valid. The restaurant company appealed to the United States Court of Appeals, and in January, 1953, the court ruled, 5 to 4, that Congress lacked power to authorize the Legislative Assembly to enact the 1872 and 1873 ordinances. The District government, with the aid of the United States Department of Justice, then brought the case to the Supreme Court, which in June, 1953, unanimously reversed the United States Court of Appeals.

The Thompson Restaurant decision had several important consequences. First, it ended segregation in the city's restaurants. Second, it established a firm constitutional basis for all state laws and municipal ordinances prohibiting racial discrimination in places of public accommodation. Third, it confirmed the constitutional power of Congress to delegate broad home-rule authority to a local legislative body for the District of Columbia, and thus greatly aided current efforts to re-establish suffrage and a local legislative body in the District of Columbia. Fourth, the Supreme Court's decision also furnished the basis for validation of another ordinance enacted in 1872, prohibiting discrimination in restaurants, hotels, barbershops, and bathing houses; and it remanded the case to the United States Court of Appeals to consider the applicability of that law insofar as it concerned restaurants.

Racial discrimination in restaurants vanished overnight without disturbance. Previously expressed fears that restaurants would lose business proved groundless. On the contrary, the Washington Restaurant Association reported an increase in business. Except for a few ambiguous instances, no restaurant or other public eating place in the nation's capital has since refused to admit and serve any person because of his race or color.

A new double-pronged attack on racial discrimination in places of public accommodation began in September, 1953, when twenty local and national organizations, under the leadership of the American Veterans Committee (AVC), jointly requested the District Commissioners to enforce three Reconstruction period civil rights laws, enacted in 1869, 1870, and 1872, which had lain unused for over eighty years. The 1869 law prohibited racial discrimination in places of public amusement. The 1870 law increased the penalty of the 1869 Act and extended the prohibition to restaurants and hotels. The 1872 Act, one of the laws involved in the Thompson Restaurant case, is described above.

The Thompson Restaurant decision, of course, had settled most of the legal issues relating to the validity of the old civil rights ordinances. There is a significant difference, however, between these laws. The 1872 and 1873 laws, enacted by the Legislative Assembly, applied to all of the District of Columbia. But the 1869 and 1870 Acts had been enacted by the "Corporation of Washington," which had jurisdiction over only the old "City of Washington," an area bounded by Rock Creek, Florida Avenue, and the Anacostia River, which together with the later-annexed area of Georgetown, comprised less than one-fourth of the District of Columbia.

This joint request of the twenty organizations, accompanied by a comprehensive legal analysis by AVC's national counsel, pointed out that although the Corporation of Washington was abolished in 1871 and the Legislative Assembly three years later, the laws of 1869, 1870, and 1872 had been continued in force by saving clauses of subsequent general legislation. The twenty organizations, therefore, asked the District Commissioners to announce that the laws would be enforced within the area to which they applied. Also, since the 1869 law stopped at the old boundary lines of the city, the District Commissioners were asked to promulgate a regulation, which they have the legal power to do, prohibiting racial discrimination in places of public amusement in the entire area of the District of Columbia.

At the end of September, 1953, operators of movie theaters announced that they were dropping all racial bars to admission. Two months later, the District Commissioners issued the long-awaited policy order establishing nondiscrimination as the official policy of the District government in connection with all personnel actions affecting District government employees, as well as all matters concerning public use of the facilities and services of those agencies. This policy order applied to all except some six of the more than ninety agencies under the jurisdiction of the District Commissioners.

Shortly thereafter, the standard nondiscrimination clause, which had been present in almost every federal contract since 1941, was ordered included in all new contracts made by the District government. Almost simultaneously, the National Capital Housing Authority announced that its public housing facilities were being integrated "without friction."

In February, 1954, the United States Court of Appeals held that the 1873 Act had repealed the 1872 law, but only with respect to restaurants, thus leaving the 1872 law in force with respect to hotels, barbershops, and bathhouses. Since then, the hotels in the District of Columbia have complied with the law.

The pace quickened in all areas of discrimination after the Supreme Court's school segregation decision of May 17, 1954.

The first agency to act was the District of Columbia Recreation Board, which had for years striven to maintain racial segregation in public recreation. Under pressure from the United States Department of the Interior, it had reluctantly agreed in 1949 to a "gradual" policy of desegregation. But its cumbersome segmentalized desegregation procedure, with public announcements of hearings, committee reports, staff studies, board polls, and so on, stimulated both the proponents and the opponents of segregation to frantic battle formations. As the pro-and the anti-segregationists pushed their views, racial tensions over the playgrounds visibly heightened. During 1952 and 1953, the Board ended segregation in only about a dozen individual playgrounds. The whole process seemed interminable, frustrating, and ragged.

On the day after the Supreme Court's school segregation decision, the Recreation Board abruptly abandoned all segregation practices in hundreds of playgrounds and other recreational facilities. Even more astonishing than this about-face was the great calm that seemed to settle over the playgrounds. The battlers for and against segregation had nothing more to fight about. From then on, the playgrounds were for play and recreation. The Board is no longer tied up with racial squabbling, and now devotes its time to improving recreation facilties for all people.

When the Supreme Court's 1954 decision was announced, President Eisenhower expressed the hope that the public schools of the District of Columbia would become a "model" for the nation. A few days later the District of Columbia Board of Education adopted a complete desegregation policy, and the superintendent of schools announced plans for an immediate beginning of the desegregation process. This was supplemented two weeks later by the announcement of the District Congress of Parents and Teachers that all racial bars to membership in the Parent-Teacher Associations were being ended. The formerly white and colored PTA's were joined in one Congress of PTA's.[3]

As the school desegregation plans developed, about three thousand Negro children were transferred to white schools in September, 1954, the teachers colleges were desegregated, separate examinations for teachers were abolished, and considerable integration of teaching and administrative personnel was achieved. During the summer of 1954, new school boundaries were announced, which applied at once to all children entering a school for the first time. The all-white Federation of Citizens Associations filed a suit in the District Court to prevent integration of the schools, arguing that the Supreme Court had not yet issued its mandate; but the suit was dismissed. Within the next two months, an additional two thousand children were permitted to transfer to the schools in their new zones.

School integration proceeded smoothly and uneventfully except for the brief period of an abortive student walkout that occurred about a month or so after the schools opened in the fall of 1954. The almost complete change from a racially segregated institutional setup to a nonsegregated one was accomplished with only this one disruption. This four-day strike in October, 1954, by some 2,500 white junior and senior high school students, was quickly brought under control. Although some credited a White Citizens type of racist organization with helping to spark this student demonstration, most observers blamed the delightful and balmy October weather, so conducive to school absenteeism, for the temporary halt in scholastic endeavors.

The prompt action of school and police authorities in ordering the students to return gave notice that professional hate-mongers would not be allowed to take control, and prevented bigotry from bringing down law and order. The incident, deplorable though it was, thus served a useful function. It tested and proved the soundness and strength of community progress toward desegregation within the framework of law.

The new public school districts, based on geographic boundaries, were applied to junior high school graduates in February, 1955. By September, the new school zones were applicable to all children except those already enrolled who wished to remain in their present school until graduation, if space was available. Many community organizations criticized this option plan, urging that all pupils be assigned to schools nearest their homes. Nevertheless, desegregation of students has proceeded rapidly and steadily. The teachers' unions have merged. The teaching and administrative staffs are being assigned without regard to the race of either the pupils or other staff members. No Negro teachers lost their jobs because of integration.

Assignments to schools are now largely determined by residence. Hence the student bodies in the District schools now reflect the racial composition of the neighborhoods, with thousands of Negro children in formerly white schools and hundreds of white children in formerly Negro schools. However, because of the persistence of racial residential segregation, plus the growing percentage of the District's Negro population, about twenty-one of the 170 schools still have all-colored student bodies, and about three have all-white student bodies.[4]

The over-all consensus is that pupils, teachers, and parents have adjusted themselves well to interracial education. Instead of fighting to force or to prevent the shift of a school building, parents and teachers of both races are co-operating to benefit all the children within the school zone. Negro teachers are accepted completely by white children, parents, and teachers. Pupils of both races are learning respect for each other, particularly in extracurricular activities, such as sports and school newspapers.

This does not mean that all educational problems arising from segregated schools are gone. Before the change-over, the Board of Education had to devote much of its time, desperately but ineffectually, to trying to relieve the hardship and inequities arising from the fixed racial lines. They shifted buildings, revised budgets, reassigned teachers, combined or closed classes, etc. They worked so hard on racial problems that they could hardly attend to educational needs, but when school desegregation did away with these racial problems, the public became aware of the educational problems.

Evidence of the markedly inferior schooling in the former Division II (Negro) schools showed up in the results of city-wide achievement tests taken by the students. Many Negro children were simply not adequately prepared for their present class level. Many children, but more colored than white children, failed to achieve the national average in many subjects. Behavior difficulties appeared at some schools, more in the high schools than in the grade schools. But not all of these problems were with Negro children alone.

Widespread debate began over the need for more remedial and special classes, and the Board of Education sought more funds to hire 180 additional teachers to overcome this accumulated deficiency. Eventually, a four-track program was instituted to raise achievement levels for the retarded students and to prevent capable students from being held back by their slower classmates.

A most pertinent comment on the effect of desegregation was made by Dr. Carl E. Hansen, superintendent of the public schools of the District of Columbia. In reporting on the District's program to the Federal Commission on Civil Rights, meeting at Nashville, Tennessee, on March 5 and 6, 1959, Dr. Hansen stated:

At once the charge was made that desegregation lowered school standards. What really happened was that we began to report achievement scores for the entire school system. The method of reporting changed, not the facts.

Since 1954, city-wide achievement medians have gone up, although the number of white pupils has decreased. This fact attests to the educability of the Negro pupil and indicates that the cultural and economic poverty experienced by many Negro pupils can be overcome to some extent by education.

Another of the charges of the white supremacy groups, that District of Columbia segregation had resulted in an outbreak of juvenile delinquency, especially among colored youth, has been answered by the statistics, too. The District of Columbia Department of Public Welfare reported that delinquency among Negro children of school age fell from 37.1 per thousand to 21.2 per thousand in the period 1954 to 1959, while the rate among white children remained constant.[5]

Many factors went into the success of the District of Columbia desegregation experience. Chief among these was the inspired leadership given by President Eisenhower, which was transmitted through his appointees, the Commissioners of the District, led by Chairman McLaughlin, to the school officials responsible for carrying out the program. From the very time of the Court's decision it was made clear that compliance with the decision was the official position of those in authority.

The immediate and total nature of the desegregation program was also important. Confronted with an accomplished fact and without time to organize effective opposition, supporters of segregation were unable to engage in delaying tactics or subject any single class or school or small group to harassment. Experience has shown that chances for success in desegregation are greater where these elements of expedition and totality are present.

Perhaps the most significant feature of the desegregation of the District's public school system is that it changed the whole focus of attention in dealing with school problems. Formerly, both the Board of Education and the public approached virtually every school problem from the point of view of how it would fit within or affect the rigid lines of racial segregation, rather than how it would achieve maximum educational advantage for the children and the community. Now the whole emphasis, by the Board, by the District Commissioners, by the PTA, by the teachers, and by the public, is on how to correct existing weaknesses and improve educational opportunity for all children, regardless of race. In sum, the District schools are now tackling the problems of education forthrightly, with dispatch, and in a way that promises to benefit all the children.

Washington is still not free of racial discrimination. In other important areas of life in the nation's capital, the barriers of racial segregation and other forms of discriminatory treatment are still present. Progress is being made only slowly in jobs, housing, and medical care. In some areas there is hardly any progress at all.

Negroes in the District of Columbia, as elsewhere, have traditionally been bunched, in the main, into the low-paid, temporary, unskilled labor group. They have had few opportunities to get into the professional, managerial, white-collar, or skilled jobs.

The job barriers are now cracking open. The local gas and electric companies have within the past three years hired colored clerical workers for the first time. At least two of the local dairies have hired Negroes as retail driver salesmen. The District Transit Company now employs Negroes as "platform workers," driving buses and street cars, an occupation which had been for many years closed to Negroes. The new climate, along with considerable prodding by citizens' groups, particularly the Urban League, and by the President's Committee on Government Contracts, headed by Vice President Nixon, finally initiated the change in policy. The President's Committee, working with the Communications Workers of America, also succeeded in persuading the Chesapeake and Potomac Telephone

Company to hire Negroes as telephone and teletype operators to eliminate discrimination in the operation of its training program.

More and more colored men and women are getting jobs in retail sales work in shops and small stores in the District of Columbia. In major retail, banking, and other business establishments, however, most of the entering jobs cannot be had by Negro workers. Although some unions are now integrated, apprenticeship and membership opportunities are simply not available to Negroes in most of the skilled-craft unions. Even where skilled Negro help is available, the men are unable to obtain construction work because the contractors hire under the union hiring-hall system, and the unions have not admitted Negroes to membership. The President's Committee on Government Contracts has protested the exclusion of Negro electricians and rodmen from jobs connected with the East Front extension of the Capitol and construction of the third House Office Building. With the powerful backing of President Meany of the AFL-CIO, a member of the President's Committee on Government Contracts, an end to this discrimination has been achieved.

Washington, as our nation's capital, of course has many government jobs in the federal and in the District of Columbia agencies. There, the outlook for the Negro is somewhat better. Discrimination in federal government jobs probably still exists, but it is much less blatant, having been for many years forbidden by law. Moreover, in March, 1955, the Civil Service Commission ordered that all forms relating to civilian personnel should thereafter be printed without any designation or question as to race. Segregated work situations and facilities, as such, no longer exist in federal government agencies.

At present, many clerical, and some professional, jobs in government are held by colored people. However, many governmental agencies are all-white, except for the traditional colored messengers. The great majority of Negroes employed by the federal government are still in the lower echelon of government jobs, working as charwomen, laborers, elevator operators, messengers, and mail attendants. Although a few of the higher positions are occupied by Negroes, it is still true that almost all important federal government business is transacted with and by white people. Neither the former Fair Employment Board in the Civil Service Commission, nor its successor, the Committee on Government Employment Policy, which President Eisenhower established in 1955, has been able to do enough to change the picture, either in the federal government or in the District government. There is in fact a continuing gap between policy and compliance.

Complaint is often made that Negroes are not qualified for the higher echelon jobs in the federal government owing to inadequate education, training, and experience. The experience factor is, of course, the deficiency of our system in not giving the Negro adequate opportunity, but the education and experience factor can be remedied where there is a will.

For example, in 1950 when I was a congressman I had a complaint that the Foreign Service of the State Department, our diplomatic service, did not have an adequate quotient of Negroes. Especially was this true, it was pointed out, since many new nations in Asia and Africa would welcome such personnel. Upon inquiry I found that the standard examination for the Foreign Service was open to all, but not enough Negroes took it or could pass it. I called in the presidents of a group of Negro colleges, led by Dr. Bond of Gettysburg College and Dr. Johnson of Howard University. They agreed to remedy this condition with their students, and the situation has shown marked improvement since.

The Nondiscrimination Policy Order adopted in November, 1953, by the District Commissioners has not materially changed the long-established racial disparities in the District government agencies. In part, this is because practices and traditions that are generations old do not yield to even the best of policy statements unless affirmative action is taken to carry the policy into practical effect. Moreover, the Policy Order is not a firm and unequivocal declaration of nondiscrimination. It specifically exempts several important District agencies. Although the exceptions of the Fire Department and the Industrial Home Schools have been removed by subsequent amendments, the Policy Order still exempts the District Training School, the Home for the Aged and Infirm (now called the District of Columbia Village), the Jail Division, and several institutions of the Department of Correction.

A grave situation, however, is created by the way in which the Policy Order is disregarded. Since August, 1954, the Order has required that the Fire Department be operated without any racial distinctions. In fact, partial integration was initiated at that time and has proved to be unrealistic. Of the twenty-four fire companies in 1954, five were all-colored (white officers were at the head of four), and nineteen were all-white. The five colored companies were approximately eighteen men over-strength, while the white companies were so undermanned as to impair their efficiency. Indeed, white firemen found difficulty in getting leave from their posts because of the lack of replacements.

Despite much prodding by various community organizations, little was done to deal with discriminatory employment until the District Commissioners, in April, 1958, issued an order establishing a Commissioners Council on Human Relations "to encourage harmonious relations among the residents of every community and to encourage the granting of equal opportunity by persons engaged in private business." The Council also was urged "to assist the Commissioners to promote, foster and encourage . . . the full and impartial application and observance of the Commissioners' policy on non-discrimination. . . ." In August, 1958, seven outstanding citizens of the District were appointed to the Council, under the chairmanship of Leon Chatelain, Jr., a respected architect who had formerly been president of the District Board of Trade. In the months that followed, the Council obtained a substantial grant of funds from a private foundation, and employed an executive director of outstanding skill. It began to deal with various problems of discriminatory employment both in the District government offices and by employers engaged in work under contracts with the District government. Although the Council has no enforcement authority, but acts only in an advisory capacity, it has played a significant role in advancing nondiscrimination in the District of Columbia. Notices posted in the offices of contractors and other employers advise that inquiries on the city's racial nondiscrimination policy in construction contracts may be made to the Council.

Negroes are now admitted into most places of public amusement in the District of Columbia. They also now participate, on an integrated basis, in virtually all sports, amateur and professional. A significant factor in bringing this about was the unanimous decision of the Municipal Court of Appeals in the test case of *Central Amusement Company* v. *District of Columbia*, decided in April, 1956, which upheld the validity of the 1869 law mentioned above, and affirmed fines of $110 imposed on the company for excluding Negroes from its bowling-alley establishment. The effect of the decision was emphasized on May 3, 1956, when the District Commissioners issued a regulation extending the requirements of the law to the area of the District of Columbia lying beyond the original City of Washington. There is good reason to believe that the existence of a uniform mandate upon all places of public amusement to admit all well-behaved persons without regard to race or color has relieved the operators of much pressure from both sides.

One of the important holdouts against desegregation in the District of Columbia is the Police Boys Clubs. This organization, established about twenty-five years ago by the District of Columbia Police Department, provided nine clubhouse facilities for some 22,000 boys. Its board of directors consists of some 125 leading citizens of the community, plus about 50 police officers with rank of captain and above—all white. Policemen were used to staff the clubs, to operate the summer camps, and to raise funds by direct solicitation from the general public. But despite the extensive integration in public facilities, the officials of the Police Boys Clubs steadily rejected the requests of numerous other community organizations.

In December, 1954, the Police Boys Clubs abruptly abandoned one of its locations in the All Souls Church (Unitarian) rather than integrate. The Unitarian Service Committee promptly filled the void by establishing its own Columbia Heights Boys Club, which now provides club facilities for hundreds of boys on an integrated basis. In 1955, the Police Boys Clubs abandoned another clubhouse in the Anacostia Park Field House rather than comply with the nonsegregation policy of the Department of the Interior. In 1956, it abandoned a third club using facilities in the integrated Brookland Public School rather than admit any Negro boys.

The controversy focused public attention on the dubious propriety of permitting policemen to solicit funds from the general public to support the Police Boys Clubs operations. In 1957, the District Commissioners prohibited the use of policemen for public solicitation on their behalf. This action, and the widespread reluctance of the public to contribute to a segregated organization, resulted in a sharp drop in contributions and compelled the organization to abandon four of its six remaining club facilities. This insistence on continuing segregation remained as a tragic example of intransigence, but because it is an exception to what is going on in the whole community, it could change at any time.

The counterpressure in matters of segregation is often attributed to the southern congressmen who allegedly dominate the District Committee of the House of Representatives. Although astute observers of the local scene feel that this is a greater fear than actuality it has been an important factor in the failure of Congress to enact the District of Columbia Home Rule Bill. This bill, which would provide a local, popularly elected government for the District, was passed by the Senate in 1949, 1952, 1955, and 1958, but in each instance, it died in the House District Committee. In July, 1959, the Senate passed a Home Rule bill for the fifth time, but once again determined effort to bypass the House District Committee, even by means of a discharge petition—a rarely used means to get a bill on for consideration, requiring the signature of a majority (219) of the members of the House of Representatives—ended in failure. A constitutional amendment to give District residents a vote in presidential elections did, however, get out of the House Judiciary Committee, was passed by both Houses, and is up for ratification by the states.

In housing, the picture is still spotty. The biggest break in the iron ring around the segregated ghettos of Washington occured in 1948 when the Supreme Court ruled in *Hurd* v. *Hodge* that racial restrictive land covenants are unenforceable. Since then, Negroes have moved into many areas of the city formerly closed to them. A great deal of voluntary interracial private housing has developed. In some instances, the arrival of a Negro family in a neighborhood has been accompanied by a flurry of "for sale" signs, only to be followed soon after by removal of these signs. But one of the most disturbing developments is the increasing trend by real estate brokers and sales-men to promote racial fears through "block busting,"—using the rumor that the entire block is "going colored" to frighten white homeowners into panic sales at depressed prices. A favorite technique in this strategy is to advertise the sales of homes in the area under the designation "colored" in the real estate columns of the local newspapers. During 1958 and 1959, about forty community organizations under the leadership of the American Veterans Committee sought to persuade news-papers to refrain from such racial listing, but they were not successful at that time.

Sometimes a neighborhood adjacent to a largely colored area will change to all or mostly colored. However, in some in-stances, the pattern of the neighborhood remains interracial. Many large apartment houses also are now interracial. All public housing has been desegregated since January, 1955.

This considerable amount of interracial residence was greatly responsible for the large degree of interracial school attendance which occurred when the schools were desegregated. These racially democratic patterns of residence in the District have provided not only the physical setting but also the emotional climate of acceptance within which the desegregation of schools, playgrounds, theaters, and other facilities has been achieved with relative convenience.

Most of the suburban areas around Washington, however, are still virtually closed to Negroes. The percentage of Negroes is consequently considerably smaller in the adjacent counties of Arlington and Fairfax, and the cities of Alexandria and Falls Church, in Virginia, and the counties of Montgomery and Prince Georges in Maryland, than it is in the District of Colum-bia. This disparity is emphasized in the younger age groups, particularly because of the modern trend toward suburban dwelling by families with young children. Together with the larger proportion of white children in private and parochial schools, it helps to explain why in the District, with Negroes forming about 52 per cent of the total population, Negro children constitute about 75 per cent of the public school student body.

Housing discrimination also affects Jews and other minority groups. An estimated fourteen residential areas in the nation's capital are open to "gentiles only" through restrictions imposed by the real estate companies which developed them. One area contains a significant number of high officials in the executive, judicial, and legislative branches of our federal government. Some of these homeowners refused to accept the restrictive clauses in the deeds to their homes and filed affidavits indicating their opposition, but others signed despite private reservations.

Medical care for Negroes in the nation's capital still remains full of inadequacies and discrimination. Only a few hospitals admit Negro patients on a nonsegregated basis. At one institution, a church-supported hospital, an injured Negro woman was denied even emergency treatment because "there wasn't any doctor available."

Although Negro physicians are now admitted to the District Medical Society, many institutions still refuse to grant them hospital privileges. This means that when a patient of a Negro physician goes into such a hospital, he can be attended only by a white doctor.

Colored people on the average have a greater need for proper medical care because of their lower income levels and more physically difficult occupations. Such discriminations weigh heavily upon them. Since bacteria know no color line, inadequate medical care for colored people, particularly in an increasingly desegregated society, directly affects all the people, both white and colored, and thus becomes a matter of community concern.

Discrimination also had to be fought in voluntary and professional organizations. The most famous case was the fight within the District of Columbia branch of the American Association of University Women a decade ago to readmit Dr. Mary Church Terrell. The wife of the founder of the Terrell Law School at Howard University, Mrs. Terrell was an outstanding Negro personality. She was a member of the Board of Education of the District of Columbia, active in many civic and welfare organizations, and at one time had been a member of the AAUW, but had allowed her membership to lapse. She had reapplied but had been rejected because of her race. Eventually the group which opposed her application split off and formed its own association. Dr. Terrell was admitted to membership in the AAUW in 1951. Now many voluntary and professional organizations admit Negroes as members without incident.

Integration has already come to the professional associations of nurses, teachers, accountants, sociologists, economists, architects, optometrists, social workers, dentists, and doctors. Both the National Press Club and the Woman's National Press Club have admitted Negroes to membership. The District Bar Association succeeded in eliminating the racial barrier in October, 1958, after several years of controversy including a court suit to nullify an earlier voice vote in favor of dropping the word "white" from its bylaws. Several dozen Negro lawyers have since been admitted to membership.

The YWCA integrated more than ten years ago, but only in the spring of 1960 did the YMCA begin to admit Negroes to general membership.

In the field of organized religion, the Catholic Church, the Unitarians, the Quakers, and the Ethical Culture Society have encouraged and achieved integrated worship and other activities. But eleven on Sunday morning is still the most segregated hour in our nation's capital, and only relatively few Negroes come into the white Protestant churches. The Washington Council of Churches, however, is free of segregation, and its Commission on Community Life devotes much effort to find "ways in which the local church could practice better race relations within its own life and community."

It is apparent, notwithstanding claims that segregation in Washington has ended, that our nation's capital is still fighting the battle of Jim Crow. The major bastions of race discrimination nevertheless have tumbled down, and the walls of prejudice are crumbling. The progress made in leveling racial barriers has been real, substantial, and rapid. These achievements, and the city's peaceful and willing acceptance of desegregation, demonstrate that the goal of true national capital is in sight. White and colored people are clearing their minds of stereotypes and fears. And within the tradition of peaceful change and mutual understanding, under the guidance of the Constitution and the laws of the land, the race line is being removed from our nation's capital.

It took law, dedicated men and women, and a favorable community opinion to make measurable progress toward equal opportunity in the District of Columbia. It is a clear pilot-plant operation showing that it can be done with benefit and blessing to the whole community, that no segment of society can remain aloof from the effort; and that society takes its impetus and form best from law.

Chapter Eleven

Discrimination and the Social Order

Americans may seek to deny equality of opportunity to fellow Americans in amazing and ingenious ways. In his home, in his living room, in the privacy of his relationships, a man may and should select his friends and guests as he wishes. On the other hand, it is contrary to sound public policy to permit discrimination on account of race, color, creed, religion, or national origin in places of public accommodation and transportation, and in the administration of justice.

This latter is the true definition of the "social order" as we use that term in the affairs of government and organized communities; it is very different from the whole complex of social activities into which pro-segregationists insist that civil rights advocates are trying to force integration. In their argument, pro-segregationists are engrossed by their fears rather than by the facts.

Twenty-three states now have statutes prohibiting discrimination or segregation in places of public accommodation, in transportation, and in the use of recreational facilities. One of the most recent states to adopt such a law against discrimination in places of public accommodation was the state of Maine, where only a short time ago a study had shown that a majority of

Maine's places of public accommodation pursued a policy of discrimination against minorities.[1]

California is another state which recently adopted a law against discrimination in places of public accommodation; the same law repealed the ban on intermarriage and also required the removal of any designation of race on marriage licenses.[2] The public accommodations section of the law in the state of Washington provides that anyone who is in the business of serving the public must make that service available to all persons under the same uniform terms. This is the same type of clause that appears in most of the state antidiscrimination laws. Many of them also provide for punishment of violations by fines and jail sentences.

This series of laws marks a trend which completely reverses the situation after the beginning of the century. There were relatively few laws requiring segregation up to 1900. One of the most important was that which required segregation on trains. This was based on a Supreme Court ruling in 1877, in the case of *Hall* v. *de Cuir* in which the Supreme Court ruled that a state could not prohibit segregation on a common carrier. The Court later ruled that a state could constitutionally require segregation on carriers. (This was in the case of the *Louisville, New Orleans and Texas Railroad* v. *Mississippi,* 1890.) The classic case for the doctrine of separate but equal accommodations— applied also to public school segregation until 1954—was *Plessy* v. *Ferguson,* 1896, in which the Court held that "legislation is powerless to eradicate racial instincts." [3]

Most of the laws in the southern states requiring separate waiting rooms in railroads and other public stations were passed within the first decade of the present century. During this period, segregation on street cars was also initiated in most southern states. Montgomery, Alabama, in 1906, was the first city to require a completely separate streetcar for colored persons.

The greatest proliferation of discrimination and segregation

laws and statutes and regulations of all kinds took place between 1900 and 1920. Some of the seaboard states even extended segregation to steamboats. In many places signs were
erected which had no sanction in the law whatever. These set
up separate entrances and exits for white and colored persons
in theaters, in boardinghouses, in waiting rooms and rest rooms,
as well as separate ticket windows at railroad stations and
separate drinking fountains. Some hospitals refused to accept
colored patients. In others, the law went into elaborate detail to
separate colored and white cases, to bar white female nurses
from attending Negro male patients, and otherwise to keep the
races apart. It was hard to say where law ended and custom
began in the separation of the races in ball parks, skating rinks,
bowling alleys, drive-in theaters, circuses, in the use of separate
telephone booths, and in some instances even the distribution
of school books. One law required textbooks to be segregated
even when they were sorted, that is to say, those used for
white children were kept in one place while those used by
colored children were put in another. In many localities the
prohibitions against mixing of the races were just as rigid
against white persons as they were against colored persons.

The emotional reaction of some southerners to the Supreme
Court decision in the school segregation cases led to an almost
fanatic search for books in local libraries which the zealots
judged to be propaganda for integration. The book hunt started
in June, 1959 with an attack on a children's illustrated story
called *The Rabbits' Wedding,* by Garth Williams. The story
describes a white rabbit and a black rabbit who lived and played
in a large forest. The black rabbit wanted to marry the white
rabbit. They had a celebration, and "all the other little rabbits
came out to see how happy they both were and they danced all
night in the moonlight. And so the two little rabbits were wed
and lived together happily in the big forest, eating dandelions." [4]

Alabama State Senator E. O. Eddins promptly shouted: "This book should be taken off the shelves and burned." In the Orlando, Florida, *Sentinel* columnist Henry Balch wrote: "As soon as you pick up the book you realize these rabbits are integrated. One of the techniques of brainwashing is conditioning minds to accept what the brainwashers want accepted."

The controversy over this book made front-page news and reached international proportions. It led to books being thrown out of southern libraries and destroyed. One, called *The Three Little Pigs,* was chosen because one of the illustrated animals was a black pig.[5] Another book, entitled *The First Book of Fishing,* in the Shreve Memorial Library in Shreveport, Louisiana, was attacked because it had illustrations of white and Negro children fishing and picnicking together.[6] A fourth, which was attacked by the Grand Dragon of the Alabama Ku Klux Klan, Robert M. Shelton, was called *Two Is a Team.* It tells the story of a Negro boy named Ted and a white boy named Paul who are playmates. The book is illustrated in color and shows the two children visiting in the homes of each other and playing with children of other races.[7]

It now seems incredible, in retrospect, that sober adults could have taken the positions they did with regard to those books. My colleague, Senator Clifford B. Case of New Jersey, in a speech delivered at the Eleventh Annual Conference of the State Commission Against Discrimination in West Orange, New Jersey, commented on this witch hunt in the following words: "If groups in Alabama and Florida succeed in stripping these children's books from library shelves, future generations will hear of them only by word of mouth. Nor is the library the only new rampart to be manned. The zoo will almost certainly be next—the days of the zebra may be numbered." [8]

Miss Inez Boone, the chief librarian of the Shreve Memorial Library, reacted to the attack on the children's books by saying: "If we're going to have a witch hunt through our picture books we may as well close our doors. Anyone who's looking for something can read it into almost any book—even the Bible." [9]

Miss Boone was upheld in her decision by her library board, but Miss Emily W. Reed, the director of the Alabama Public Library Service Division, had a more difficult time. She was attacked by the Citizens Council of Montgomery, Alabama, for distributing a reading list containing the titles of some ten or twelve books which allegedly promoted integration. Charges that the state was permitting pro-integration literature to be distributed in school libraries brought a denial from the school superintendent. Miss Reed said that the list of recommended books which she had circulated had been compiled by committees of the American Library Association. But one of the books on her list, the story of the Montgomery bus boycott, called *Stride Toward Freedom,* was written by the Negro leader of the boycott, Rev. Martin Luther King, Jr., and Alabama legislators were reported considering a bill which would have deprived Miss Reed of her position. Some months later Miss Reed accepted an appointment as consultant in adult education in the District of Columbia Public Library.[10]

In Mississippi, state Senator Wilbur Hooker and former Representative Ed White of Lexington, Mississippi, accused the University of Mississippi Library of using a $500 grant and university matching funds to buy books dealing with race problems. They charged that every book purchased favored integration, while pro-segregation books were kept in the stacks, for which a permit was needed. Fortunately, the state college board expressed confidence in the university authorities and declined to enter the controversy.[11]

These aberrations inspired one southern wit to write to the *Arkansas Democrat* of Little Rock, complaining about the refusal of his white coon dog to hunt with his black coon dog. He asked the newspaper whether he couldn't go to court and get an injunction which would compel his dogs to hunt together.[12]

Much more serious was the Red Chinese radio in Peiping, which had a field day with these stories of prejudice. Said Radio Peiping: "A segregationist in Miami, Florida, demanded that the book called *The Three Little Pigs* be taken off the public shelves in Florida because in some editions the pig, smart enough to outwit the wolf, is black, while the one that gets eaten is white." [13] These and other comments by Peiping were broadcast to the vast colored populations of Asia and South America.

The extent to which the segregation fever has infected otherwise sane and sober citizens is perhaps best illustrated by the following story. It seems that a Negro started to enter one of the largest churches in a southern city when he was stopped by a policeman at the door. The policeman said: "You can't go in here. Don't you know this is a white church?" The Negro replied: "Oh, that's all right. I'm the janitor." The officer considered this reply for a moment, then said: "Well, all right. But you better be sure. Don't let me catch you praying while you're in there!"

The attack on the books reflected the deeper tensions beneath the surface. Racial tensions, built up over a period of years in such places as Little Rock, Arkansas, and Montgomery, Alabama, exploded finally in the shocking school desegregation disorders and in a spectacular bus boycott. In Montgomery, in 1955, the refusal of one Negro woman to obey a public transit bus driver's order to give up her seat for a white passenger triggered the whole situation, and led to a city-wide protest movement that attracted international attention. The idea of protesting racial discrimination by boycotting bus transportation spread to Florida and as far away as the Union of South Africa, where in such cities as Port Elizabeth and Johannesburg dramatic bus boycotts involving more than 50,000 Africans were carried on for over three months.

The Montgomery bus boycott under the leadership of Rev. Martin Luther King, Jr., lasted for almost two years, and was accompanied by a considerable amount of violence. Negro churches and homes were damaged by bombs, automobiles were overturned, and transit buses were fired upon. For a time the Montgomery City Board of Commissioners suspended all operations while efforts were made to break up the car pools used by Negroes in their boycott. The violence and litigation were ended by the United States Supreme Court decision on November 13, 1956, that state laws and city ordinances requiring segregation on public buses were unconstitutional.[14] This decision destroyed the last bit of justification for the "separate but equal" doctrine —which had hung on so tenaciously in transportation—first enunciated by the Court itself in 1896 in the case of *Plessy* v. *Ferguson.*

Segregation in public transportation in other southern cities and states is now gradually being discontinued, although a series of rear-guard actions was fought in the lower federal courts following the Supreme Court decision. In every case, however, the Court held that the local segregation statutes were unconstitutional. Atlanta was one of the last southern cities to continue to compel separate seating of whites and Negroes in public transportation, yielding finally to a federal court order in January, 1959. However, out of habit, many Negroes still continue to sit in the rear of buses and trolleys.

The struggle against segregation in public transportation has also resulted in federal court actions halting discriminatory practices on railroads and in dining cars. However, a survey by the Southern Regional Council in July, 1959, covering twenty-one southern cities, indicates that discrimination in public accommodations, particularly those related to transportation, will give way slowly, and only under constant pressure.

Segregation barriers in the waiting rooms of airline terminals and railroad stations in these cities have been dropped, but they still persist in bus stations everywhere except in Richmond, Greensboro, and Norfolk. The Interstate Commerce Commission held, in November, 1955, that segregation of interstate passengers is unlawful, and some bus stations, therefore, have set aside special segregated waiting rooms for intrastate passengers! Rest rooms in most railroad stations and airports are no longer segregated, but the practice reportedly continues in many airports, including at least five built with federal aid: Montgomery and Birmingham, Alabama; Meridian and Natchez, Mississippi; and Tallahassee, Florida. Efforts to block federal aid in the building of air terminals encompassing such facilities have so far failed.

None of the bus terminals in the survey has unsegregated restaurants, but railroad stations in five cities serve Negroes at unsegregated lunch counters, and seventeen air terminals claim to have dropped segregation altogether in their restaurants.[15] As recently as January 6, 1960, however, the Atlanta Airport Restaurant was ordered by the Federal District Court to remove screens and other forms of racial discrimination. The action had been brought by H. C. Coke, a Birmingham insurance man, who asked for an injunction to halt the practice of seating Negroes behind a screen at the restaurant.[16]

A wave of demonstrations against segregation in North and South Carolina cities, as well as in Virginia and Florida, was launched by Negro students against segregated lunch counters in chain stores, in February, 1960. In each case, Negro students occupied lunch-counter seats and asked to be served. Store managers replied by closing their doors. The demonstrations started on February 2 in Greensboro, North Carolina, and spread rapidly to Raleigh, Charlotte, and Rock Hill, South Carolina, to Hampton, Virginia, to Deland, Florida, and to other cities. The boycott was supported in New York City by Negroes who picketed the chain stores in that city.

Police broke up sit-down demonstrations in many cities by large-scale arrests. In Montgomery, Alabama, Savannah, Georgia, and Orangeburg, South Carolina, demonstrators were fined. In Marshall, Texas, police dispersed a crowd of Negro demonstrators by training fire hoses on them. The right of public assembly was honored by police all over the South more in the breach than in the observance.

As Easter approached, Negro leaders called for a boycott of businesses which practiced segregation. Announcement of the boycott of major stores was made in Jackson, Mississippi, in Little Rock and Pine Bluff, Arkansas, and in cities in Georgia, Florida, South Carolina, Tennessee, and Virginia. Southern businessmen threatened to fire Negro employees in retaliation if the boycott went into effect. Meanwhile, sympathy demonstrations were staged by students at Yale, Harvard, M.I.T., and Michigan; at Oberlin and Wesleyan (Connecticut), students collected funds to help pay court costs of Negro demonstrators.

The coming of industrialization to large areas of the South is bringing about new relationships, and in combination with the opening up of facilities to Negroes for higher education, it is gradually changing the social order. The South cannot remain unaffected by the general climate of the United States favoring equality of opportunity for all peoples, by the antidiscrimination statutes in eighteen states; by the Supreme Court decisions in cases involving the public schools, public transportation, recreation parks, municipal golf courses, and other cases declaring separate but equal facilities to be an evasion of the constitutional guarantees of equal protection of the laws. The federal courts have given a broad rather than a narrow interpretation to laws rejecting discrimination and racial segregation in places of public accommodation. Their decrees bar segregation in such places as city swimming pools, dance halls, public laundries, retail shoe stores, beauty parlors, and similar places of public service.[17] In many cities, however, policies remain unclear and ambiguous.

While discriminatory practices showed a noticeable decline as compared with previous years, an increasing number of cities have enacted ordinances itemizing long lists of public facilities where racial or religious discrimination is prohibited. Nevertheless, incidents have occurred involving distinguished foreign visitors, which have caused untold damage to the prestige of the United States. One such embarrassing incident took place in Kansas City at the end of July, 1959, when the secretary general of the Nigerian Civil Service Union, touring the United States with a group of other international labor leaders, entered a downtown Kansas City cafeteria. He was one of a group of ten union leaders who were on a nationwide tour of our factories and cities. The Nigerian labor leader, Alaba Kalejaiye, was allowed to eat his food in the cafeteria, but was told by the manager not to return. One of the men in Mr. Kalejaiye's company later remarked: "We feel quite bitter about this. We all deeply resent the treatment of Mr. Kalejaiye and feel that this incident has spoiled our visit here." Washington offered an official apology which explained that the incident was "in no sense typical" of the United States, but it could not wipe out the damage done to our prestige.[18]

Foreign diplomats resident in the nation's capital have also been embarrassed by racial discriminatory practices, especially in their search for recreation. Early last summer, a Chinese research specialist and his family were turned away from two Chesapeake Bay beaches, and a few weeks later five natives of

India, three of whom were members of official missions to the United States, were refused admission to two Maryland beaches near Annapolis.[19] One of the members later said: "It was a very unpleasant experience. I had never realized before that foreigners could be treated this way only thirty miles from Washington."

Vacation resort hotels in New York and other areas of the country have frequently sought to evade laws prohibiting racial or religious discrimination by referring to themselves as private clubs and featuring in their advertising that their facilities were available only on a membership basis. Bona fide private clubs are not affected by civil rights legislation, but investigation disclosed considerable misrepresentation in order to evade the law. Complaints in New York were filed with SCAD, which found that some of these so-called private clubs were in fact public places with discriminatory admission policies.

One of the most notorious of these cases involved the Castle Hill Beach Club in the Bronx. Hearings were held in December, 1953, by SCAD on complaints brought by two Bronx residents who claimed that they had been denied admission because of their color. The club maintained that it was a private organization and not a place of public accommodation subject to the jurisdiction of the Commission. After investigation, however, SCAD ruled that the swimming pool operated by the club was a place of public accommodation within the meaning of the law, and not a private club. This ruling was upheld by the New York Court of Appeals, the state's highest court, on April 11, 1957, after it had been maintained by two lower courts.[20]

Another prominent case involved the exclusive Lake Placid Club in upstate New York, which had advertised that its facilities were available for conventions and conferences. After conferring with SCAD, however, the club decided that it wanted to retain its completely private character and therefore agreed to desist from such advertising.[21]

The most shocking instance of discrimination was provided by the West Side Tennis Club in the Forest Hills section of New York City. This is the place where the national tennis championship matches and the Davis Cup matches have been held, traditionally, since the beginning of the competition over forty years ago. The Club attracted world-wide attention in July, 1959, when it refused membership to Ralph J. Bunche, Nobel Peace Prize winner and undersecretary of the United Nations, and his fifteen-year-old son because they were Negroes. The United Nations official had applied for membership on the basis of a recommendation by George Agutter, the Tennis Club professional who had been training Dr. Bunche's son, Ralph, Jr.

On learning that his application would not be welcome, Dr. Bunche made the following statement:

Neither I nor my son regard this action as a hardship or humiliation. Rather, it is a discredit to the club itself. It is not, of course, in the category of the disfranchisement, deprival of other rights, segregation and acts of intimidation suffered by many Negroes in the South and of discrimination in employment and housing, suffered by most Negroes in the North as well as the South. But it flows from the same well of racial and religious bigotry. It confirms what I had often stated, namely, that no Negro American can be free from disabilities of race in this country until the lowliest Negro in Mississippi is no longer disadvantaged solely because of race; in short, until race prejudice has been everywhere eliminated, I am, in fact, glad to have this unpleasant but necessary lesson made real in this way to my son.[22]

On the floor of the Senate I said that the Club is not a private living room with tennis courts attached, but that by virtue of the national and international competitions held there, on which the eyes of the world are focused, it is a national institution as well.[23]

The Club's action was roundly denounced by New York City officials as well as by numerous civic leaders and organizations. The City Commission on Intergroup Relations announced that it would investigate the situation.[24] Proposals to transfer the Davis Cup matches were under serious consideration. To stem the uproar, the Club's Board of Governors expressed its regret over the embarrassment caused by the incident and announced that its president had resigned.[25] It denied that there had ever been any provisions in the Club's constitution or bylaws barring a candidate from membership because of race, creed, or color. However, the Board was not able to produce any Jews or Negroes who were members of the Club. It stated that any membership applications from Dr. Bunche or his son would get courteous and prompt attention.

Dr. Bunche accepted the apology and said that while he did not seek membership for himself, he would take up the question with his son.

Because of Dr. Bunche's reputation, the incident assumed international importance. Moscow radio, of course, capitalized upon the situation to attack the United States in the following language. In a broadcast in Russian on July 22, Moscow said:

It is a well-known fact that discrimination against the colored races is an integral trait of the American way of life. This applies even to those Negroes who through exceptional circumstances obtain high posts, and whose names are used to publicize the so-called racial equality in the United States.

The radio gave an account of the incident and quoted the statement of Dr. Bunche.

Radio broadcasts from Peiping and other Communist capitals echoed the Moscow line. Cairo beamed it to its vast African audience.

Surveys of social clubs in the New York metropolitan area, which were made subsequent to the Ralph Bunche incident, show that in Long Island and Westchester and New Jersey discrimination is the rule. The largest private club in the city, which was investigated by the New York City Commission on Intergroup Relations, excludes almost all Jews and Negroes from membership. A few clubs had some Jewish members, but none of them had Negro members.

A famous case in 1954, which dramatized the fight against resort discrimination, involved the Camelback Inn in Phoenix, Arizona. In that year, the National Association of Attorneys-General had scheduled their convention in Mississippi and had asked Attorney General Herbert Brownell, Jr., to be their keynote speaker. The Attorney General of Mississippi, however, publicly stated that Mr. Brownell would be unwelcome in Mississippi because of the position he had taken against public school segregation.

The National Association of Attorneys-General thereupon decided to move their convention to the Camelback Inn. This hotel, however, regularly followed a "Christians Only" policy, and when this fact was exposed by the newspapers, a number of officials—including my successor as attorney general of New York, Judge Louis J. Lefkowitz—at once publicly stated that they would not attend the convention. The response of the National Association of Attorneys-General was to cancel the Camelback reservation because of the resort's "rigid policy of 100 per cent Gentile clientele," and to schedule its meeting at the famous Greenbrier Hotel in White Sulphur Springs, West Virginia.

Since most business and professional groups who hold conventions include Jews, the Camelback Inn publicity resulted in a number of cancelations by groups planning to hold their meetings at the Inn.[26] It also revealed that in order to get the lucrative convention business, some hotels were using a double standard of admission. A convention scheduled by the Maine Medical Association canceled its reservations at a hotel because of a discriminatory policy, though the Association's membership of 700 physicians included less than 5 per cent who were Jews.

The spectacular growth of the convention business and the

refusal of the organizations sponsoring conventions to abide by the pattern of religious and racial segregation and restrictions have resulted in striking changes, particularly in key southern cities. Organizations have sought to hold their conventions in places where their members would not be embarrassed. One of the foremost national organizations to take a stand against meeting in cities where Negroes are excluded is the American Association for the Advancement of Science, one of the world's largest scientific groups. Another prominent group is the Southern Historical Society, whose members have urged it to refuse to convene in cities where segregation is practiced. Dr. Louis E. Jones, of the well-known Tuskegee Institute, called on Negroes to boycott the scheduled meeting in Atlanta of the Southern Sociological Society in April, 1960, because of segregation practices. The United States Conference of Mayors shifted its convention from New Orleans to Miami Beach in 1958 after its officials had been notified that Negro delegates could not stay at hotels for whites and could not attend meetings held in them.

In Louisville, Kentucky, all but one hotel will now house mixed conventions. Some still are hesitant if there are more than just a few Negro members. New Orleans, Atlanta, and Birmingham are about the only major holdouts among the large cities. However, no matter how encouraging these developments may appear, it is a far cry from the integrated conditions that exist in northern cities.

In the past, most southern hotels admitted Negroes to meetings, but they have been barred from the banquet hall and they have also been forced to seek rooms in Negro homes. Today, however, hotels in at least five southern convention centers will provide accommodations for groups with a sprinkling of Negro members, and also make available their dining facilities. Even those hotels which once had practiced "bootleg integration," that is, by making no issue about serving mixed dinner meetings, are now prepared to do it openly.

Some of the most striking advances in eradicating segregation barriers have been made in the fields of sport and theater. Negro athletes have always been recognized despite discrimination practices; one of the most spectacular demonstrations of American determination to wipe out this evil came in the Olympic Games of 1936. These were held in Berlin, and in defiance of the Nazi theory of racial superiority, which was gaining peak momentum, the United States team included Jesse Owens, a Negro, and one of the greatest athletes of his generation. Owens won the 200-meter run and the broad jump, and also was lead-off man in the champion 400-meter relay team.

For business reasons, major league baseball was always on the lookout for good Jewish ballplayers, but it had an unwritten agreement to exclude Negro athletes, until 1947 when Jackie Robinson joined the Brooklyn Dodgers. The increasing numbers of Negro fans attending the games, however, as well as the outstanding skill of athletes in the Negro leagues, prompted baseball managers to sign up Negro players. Within two years after Jackie Robinson joined the Dodgers, nine other Negro players had been signed up; Sam Jethroe by the Boston Braves; Dan Bankhead, Roy Campanella, and Don Newcombe by the Dodgers; Monte Irvin and Henry Thompson by the New York Giants; and Larry Doby, Luke Easter, and Satchel Paige by the Cleveland Indians.

Today, Negro players are so much a part of the baseball scene, and integration is so completely accepted, that neither fans nor management are aware of the problems and difficulties this issue once caused. Jackie Robinson and the Negro players who were signed up after him had to face and overcome all kinds of discrimination and prejudice. They got along very well with their teammates but had to overcome the discriminatory policies of hotels, restaurants, and training camps in the South. In some towns they were allowed to share rooms with the rest of the team, but not their meals; in other places they had to find Jim Crow sleeping accommodations. In the South they had to face threats from the Ku Klux Klan, other prejudiced elements among the townspeople, and legal action. But baseball managers refused to be cowed. Negroes played in the exhibition games, and the fans came in large numbers anyway.[27]

Prejudice against Negroes in basketball is limited to the South; there is no discrimination in the professional game. In professional football, Negroes have participated for many decades, but college football is plagued by discriminatory practices on southern gridirons. Chiefly affected are post-season bowl games; the issue is avoided in season games by scheduling interregional games to be played on northern fields.

Boxing does not discriminate among fighters; but in many southern cities, mixed bouts are prohibited by law.[28] Boxing frequently does play up a fighter's color, religion, or national origin for box-office reasons. A strong chauvinistic appeal is regarded as good business. And in tennis, players of many races and nationalities have participated in the Davis Cup and other championship tournaments, but it was not until 1956 that a Negro player successfully won through to a championship. Althea Gibson became the first Negro to achieve this distinction when she became the women's singles champion. Although many tournaments are open affairs, many tennis clubs where players are developed do not admit Negroes or Jews to membership.

Marked progress has been made in the theater in eliminating two major forms of prejudice. The removal of offensive stereotypes has a long history, and it is not yet concluded. The comic Jewish stereotype, which originated in the medieval period and survived down to our times in burlesque and vaudeville, has practically disappeared. Stereotypes of the savage Indian, the crafty Oriental, the murderous Hindu and the obsequious mammy and Ole-Black-Joe minstrel-type Negro are gradually being dissipated in the light of realities. The theater, movies, and television all have produced realistic portraits of considerable dramatic value of men and women of differing races and creeds.

In all these media, Negro performers are employed with relatively few instances of discrimination. Actors Equity, the Dramatists Guild, and the League of New York Theaters issued a joint statement on January 27, 1960, reporting substantial progress in the integration of Negro performers in Broadway shows. It said: "There have been significant examples of the integration of Negroes and other non-Caucasian artists in all the media of the performing arts. In each instance, the realities have been more faithfully served and the theater has been vitalized." [29]

As a sign of this progress, Equity, which had a committee to deal with problems of integration, broadened its name and scope to Special Committee for Ethnic Minorities in the Theater. Several shows on and off Broadway in 1960 are employing many Negro and Oriental members of Equity. In the musical field, increased opportunities for Negro musicians were noted by the Urban League of Greater New York, which reported in 1959 that more than a dozen local symphonic groups, an equal number of show orchestras, and almost as many television orchestras were hiring musicians without regard to their color. [30]

It is in the administration of justice that some of the most flagrant instances of discrimination have taken place, and the Federal Commission on Civil Rights, which has been conducting an investigation, has turned up what its chairman has described as "shocking" abuses.

The most vivid evidence of the way accused men can be deprived of their rights is provided by the Mack Charles Parker lynching case in Mississippi. Parker, a twenty-three-year-old Negro truck driver, was being held in the Pearl River County jail in Poplarville, Mississippi, on charges of raping a white woman. He had not been tried or identified by the victim. Nevertheless, he was forcibly removed from the jail by a lynch mob and shot to death on April 24, 1959, two days before he was scheduled to be tried. His body was found in the Pearl River nine days later by agents of the Federal Bureau of Investigation.

In November, the FBI submitted a 378-page report of its investigation to Governor J. P. Coleman of Mississippi. This report, kept secret, was turned over to the district and county prosecutors when the Pearl River County grand jury met that month, but it was never submitted to the grand jury. No FBI agents were called to testify, although the Department of Justice had notified local officials that it was preparing to bring in the evidence. And the grand jury adjourned on November 5 without returning any indictments in the Parker lynching.

Some time later it was learned that the long-secret FBI report named twenty-three white men as "known and suspected" participants in the lynching, and contained factual statements by at least three farmers involved in pre-lynch meetings.

United States Attorney General William Rogers offered the opinion that no federal prosecution could be successfully maintained. Federal action could be taken only under the Lindbergh kidnaping law if it could be proved that the victim had been transported across state lines, or under the Civil Rights Act of 1871, which permits federal prosecution only if state officials are involved in the commission of the crime. The inadequacy of these statutes to deal with this tragic situation underlined the need for federal jurisdiction in lynching cases. The classic federal antilynching bill—which has gotten nowhere in the Congress to date—makes it a federal crime (1) to deprive any person—either directly or indirectly—of his right not to be deprived of life, liberty, or property except by due process of law; or (2) for any federal or state official to fail to carry out his duty to prevent such lawlessness. Violators are subject to heavy fines or prison terms.[31]

In January, 1960, another attempt to secure indictments in the Parker lynching case ended in failure when a twenty-one-man federal grand jury in Biloxi, Mississippi, which included one Negro, returned a finding that no basis existed for prosecution. Thirty-two witnesses were heard, including some of the principal suspects. Twelve affirmative votes would have been necessary to return an indictment, and the grand jury's failure to do so ended any possibility of prosecution.

Juxtaposed to this failure to act in the Mack Charles Parker case must be placed the case of Robert Lee Goldsby, another Negro, whose conviction and sentence of death for shooting a white woman in Vaiden, Mississippi, in 1954, was set aside by the federal Court of Appeals for the Fifth Circuit and sustained by the United States Supreme Court. Goldsby's conviction was reversed on grounds that Negroes had been systematically excluded from voting and therefore also from the jury rolls, which were chosen from the list of registered voters. The jury which tried Goldsby thus was judged to have been unconstitutionally constituted. Goldsby was subsequently tried again, in December, 1959, and convicted, after the trial was transferred to Jackson, Mississippi, where Negroes are called for jury duty, although in very small numbers.[32]

The belief has been widely prevalent that Negroes are given heavier penalties than white persons on conviction for similar crimes in the South. But in Florida in May, 1959, the effect of current civil rights developments may have begun to be felt. In one county a Negro youth was tried, convicted, and sentenced to a long prison term on charges of raping a white woman. Almost at the same time in Tallahassee, in a sensational trial, four white youths were convicted on charges of raping a

Negro coed and were sentenced to long prison terms. Although the conduct of the court was above reproach, and the sentences commensurate with the evidence, the Communist press and international radio seized the opportunity to accuse the United States of maintaining a double standard of justice, charging that if the boys had been Negroes they would have received the death penalty. Considerable stress was placed upon the fact that Negroes have been executed for rape but no white rapist has been similarly doomed.

Popular impressions of abuse in the administration of justice are reinforced by such shocking instances as the sentencing of a twelve-year-old Negro boy in Pikeville, Tennessee, to thirty-five years' imprisonment in September, 1959, for the rape of a seven-year-old white girl. The boy, James Westmoreland, of Nashville, is alleged to have confessed. Reports of police brutality to Negro prisoners come from points as widely distant as Los Angeles, California, and Maryland, near the nation's capital; and while they may be disputed and denied, some evidence of discrimination remains. However, federal court insistence on the constitutional rights of accused men, and public support for equality of justice, is bringing about a greater sensitiveness to discriminatory practices in police and court actions, and substantial progress in their elimination. A striking case to illustrate this point is the Mallory case in Washington, D.C., a case that has resulted in an insistent demand for Federal legislation to overturn a U.S. Supreme Court decision. For in that case the court reversed a conviction for rape of Mallory, a Negro, because the confession was obtained by police questioning while Mallory was being held in a police station overly long before being arraigned before a magistrate and informed of his rights.

Chapter Twelve

The Reaction Abroad

South Africa's effort to repress its colored population and maintain a policy of apartheid has resulted in riots, tragedy, and a sharpening of racial self-consciousness throughout Africa. When Sékou Touré, president of the newly independent African Republic of Guinea visited the United States in the fall of 1959, he expressed a desire to see one of the southern states where racial difficulties had occurred. He was invited to visit North Carolina, not a "hard-core" state, but a state nevertheless with its share of trouble over integration and civil rights.

In North Carolina the African leader and his party were the guests of Governor Luther Hodges, and were feted by both white and Negro leaders at banquets and gatherings; significantly, the guest lists included white political personalities with constituencies which were traditionally sensitive to "mixing of the races." President Touré also visited a Negro college, where he received an honorary degree, and the Mutual Life Insurance Company, the world's largest Negro-owned-and-operated insurance concern.[1]

The President of Guinea—who in his youth had received Communist indoctrination and training in Moscow and Prague

—left North Carolina impressed. "We prefer fraternity to charity," he had told the National Press Club in Washington. For he knew that substantial social and economic collaboration between the United States government and the new governments of Africa, which he had discussed with President Eisenhower and Secretary of State Herter, could best be achieved on a partnership basis rather than on the basis of patronizing or philanthropy. The former African colonies and dependencies, now newly sovereign, are very sensitive to any indication that they are not being treated as equals. The Soviets know this, and have shown their awareness not only by their propaganda but by the indoctrination they have given impressionable young African students in the U.S.S.R.

The insistence of President Touré on visiting the South, his favorable reaction to what he saw and the treatment accorded him there, are almost textbook illustrations of the declaration made by President Eisenhower in his January, 1959, State of the Union Message. He said:

If we hope to strengthen freedom in the world we must be ever mindful of how our own conduct reacts elsewhere. No other nation has ever been so floodlighted by world opinion as the United States is today. Everything we do is carefully scrutinized by other peoples throughout the world. The bad is seen along with the good. Because we are human we err. But as free men we are also responsible for correcting the errors and imperfections of our ways.

The shortcomings or colonialist traditions of other nations cannot be considered properly as any basis for our policy in the United States, for the world has come to expect more of us. The American Revolution and the Declaration of Independence of 1776 have traditionally served as an inspiration to lovers of liberty and independence everywhere; the leadership of the free world has devolved upon us by virtue of our productive power and the nature of the cold-war struggle. And freedom and prejudice cannot serve together as handmaidens in the household of liberty.

Race relations in the United States epitomize to millions throughout the world the validity of the concepts of the constitutional democracy which we preach. Continuance of segregation and discrimination in our country has cost and continues to cost us as much in terms of our strength in winning the struggle for freedom in those places where it counts—with the two-thirds of the people of the free world whose skins are yellow, brown, or black—as have all the U.S.S.R.'s earth satellites and moon probes combined. Our difficulties, often as dramatic as the crisis in Little Rock, the bombings of schools and churches, or the Mack Charles Parker lynching, reflect adversely on the prestige and authority of the United States. Serious doubts are raised over our ability to lead and retain "on our side" the peoples in the so-called uncommitted nations in south and southeast Asia, the Pacific, the Middle East, and Africa.

There is little argument to the contrary—even among convinced southerners—that the way these millions go may decide the cold war as decisively as any other single factor. Harry Golden, the witty editor of the *Carolina Israelite,* has well pointed out:

The American people as a whole are becoming more mature about civil rights, which is why more injustices appear in the newspapers. . . . We need more than the military bases and missiles. Read the editorials out of India, Ghana, Kenya, Ceylon, and Jakarta, and you will not find a sentence about foreign aid, military bases or electrical appliances. The editorials are about first-class citizenship and human dignity. Civil rights have become important to the world and to America. . . . These are the things watched by the uncommitted nations—and we must gain the confidence and trust of these uncommitted nations or lose the world. It is as simple as that.[2]

Within the United States the political coming-of-age of non-white communities is reflected in the growing number of representatives in government. Hawaii, with its predominately Oriental population, has become our fiftieth state, and has sent the first members of Far Eastern ancestry and race to the Congress in Washington: Senator Hiram Fong, who is of Chinese descent, and Representative Daniel K. Inouye, who is of Japanese descent. These men take their seats beside a Hindu congressman, Representative D. S. Saund of California, and four Negro members of the House of Representatives, Representatives William L. Dawson of Illinois, Charles C. Diggs, Jr., of Michigan, Robert N. C. Nix of Pennsylvania, and Adam Clayton Powell of New York.

Senator Hiram Fong of Hawaii visited communities in fourteen Asian nations, bringing to them the message that the United States is still the land of equal opportunity where he, the son of a Chinese field laborer and an indentured servant, could become a wealthy man as well as the first United States senator from his state. Judge Saund of California has visited India where he was born, providing by his very presence a convincing answer to false Communist tales of wholesale American prejudice and discrimination. A distinguished American Negro, John Howard Morrow, has been named United States ambassador to Guinea; he is one of many Negroes who have become active in strengthening our ties with the nascent nations of Africa.

I am convinced that in the present struggle for the survival and victory of the ideals of freedom, it is just as important for us to meet the challenge of discrimination and segregation at home, successfully and in time, as it is to meet the economic and propaganda challenges of the cold war. We cannot deal with only one single issue at a time; the facts of international life present us with a whole complex of challenges, each of major importance and interdependent with the others.

In areas where the struggle for racial equality has not progressed, such as in the Union of South Africa with its policy of apartheid (the legally enforced doctrine separating the races), our policy is most important. In response to a specific inquiry I made, the United States State Department recently informed me that the United States embassy in South Africa has been able to hold several different social functions without government interference which were attended by American and African Negroes, sometimes as guests of honor.

This persistence in democratic practices and quiet insistence on pursuing the traditional American policy of equality even in the midst of intolerance did not in the least disturb our good relations with the Union of South Africa or its citizens. One can well imagine, however, what the impact in President Touré's Guinea and in other countries would have been had we followed the local South African custom of race separation.

The United States must continue to make unalterably clear through every appropriate means at its disposal our disagreement with any national policy which legislates inequality. The Congress recognized this when it incorporated into the Mutual Security Appropriation Act, 1960, a provision to the following effect:

SEC. 113. It is the sense of Congress that any attempt by foreign nations to create distinctions because of their race or religion among American citizens in the granting of personal or commercial access or any other rights otherwise available to United States citizens generally is repugnant to our principles; and in all negotiations between the United States and any foreign state arising as a result of funds appropriated under this Act, these principles shall be applied as the President may determine.

This provision was the outgrowth of the refusal by Saudi Arabia to allow United States soldiers of the Jewish faith to serve at the American air base at Dhahran. As the hearings before the Senate Committee on Appropriations and other reports subsequently brought out, there also existed instances of discrimination in other countries against Americans who were Negroes or Jews.[3] Americans have been the subject of discrimination by foreign countries before. More than one hundred years ago certain Swiss cantons sought to prohibit the entrance into their territory of American citizens who were Jews. Senator Lewis Cass of Michigan expressed the sentiment of the Senate over this proposed treaty when he informed a constituent in 1885:

> The invidious distinction contained in the treaty with Switzerland, between American citizens, granting rights to Christians which are withheld from Jews, was not ratified by the Senate; such a principle will never receive the sanction of this body.

In 1885, our country was compelled to assert vigorously its refusal to permit a foreign government to discriminate against American citizens. This time, the situation revolved about the appointment of Anthony M. Keiley, a former mayor of Richmond, Virginia, to be minister plenipotentiary to Austria-Hungary. The Austrians refused to accept this distingiushed Virginian because his wife happened to be Jewish. The letter sent to the Austrian government by Secretary of State Thomas F. Bayard on May 18, 1885, is a priceless document, a masterful statement of policy; it says in part:

> It is not within the power of the President nor of the Congress, nor of any judicial tribunal in the United States, to take or even hear testimony, or in any mode to inquire into or decide upon the religious belief of any official, and the proposition to allow this to be done by any foreign government is necessarily and a fortiori inadmissible.
>
> To suffer an infraction of this essential principle would lead to a disfranchisement of our citizens because of their religious belief. . . . It is not believed by the President that a doctrine and practice

so destructive of religious liberty and freedom of conscience, so devoid of catholicity, and so opposed to the spirit of the age in which we live can for a moment be accepted by the great family of civilized nations or be allowed to control their diplomatic intercourse.

Certain it is it will never, in my belief, be accepted by the people of the United States, nor by any administration which represents their sentiments. . . . Into the religious belief of its envoy or that of any member of his family, neither this Government nor any officer thereof, as I have shown you, has any right or power to inquire, or to apply any test whatever, or to decide such a question, and to do so would constitute an infraction of the express letter and an invasion of the pervading spirit of the supreme law of this land.

The matter was not dropped with this letter. Mr. Keiley resigned without serving, and for two years thereafter the United States did not appoint a minister to Austria-Hungary.[4]

There is a third great precedent supporting the principle which was restated in the amendment to the Mutual Security Appropriation bill. We had a commercial treaty with Czarist Russia which dated back to 1832. Under it, the rights of American citizens to equal treatment and opportunity were clearly set forth. But Russia repeatedly violated this provision of the treaty, and our government tried for more than forty years to get her to stop. We protested in 1890, and for two decades thereafter, in attempts to get Russia to admit Roman Catholic priests and Protestant missionaries, and to recognize the passports carried by Americans of the Jewish faith. A great deal of money in investments and annual trade was carried on under this treaty. It was a considerable factor in our foreign trade at that time.

Nevertheless, public indignation reached such a pitch that on December 4, 1911, a resolution providing for the abrogation of the treaty of 1832 was introduced into the House of Representatives. On December 5, the same resolution was introduced into the Senate. It was adopted by the House on December 13 by a vote of 301 to 1. Two days later, President Taft terminated the treaty with Russia, and on December 19, the Senate unanimously approved the President's action.[5]

In the case of Czarist Russia, as in the controversies with Switzerland and Austria, we had to meet a Jewish question or a Roman Catholic question or a Protestant question. What we had to decide was whether or not our government would permit another government to read into a treaty exceptions which do violence to the spirit of our Constitution and to the rights of all Americans.

Similarly, in the 84th Congress, disturbed by discrimination by Saudi Arabia and other Near East countries against Americans of the Jewish faith, the Senate on July 25, 1956, adopted a Resolution in the same tradition, introduced by Senator Herbert H. Lehman of New York. It reads as follows:

Whereas the protection of the integrity of the United States citizenship and of the proper rights of the United States citizens in their pursuit of lawful trade, travel, and other activities abroad is a principle of United States sovereignty; and

Whereas it is a primary principle of our Nation that there shall be no distinction among United States citizens based on their individual religious affiliations and since any attempt by foreign nations to create such distinctions among our citizens in the granting of personal or commercial access or any other rights otherwise available to United States citizens generally is inconsistent with our principles: Now, therefore, be it

Resolved, That it is the sense of the Senate that it regards any such distinctions directed against United States citizens as incompatible with the relations that should exist among friendly nations, and that in all negotiations between the United States and any foreign state every reasonable effort should be made to maintain this principle.

Later that year, both major parties adopted in their platforms planks affirming their stand on this issue. The Republicans said:

We approve appropriate action to oppose the imposition by foreign governments of discrimination against United States citizens based on their religion or race.

The Democrats said:

We oppose as contrary to American principles, the practice of any government which discriminates against American citizens on grounds of race or religion. We will not countenance any arrangement or treaty with any government which by its terms or in its practical application would sanction such practices.

We cannot expect the peoples of the free world—especially that great preponderance whose skins are black, brown, or yellow—to be familiar with American cars, American jazz, and American movies and yet remain ignorant of the state of equality of opportunity among the peoples of the United States.

In the fourteen years since the conclusion of World War II, twenty nations have achieved national independence; of these, nineteen have populations which are predominantly nonwhite. And in 1960 and 1961, some six additional African states will become sovereign. Robert Freeman, an American Negro doing business in Ghana, reported: "Ghanaans sometimes ask us about race relations in the United States. They say: 'We've got our freedom, when are you going to get yours?' " [6]

The crisis in Little Rock over public school desegregation, in 1958, is a dramatic illustration of the impact of our handling of domestic race problems on our image abroad. The worldwide interest in this case gave the Communists a field day at our expense while the non-Communist press also reflected in varying degree the adverse reaction and damage to our prestige. But when the United States government sent in troops to prevent anarchy, the world approved, and our prestige gained greatly because we were trying, even though we did not then succeed in enforcing school desegregation widely in the South.

On the walls of Italian towns, native Communist parties

plastered pictures showing a Negro child being escorted to a Little Rock school by a colored adult amid the jeers and threats of a surrounding mob of whites. Under it was the caption "Capitalist World." Beside it was a picture of a Negro and a white youth together, arm in arm, labeled "Socialist World."

In India, a key nation in the cold war, reports were featured prominently by the influential *Times of India* under the headlines: "Negroes fired on in Little Rock. Incidents increase in racial riots." One photograph was captioned: "United States School Integration Dispute. Armed men cordon off white school. Racial desegregation in Arkansas prevented."

The reaction in Ethiopia was shown by the newspaper *Voice of Ethiopia,* which reported that a white mothers' league had been formed at Little Rock. The paper said the white mothers hoped "to see Governor Orval Faubus of Arkansas and urge him to close the school, to which Negroes have been admitted under Federal armed guard for the past three days."

Considerably more hostile was the comment in the newspaper *Al Ra'id* of Tripoli, Libya, which wrote: "White Americans have hatred for the colored peoples. This situation counteracts the millions of dollars which the United States spends each year in Africa and Asia." In Nigeria, the *West African Pilot* said: "The Little Rock incident has shown that the United States has no moral claim to be the leader of Western democracies."

At the other end of Africa, the *Sunday News* of Tanganyika declared: "It must be ironical that the United States, which has championed the cause of liberty of the individual throughout the world, should have shown so much dissent within its borders. . . ."

The Egyptian press and radio gave full vent to their anti-Western feelings, and in numerous broadcasts to Africa, Cairo radio poured out a torrent of invective. Typical was a broadcast in Swahili, which said: "The white people, the aggressors, usurpers of our rights, suckers of our blood, and savages, are the first to draft laws and they are the first to break them. The Americans speak about a government of the people, by the people, and for the people, but the Americans do not regard the Negroes and the nonwhites in America as human beings like themselves. . . ."

The controlled Baghdad press and radio also were hostile. Arabs read in the *Iraq Times:* "Negroes: President called in Attorney General. Whites continue their segregation fight." In the key southeast Asian nation of Indonesia, the *Times of Indonesia* told its readers: "Central High School integrated under protection of bayonet." And quoting Radio Moscow: "It is hard to realize that this is taking place in a country preaching herself of civilization, in a country proclaiming its democratic liberties for all to hear."

Japanese newspapers reported the Little Rock happenings objectively, but editorial comments contained a tone of mild reproach, as in the following: "It is an abnormal scene by armed forces under the order of a governor."

The story was much the same in Western Europe. From Sweden the following comment was typical: "The wave of hate-inspired actions now rolling over a number of America's southern states can only be characterized in one way—they are a shameful and deeply humiliating stain on the escutcheon of that country."

West Germany warned: "The times of the Ku Klux Klan and of lynching appear to be returning." And from Rome, *Il Quotidiano,* the organ of the Roman Catholic Action Movement, stated that the situation "does not bring honor to the greatest democracy in the world."

The encouraging note in the reaction of the world to Little Rock was clear, and it points the way to the future. It is the understanding of the difficulties of a democracy involved in the race problem, which was manifest in public opinion outside the Communist bloc. It was well expressed in a page-one editorial in the *Times of Indonesia,* typical of other such expressions, which summed up even the token integration in the public schools at Little Rock by saying: "To us it is a personal triumph for President Eisenhower, a reaffirmation by Americans of their faith in the democratic system of government and a heartening example of human progress under the rule of law."

From the *Voice of Ethiopia,* the daily organ of the Ethiopian National Patriotic Association, on August 30, 1957, there came the following recognition of American efforts to assure equality for all its citizens:

The United States is to be congratulated on its courage, its patience and its enterprise in tackling a vexatious and deep-rooted problem intelligently. She has been fortunate in her leaders, who have had the temerity to assail the deep South, stronghold of segregationalism. She has been fortunate in having citizens in the South who have faced the problem with courage and, fighting public opinion, have bit by bit won their fight for integration. What is happening across the Atlantic is a splendid example for South African leaders to follow. A man is a man for all that, and all that, whether he be black, white, yellow or copper skinned.

I am convinced that these notes of encouragement demonstrate the reservoir of basic good will that the United States has succeeded in building up throughout the world, good will that leads to understanding that we have a serious problem regarding civil rights. They show a willingness to adopt a policy of waiting to see if and how we will act adequately to solve that problem. The world is willing to judge us by our genuine abhorrence of bigots and bigotry, and to give due credit to our national efforts to correct the wrongs of discrimination and segregation and attain the goals of democratice practice to which we aspire.

In calling attention to racial disorders and discrimination in the United States, the Communists have endeavored to "expose" as false the democratic American way of life, contrasting it with pictures of idyllic existence for racial and national minorities within the Communist world. Such incidents as the 1951 Cicero, Illinois race riots; the Emmett Till kidnaping case; the recent Mack Charles Parker lynching, and other examples of racial conflict have all furnished grist for the Red propaganda mill.

The creation by the Communists of an image of violence and discrimination in the United States was put to good use by them during the unsuccessful Hungarian revolution, when Soviet brutality was laid bare to the world. During the United Nations debate on the Hungarian resolution, Soviet propaganda efforts to smear the United States were intensified, reviving old horror stories and editorializing on racism in this country, pointing out that the United States did not come into the world tribunal of nations with clean hands when it criticized the Soviet Union for its excesses of cruelty in Hungary. United Nations delegates from Asian and African nations were told that in the very land where the United Nations had its headquarters "people of your color are being persecuted."

The Russians have used racial incidents in the United States not only to try to divert world attention from their own totalitarian terror but also to discredit the West and to aggrandize the Communist system. This propaganda is particularly damaging when it is fed by recurrences of racial violence.

In the competition for Africa, especially for the new nations south of the Sahara, the Communist effort is rapidly expanding. Trade missions, technicians to supervise Communist projects, and loans and grants accompanied by political agents have been poured into Africa. Since the beginning of the year their efforts have been reinforced by Moscow radio broadcasts in Swahili, a new language in the Kremlin's propaganda arsenal. Moreover, under a student exchange program, hundreds of Africans are attending universities in the Soviet Union, Romania, Czechoslovakia, Bulgaria, East Germany, and Hungary. Others are receiving Marxist indoctrination in China, a country which is particularly active in the North African countries. Moscow broadcasts in English to South Africa make frequent reference to "reactionary racists" in the United States. A broadcast on January 4, 1960, said: "Racism thrives in the United States itself. . . . American racists who pass discriminatory laws in their own country against Negroes also remain racists in foreign policy and in every way support their fellow whites in Africa."

Under these circumstances the influence of the United States as a peace leader becomes distorted with each new outburst of racial bias. Resentment, which is strong against European "imperialism," can easily be stretched by Communist propaganda to include the United States. A long-range program with vastly increased economic and technical aid will be much more effective if we can reduce our racial problems to dimensions which can be handled without violence and injustice.

Attacks upon the United States based on instances of racial discrimination are confined not alone to the Communists—they have helpers, too. The Cuban radio, under the Castro regime, has denounced Americans on the score of prejudice; in Africa and the Middle East, Nasser's Cairo radio has taken full advantage of every available racial incident.

It is the suspicion that our devotion to democracy and equality in the United States in practice is less sincere than our words that highlighted the Communist campaign in the case of the Rosenberg traitors, when Moscow alleged falsely that anti-Semitism was the prime factor in the conviction and subsequent execution of Julius and Ethel Rosenberg. Throughout Europe, newspapers, national leaders, and prominent citizens paralleled the Communist line that there had been a gross denial of justice in the United States. In Western Europe, even the conservative press has been sharply critical whenever racial incidents take place in the United States. The adverse public image of the United States in matters of race relations thus played into the hands of the Soviet propagandists in an instance where the allegations were without basis in fact: people were conditioned to believe the worst.

The Federal Commission on Civil Rights summed up the problem when it said: "There is no single domestic policy of the United States which has a more adverse impact on the standing of the United States in the world than our failure up to date to measurably meet and deal with the problem of racial discrimination."

The United States is not alone in facing problems of native prejudice. Other nations carry this burden on their national conscience. In Ceylon, two million Tamils form a national and linguistic minority that allegedly suffers discrimination at the hands of the six million Singhalese majority. Indonesia is reported to have imposed severe discriminatory measures on its Chinese minority, restricting their occupations and places of residence.

The toll of Muslim suffering in Hindu India and the persecution of Hindus in Muslim Pakistan, which occurred when Great Britain pulled out and the Indian subcontinent attained independence in 1947, will never be fully known. The slaughter of innocents on both sides, it is reported, ran into the thousands, and great numbers of Hindus and Muslims were forced to flee across their respective borders; many of these unfortunates are still homeless and unsettled. The refugee settlements in Pakistan, for example, are still an aching and very visible tragedy. Protestants experience difficulties in Spain, as do Catholics in Sweden, while Jews have been expelled from their homes in Egypt and other Middle East countries. The Soviet Union and its satellites have periodically launched anti-Semitic campaigns. Nor can the conscience of mankind ever fail to recall the terrible official policy of anti-Semitism in Nazi Germany, where six million Jews—as well as countless non-Jewish political nonconformists —were murdered before Hitler's Third Reich was extinguished forever.

Apartheid in South Africa, the policy of strict racial segregation, provides one extreme of the African picture, at the other end of which are the strong feelings against the whites in parts of black Africa, especially in some areas still in colonial status. In the latter, anticolonialism manifests itself in antiwhite feeling. For example, the Mau Mau terror in Kenya was strongly racist in character. Racial feelings run strong in the Belgian Congo and in the Federation of Rhodesia and Nyasaland. In December, 1959, the Fiji Islands in the Pacific experienced a riot, with Indians and Fijians shouting, "Down with the whites."

In the Union of South Africa the racial conflict has about reached the deadend of tragedy and ridiculousness at the same time. The massacre at Sharpeville, where police opened fire on a peaceful crowd on March 21, 1960, and killed seventy-two men and women, shocked the conscience of the world and led to the calling of a special session of the United Nations Security Council by its chairman, U.S. Ambassador Henry Cabot Lodge, Jr. A resolution urging South Africa to "abandon its policy of apartheid and racial discrimination" was passed without a dissenting voice on April 1, and United Nations Secretary General Dag Hammarskjöld was designated to ask South Africa to modify its apartheid policy.

The attempt by a white farmer to assassinate Hendrik Verwoerd, prime minister of South Africa, at a fair in Johannesburg on April 9, 1960, climaxed a month-long struggle by nonwhites against a system of police passes which they are required to carry. Negroes destroyed their passes and called a work stoppage which was highly effective. Nationalist government police raided native quarters using whips, clubs, revolvers, bayonets, and armored cars in a determined effort to force the Africans back to work. Economic pressures mounted and businessmen appealed to the government to modify its stand as the boycott stiffened. Most African leaders were arrested, and the two leading African organizations, the African National Congress and the Pan-Africanist Congress, were outlawed. But despite the protests and the shootings, the government defended its policy and adopted stiff emergency measures despite warnings that the consequence might be more bloodshed. A peaceful solution to this racial conflict seems farther away than ever.

Yet even South Africa is beginning to recognize the effect of domestic prejudices on its foreign relations. A South African minister found it expedient, in the interests of trade, to make an unprecedented visit to the Negro Republic of Ghana, in a manner entirely inconsistent with his own country's practice of apartheid.

Leopoldville, in the Belgian Congo, where race relations have been strained, adopted an ordinance on November 16, 1959, which forbids the establishment of special sites or areas reserved for certain races or ethnic groups in shops, institutions, and public places.

And in Spain, where American aid has been rapidly increasing, concessions have been made to Protestant religious worship primarily as the result of the United States government's good offices.

Communist agitation, which stirred up anti-American feeling in Western Europe immediately following World War II and produced "Yankee go home" signs on European walls, was defeated by the strong ties of blood and culture between Americans and the people of Europe. The American dream of democracy and equal opportunity is a major factor, also, in the awakening peoples of Asia and Africa. Whether we shall be able to hold their confidence and friendship depends in great measure on how we conduct ourselves at home. The increasing importance of the nonwhite world in Asia and Africa places our domestic group-relations problems in a perspective entirely different from that of just two decades ago, before World War II.

Yet overriding all the practical considerations of prestige, security, trade, and free-world leadership, there is the moral issue which asserts the sanctity and dignity of man. It is the declaration and the promise inherent in the United Nations Charter and the United States Constitution. We have moved slowly through the centuries to meet this issue, gradually accepting the responsibility which we assumed 180 years ago when we declared that all men are created free and equal. We have made tremendous strides in the struggle against religious and racial prejudices, particularly in the last decade when the need for the sanction of the law in meeting the issue of race and color discrimination became widely recognized. But we have a long way still to go, and we have begun to run out of time.

A world that combines an aggressive Communism, an awakening and largely neutralist non-Communist Asia, an emerging Africa, a proud nationalism in Latin America, and a Negro population in the United States, makes domestic segregation and discrimination intolerable. We must move forward with "all deliberate speed" in the fight against racial and religious discrimination. Our country must stand to all the world as a living affirmation of the rights of man—for this was the ideal of its Founding Fathers, as it is the ideal of their nearly 180,000,000 successors.

Chapter Thirteen

A Closing Scene in an Opening Drama

In 1960, civil rights became the number one domestic issue before the Congress. It is also, as we have seen, an issue supercharged with international implications. Peace requires populations which are educated to believe in the priceless heritage of freedom. But, in a free world that is more than two-thirds nonwhite, racial segregation or discrimination is inconsistent with freedom. To give validity and content to our struggle for freedom in the world, we must carry on the battle against racial segregation or discrimination at home with equal vigor. Those of us who have been fighting hard for adequate civil rights legislation at home have frequently been told: "Just give education a chance and it will do the job. Don't try to pass laws." To advocates of that view, I would say that it is a fine position if something happens, but a very inadequate position if nothing happens.

If the voting conditions which, according to the Federal Commission on Civil Rights, exist today in at least thirty-two counties in five states of the United States were to prevail in the predominantly nonwhite areas of the free world, about 5 per cent of their population of well over one billion people would be able to vote in their own national elections. Such a total vote in these countries of the non-Communist world, whose population is already six times that of the United States, would not even add up to the number of United States voters in the 1952 or 1956 national elections.

No section can hope to remain strong enough to sustain democratic institutions for long when only one out of every twenty of a group of its citizens can go freely to the polls. Instead of allowing discrimination to limit the size of our electorate, we must see that every citizen has the maximum opportunity to back the candidate of his choice at the polls, as well as the freedom to develop his talents and, through education, to train for, and work at, the kind of job for which he is best suited by his skills.

In his State of the Union message to the second session of the 86th Congress, President Eisenhower recommended the bill sent down by the Administration almost twelve months before, and certain proposals of the Federal Commission on Civil Rights contained in its September, 1959, report. He called upon Congress to signal to the world, by its action on this legislation, that "our government is striving for equality under the law for all our people." Because 1960 was a national election year, it was of paramount importance that every eligible citizen be encouraged to register and vote. President Eisenhower said in his message: "The right to vote has been one of the strongest pillars of a free society . . . our first duty is to protect this right against all encroachment."

On February 15, 1960, the Senate took up the matter of civil rights. This was the day scheduled for the purpose by the Senate majority leader, Senator Lyndon Johnson, at close of the previous session of the Congress. On September 14, 1959, he had said: "I serve notice on all Members that on or about twelve o'clock on February 15, I anticipate that some Senator will rise in his place and make a motion with regard to the general civil rights question." Subsequently, I had suggested an order of priorities on the proposals before us. It was necessary to remove the obstacles to the enjoyment of those civil rights we had undertaken to implement with the active authority of the federal government. These included voting rights, desegregation of the public schools, and assurances that contractors on government orders would offer equal opportunities for employment for all.

I gave high priority to public school desegregation notwithstanding the general emphasis on congressional legislation to secure the voting right. Equality of opportunity in education had been found by the Supreme Court, a coequal branch of our government, to require particularized attention in order to produce equal opportunity. It was entitled, I believed, to receive equal priority with the voting right and to be backed by appropriate legislation in the federal establishment.

There were additional measures which dealt with elementary aspects of public order that demanded our attention—against lynching and hate bombing. There was an anti-poll tax provision and a vital amendment authorizing intervention by the United States attorney general in civil suits to secure civil rights to individuals.

Before the Senate were two responsible package bills, one the Administration's measure backed by the President, and the other one supported by the majority leader, Senator Johnson. They were distinguished by their similarities and their differences. They were similar in seeking to assure the voting right and to make a federal crime of bombings intended to intimidate the opponents of racial segregation. They were dissimilar in that Senator Johnson's bill did little or nothing about segregation in the public schools or in employment by government contractors. The Administration's bill did something about both—much more about employment by federal government contractors than about public school desegregation. In procedures for enforcement there was also a fundamental difference. The Johnson bill relied on a newly created Federal Mediation and Conciliation Service which would operate locally in the civil rights field much as a similar service did in the labor-management field. It seemed to me essential to affirm the civil rights before we could conciliate those who denied them.

The Federal Commission on Civil Rights in September, 1959, had recommended the appointment by the president of federal registrars who would be authorized to register voters in the necessary areas. However, no provision of this kind appeared in the Administration's bill. On February 5, Attorney General William Rogers proposed to the Senate Committee on Rules and Administration a system of voting referees to be chosen by an alternative method—appointment by district courts. These voting referees would register voters who had been discriminated against, and see that they were allowed to vote. This provision ultimately became the most significant element of the Civil Rights Act of 1960.

In an effort to utilize both proposals, Senator Douglas and I introduced an amendment to provide for the registrar method in federal elections and for the referee method to apply in all elections, state and federal, when the registrar method did not work.

The normal course was expected to be the registrar method; under it the greatest number of persons could be registered most efficiently. Only in unusual cases where hard-core resistance was met or expected would the voting referee method be employed, thus putting the courts in a position to pass upon every disputed registration and to punish violation of its orders as a contempt of court.

Findings prior to the appointment of a registrar were to be

made by the president. He could employ any agency, including the Federal Commission on Civil Rights or the attorney general's office, to give him the basis for a finding that a denial of the opportunity to vote existed for a specified group of citizens within a specified area—an election district, a county, or a congressional district. Then the president could act, based on this determination.

The need for this kind of law was based on the findings of the Federal Commission on Civil Rights, which showed a most deplorable pattern of the denial of voting opportunities to hundreds of thousands of American citizens, in community after community of our southern states, by various pretexts and devices. There had been mass disfranchisement. Therefore, we needed machinery to give us the means for mass enfranchisement.

In answer to questions asked on the Senate floor by Senator Herman Talmadge of Georgia regarding the right to vote, I pointed out that the Fifteenth Amendment, adopted as a part of our hallowed Constitution, specifies voting, and states that the right to vote shall not be denied by the United States or by any state. It seemed to me that the members of the Congress had a duty to see that the promises of our Constitution are redeemed; and that I, like other senators, had made a promise to the people of the United States of the most solemn kind in respect to voting rights.

The destruction of voting records was another question that had arisen in this connection. It had been a very serious obstacle in the administration of the Civil Rights Act of 1957. There were ample illustrations in the report of the Federal Commission on Civil Rights. An Alabama law (17 Alabama Code, 31), for example, provided that voting-registration records were not public records and that registrars might dispose of records pertaining to unsuccessful applicants. This meant that it would be impossible even to find the evidence of a denial of voting opportunity.

The Administration's bill on this subject provided for the retention and preservation of voting records by federal officials for three years—in the law it became 22 months—and made it a crime willfully to destroy any such records. It gave the attorney general the right to inspect and copy such records upon written demand.

The basic question before the Senate was the time-honored one of civil rights. Would the South's senators filibuster successfully? This weapon of extended talk had proved fatal to civil rights legislation for ninety years, up to the passage of the Civil Rights Act of 1957, and even then had been effective enough to hold us to a diluted bill confined to only one civil right, voting. Now it was again to be put to the test. Perhaps we could have no quarrel with the senators from the South who felt that they had to utilize every parliamentary opportunity and device available to them to block any and all civil rights legislation. But we could ask those who were for some measure of change not to permit the filibuster to frustrate passage of a just and adequate civil rights law which a majority of senators considered essential to maintaining the validity of the Constitution for every American.

It was essential that this majority make every effort to provide an opportunity for full and free debate, the high tradition of the Senate. But it was neither essential nor wise to permit the terms of the legislation to be dictated by the expediency of avoiding a vote as to whether to close debate. This would amount to preserving for a minority the power over legislation which is inherent in the threat of the filibuster. Yet this is about what happened.

The question pending before the Senate was an amendment

offered by Senator Everett Dirksen of Illinois, the minority leader, to a House bill, H.R. 8315, authorizing the secretary of the army to lease a portion of Fort Crowder, Missouri, to Stella Reorganized Schools R-I, Missouri. The amendments to this non-controversial measure incorporated the Administration's civil rights package. Thereby they bypassed committee consideration and the likelihood that under normal committee procedure, the Senate's Judiciary Committee would again prove to be the graveyard of civil rights legislation.

I narrowed down most of my own forty-one proposals for civil rights legislation to eight amendments to the Dirksen Amendment to regularize Senate consideration of the issue. With Senator Paul Douglas and eight other colleagues as co-sponsors, I laid these before the Senate.

No amount of inveighing against unusual procedures could obliterate what the public now understood to be the situation. To limit the required law to the voting right was not enough; the voting right had the greatest support. But this did not change our duty—to address ourselves to the areas of segregation and discrimination in which law was needed to correct violations of the Constitution.

There was much speculation whether the round-the-clock Senate sessions would frustrate the civil rights proponents or wear out the opponents.

I did not consider this a parliamentary game. The 1954 decision of the Supreme Court in the public school desegregation cases and the report of the Federal Commission on Civil Rights had ended for all time the myth that a basic change in race relations is the result of education and the passage of time alone; law was seen to be essential. Every Senator who slept on a cot in the Senate building night after night and who answered quorum calls at awkward hours in the round-the-clock sessions setting a Senate record of 125 continuous hours, must have felt that this campaign was not a vain, annoying exercise, but essential to the interests of our country.

The main reason for the round-the-clock sessions was to give the proponents and opponents of the civil rights legislation an opportunity to make all their arguments on the bills consistent with the Senate's July adjournment timetable. Those of us who were for effective civil rights legislation were confident that the affirmative benefits of the round-the-clock debate would be to fix the attention of the country on civil rights legislation as never before, and therefore, because we had confidence in our case, to assure a better bill. We also believed that the extraordinary sessions would serve, if they were needed, as the background for an effort at cloture of debate by the necessary two-thirds majority.

After the civil rights measures had been under debate for two weeks plus one week of round-the-clock sessions (the equivalent of two weeks of our normal sessions) or a total of the equivalent of thirty days, the need for invoking cloture became evident. Otherwise the Senate would be immobilized indefinitely by a minority in opposition, through the utilization of its own rules. The motion for cloture itself was presented on March 8, 1960, by Senator Paul Douglas and myself and twenty-nine other senators. The move was made to help bring the Senate to its constitutional duty, that is, to vote.

I was under no illusions about the possibility of success. The last time cloture had been effected successfully was in 1927. In the forty-one years since 1919, when a rule on cloture was first adopted, there were only three successful cloture motions in the Senate, and none on civil rights had ever been successful.

On Thursday, March 10, the cloture motion came to a vote. To those who described our position as premature in presenting this motion, we pointed to the fact admitted by all proponents of civil rights legislation that if there was to be a meaningful bill the debate would not be ended until cloture was imposed. If there was to be a watered-down bill, our chance to alert the country would come on the cloture vote. The opponents of this legislation had not hesitated to bring the machinery of the Senate to a halt. Committee meetings and all other operations had been held up. Appropriation bills had been delayed because of this filibuster. And as far as shutting off debate was concerned, even after the more than 250 hours which had been spent on the bill by the Senate, there would still be 100 hours of debate—one hour for each Senator—if the cloture motion were approved.

The vote on the cloture motion was taken in an atmosphere of great drama. The result was 42 yeas and 53 nays. The cloture motion, therefore, was rejected. The fact that not even a majority voted for cloture showed the temper of the Senate. A majority preferred a bill which might be tolerated by the South even if the South could not agree to or accept it. A majority preferred that result to imposing cloture. For the moment, the opportunity was lost to break forever the blocking power—perhaps even veto power—of the South over civil rights legislation.

Immediately after the cloture motion was filed, the round-the-clock sessions were called off, and, as soon as cloture failed, the way was cleared for sending a mild and skeletonized bill on civil rights, which had in the meantime passed the House of Representatives, to the Senate Judiciary Committee, with instructions to report it back to the Senate in five days. From then on, the die was cast for a mild and limited civil rights bill in 1960.

It was noteworthy indeed that the Administration's bill, although it did not pretend to be a "strong" civil rights bill, did have this feature: four of seven sections, related to problems of desegregation in public school education and in jobs—and in only two of the sections to voting rights.

Whether any 1960 civil rights bill was really meaningful civil rights legislation depended on its recognition of the Supreme Court decision regarding desegregation of the public schools and on its provision for the enforcement of court orders to implement that decision.

Attacks on the Supreme Court had given the one-sided impression to many Americans, and to many others in the world, that there was no appreciable backing in the congressional branch of our federal government for the public school desegregation decree of the Supreme Court. Some had argued that these provisions were not the law of the land. It was said that the written words of the Constitution as construed by each state, rather than the interpretation of them by the Supreme Court, were the supreme law. It seemed to me that the time had come to make clear that the Congress of the United States supported the orderly processes of government, and that according to the orderly processes of government the Constitution as interpreted by the Supreme Court is the supreme law of the land.

This was the fundamental end-effect of that part of the Administration's package which I regarded as essential. It proposed that Congress find that the Supreme Court's decree in the school desegregation cases was the law of the land, a law that must be obeyed. It implemented this policy decision by making it a crime to interfere with a court order to enforce the civil right to attend a desegregated public school and by giving certain technical and financial assistance to school districts seeking to desegregate.

In a situation like that in Little Rock in 1958, there had been great difficulty in apprehending the leaders of a disorderly mob defying the court's injunction against segregated public schools. By establishing that interference with court orders was a crime, we would give the United States the ability to deal with such public anarchy. It would also enable the FBI to move in to reduce the danger of public disorder.

This much found its way into the 1960 law but was made applicable to all court orders in any type of case, which may one day create other problems; the provision for technical and financial assistance to school districts which wished to desegregate failed to pass.

It was very clear from what had happened to school desegregation in the Deep South—with outright defiance in five states and only token recognition in five others after six years—that there was absolutely urgent need for some authority in the attorney general to institute suits for public school desegregation. Although this so-called Part III was turned down by the Senate in 1957 and again in 1960, the need continues and will continue for years to come. There are fifty federal statutes in which suits for injunction may be brought by officers of the federal government to carry out the purpose of the laws and which protect the individual citizen in certain of his rights.

If Congress did give the attorney general this authority it would not only include the popularly discussed civil right to attend a nonsegregated public school but also the civil rights to enjoy other tax-supported facilities without segregation: libraries, swimming pools, beaches, golf courses, and parks; the opportunity to ride on desegregated buses, trolley cars, and trains and to use desegregated terminals and waiting rooms; and the right to enjoy equal treatment in the courts and the unintimidated right to institute suits in a court of law—to name some of the more basic civil rights.

A Supreme Court decision handed down on February 29,

1960, *in re* Raines, related directly to the effort to give the attorney general this authority. The relevant part of the Court's decision said:

It is urged that it is beyond the power of Congress to authorize the United States to bring this action in support of private constitutional rights. But there is the highest public interest in the due observance of all the Constitutional guarantees, including those that bear the most directly on private rights, and we think it perfectly competent for Congress to authorize the United States to be the guardian of that public interest in a suit for injunctive relief.

A concerted effort is under way in the southern states to hamper and stop those who, like the NAACP, would help civil rights litigants. Litigants in those states are neither rich nor familiar with legal procedures; they are generally humble people seeking elementary rights. The effort has been made, for example, by the enactment of antibarratry statutes in Arkansas, Georgia, Mississippi, South Carolina, and Virginia, to increase the difficulties faced by any litigant and to place in grave jeopardy lawyers who helped a particular litigant to institute a suit. Not only does the usual civil rights litigant need guidance, he needs, especially, financial help. To get an order for desegregation of a public school is usually estimated to cost up to $18,000 per pupil affected—an impossible burden for almost any litigant. Let us not forget that in these cases in southern states, the litigant faces not only local hostility or worse but also the attorney general of the state and his legal staff with the state's treasury financing the defense.

Included in the Administration package was the so-called antibombing legislation which did become law. My colleague from New York, Senator Kenneth B. Keating, had the initiative during his 1958 campaign to suggest that he would go to the southern states where the bombings had taken place. He invited me to accompany him, to talk with the governmental officials concerned. When we returned, we were of one mind that an antibombing law was essential. Fifty-five senators were sponsors of antibombing bills.

The Administration package provided for punishment for flight across state lines to avoid prosecution for destruction of educational or religious structures. To this was added, by Senator Keating's amendment, punishment for the interstate transportation of explosives intended to be used in such bombings. Penalties for interstate flight were fixed at a fine of not more than $5,000, or imprisonment for not more than five years, or both.

The Administration package bill also dealt with the educational needs of children of armed services personnel on duty in states with segregated public schools. According to a compilation which I had had made, the children of 38.3 per cent of the United States armed services personnel were living in such states. Where a school was closed to avoid desegregation the commissioner of education was authorized to provide for the education of these children. But I proposed also that the children of armed services personnel should not be required to attend segregated schools. This may be controlled administratively on military reservations, but there should be legislative sanction to provide schooling for such children in areas where they may otherwise be compelled to attend segregated schools.

Another proposal in the Administration's package bill concerned the Commission on Equal Job Opportunity under Government Contracts. This provision failed entirely, yet it would seem elementary that where employment is afforded as a result of expenditure of the taxpayers' money by the United States, employment opportunities should be afforded equally without regard to race, creed, or color. This is no small matter; the United States executes about 3½ million prime contracts a year, expending about $15 billion in the process. I was informed that since August, 1953, when the present Committee on Government Contracts—now headed by Vice President Nixon—was created, it had received about one thousand complaints. It has tried to adjust complaints, largely through conference and mediation.

The lack of a statutory base, however, results in the Committee's having no real staff of investigators or attorneys; its status can always be questioned. It must rely for its compliance work almost solely upon the contracting agencies. It has no sanction for noncompliance except the potential risk of a non-complying contractor of being barred from further government business.

The Administration bill gave the Committee legal status so that it would receive the authority and the appropriation to which a properly constituted agency is entitled. In 1945, the Russell Amendment, named for our colleague Senator Richard Russell of Georgia, barred agencies created by Executive Order from existing for more than one year unless they received a legislative appropriation. This killed the Committee which had been functioning in 1946, and has since inhibited the setting up of the present Committee in a truly effective way.

There was no antilynching bill in the Administration's proposals, but a number of bills on the subject, including the Javits-Douglas bill, were pending in the Senate. Lynching is condemned by everyone, but the Mack Charles Parker lynching in Poplarville, Mississippi, in 1959, showed the complete frustration which can come in the legal process of punishing those who are guilty. The intervention of the FBI in such cases is left almost entirely to local-government request and discretion. Yet the crime is certainly one that involves the United States within the spirit of the Fourteenth Amendment's guarantee of equal protection of the laws.

It is said that lynching is nowadays a rare occurrence. It also should be said that any lynching, however rare, is a blot of shame on the honor of the United States.

The bill passed by the House, which came over to the Senate toward the end of March, 1960, contained only five provisions. It made interference with court orders for public school de-segregation a crime; prohibited racially inspired bombings; provided for the schooling of children of armed forces personnel in areas of segregated school systems; ordered the preservation of voting records by state officials; and established court-appointed voting referees.

On April 8, the Civil Rights Act of 1960 was passed by the Senate, by a vote of 71 to 18. It contained sixteen amendments to the bill passed by the House in March. The defeat of the important amendments which my colleagues and I presented showed clearly that what a majority of the Senate was willing to do with regard to a civil rights bill in 1960 was about what the South might tolerate—though, of course, it would not approve. The Senate made clear that, essentially, it wanted to assure further the opportunity to vote, free of racial discrimination.

In summary, its provisions were these:

It became a federal crime to use threats or force to obstruct any order of a federal court.

It became a federal crime to flee from one state to another to avoid prosecution for "hate bombings"—the bombing of any structure or building, including schools, churches, homes, and places of business; it was also made a federal crime to transport explosives for such bombings in interstate commerce.

It required that voting records pertaining to federal elections be preserved for twenty-two months, and made them available for inspection by the Department of Justice.

It permitted the federal government to provide schooling for children of members of the armed services, where local schools were closed to avoid compliance with the Supreme Court's decree against public school segregation. It amended the Civil Rights Act of 1957 to provide for the appointment by federal courts of "voting referees," who would register under court orders persons whom local officials had deprived of the right to register or vote because of their race or color.

The civil rights problem is not a partial thing; all its parts are inseparable. Disrespect for law can have an epidemic effect. It is a communicable disease.

Outside the Senate door, as an alternative to law, hover anarchy, violence, and injustice. Sit-ins in Chattanooga, Tennessee, by Negroes demanding equal services at lunch counters erupt into a racial riot. Similar demonstrations are reported in North Carolina cities—Greensboro, Fayetteville, Highpoint, Raleigh-Durham, Winston Salem, Charlotte and Concord—and also in Richmond, Portsmouth, Whaleyville, and Hampton, Virginia; Tallahassee, Florida; Nashville, Tennessee; and Rock Hill, South Carolina.

Although neither violence nor breaches of the peace can be condoned, they are symptomatic of the refusal of men and women to accept a suppressed status. In this day and age, American citizens—especially the young—whatever their color, find such a status to be intolerable.

Will the student sit-ins grow stronger or will they wane and disappear? Will the awakening natives of South Africa be forced to violence or win concessions or will they accept conditions of status quo? Will the ferment elsewhere in Africa below the Sahara be satisfied by regional nationalisms or is it evidence of a world-wide stirring of the colored peoples? All these questions will decide future events in our own South. For we in the Congress missed the opportunity in 1960 to pass legislation that would help the United States to lead.

Congress failed in 1960 to enact into law those added provisions which would help further to head off racial disorders before they occur. We failed to give the Attorney General authority to institute suits in representative civil rights cases, thereby giving tongue to every man's legitimate grievance. Where the law prescribes the remedy, there is more likelihood that the law will be accepted.

The civil rights proponents failed in 1960 because, first and foremost, the people were not aroused enough. Senators received little mail on the issue. The Republicans in the Congress, who must furnish almost united support in view of the sectional split among the Democrats, were not united enough; the administration, though commendably active, was not militant enough; the northern liberal Democrats had neither enough votes in the Congress nor the support of the Democratic majority leaders in either house; and finally, the present cloture rule in the Senate does not work as the modern needs of our country require that it work.

Many predict that racial tensions in America will get worse before they get better. I am well aware of these predictions and of the possibility that they could be correct, but I still have great faith in the resourceful genius of our country. When public indignation is raised in America there is no denying relief. To save ourselves—and do it just in time—there must be those who will not permit themselves to be still and compliant or permit their fellow-Americans to be complacent in the face of the incendiary injustices of discrimination and segregation which persist in our society.

Notes

Chapter One

1. N. C. Belth, ed., *Barriers: Patterns of Discrimination Against Jews* (New York, 1958), p. 10.
2. *Statistical Abstract* (1957), p. 315. See also Report of the National Urban League, showing percentage increase from 1950 to 1958 in earnings of white and Negro workers, in *New York Times,* Apr. 10, 1960.
3. *Five Years of Progress: 1953-1958.* A report to President Eisenhower by the President's Committee on Government Contracts, (Washington, D.C., 1958).
4. Associated Press dispatch, in the *Washington Post,* July 31, 1959.

Chapter Two

1. Felix Frankfurter, "The Bold Experiment of Freedom," *Menorah Journal,* XXXVIII, 1, p. 3.
2. Alfred H. Holt, *American Place Names* (New York, 1938).
3. John Spencer Bassett, *A Short History of the United States* (New York, 1925), pp. 151-52. See also Abram Vossen Goodman, *American Overture: Jewish Rights in Colonial Times* (Philadelphia, 1947), pp. 146 ff.
4. Goodman, *op. cit.,* p. 40.
5. *Ibid.,* p. 119.
6. *Ibid.,* p. 159.
7. Harry Simonhoff, *Jewish Notables in America* (New York, 1956), p. 218.
8. Part I, Article 6, Clause 3.
9. Bassett, *op. cit.,* p. 462.
10. Sylvia K. Selekman, "A Wave of the Past: Lessons of the Anti-

Catholic Movement in the United States," *Menorah Journal*, XXXI, 1, pp. 18 ff.

11. Charles A. Beard and Mary R. Beard, *A Basic History of the United States* (Philadelphia, 1944), pp. 418-20.
12. Bassett, *op. cit.*, pp. 776-77.
13. Bertram W. Korn, *American Jewry and the Civil War* (Philadelphia, 1951), pp. 56 ff.
14. *Ibid.*, pp. 121 ff.
15. *Ibid.*, pp. 158 ff.
16. Lee M. Friedman, *Jewish Pioneers and Patriots* (Philadelphia, 1942), pp. 271-77.
17. Anita Libman Lebeson, *Pilgrim People* (New York, 1950), p. 397.
18. *Ibid.*, pp. 385-86.
19. *American Jewish Year Book*, XLII, pp. 284-90.

Chapter Three

1. Gunnar Myrdal, *An American Dilemma: The Negro and Modern Democracy* (New York, 1944), p. xliii.
2. John Spencer Bassett, *A Short History of the United States* (New York, 1925), p. 109.
3. *Ibid.*, pp. 350-52.
4. *Barron* v. *Baltimore,* 7 Peters 243 (1833).
5. Act of April 9, 1866, 14 Stat. 27.
6. 14 Stat. 50 (1866).
7. 14 Stat. 546 (1867).
8. 16 Stat. 140; 16 Stat. 433.
9. Act of April 20, 1871, 17 Stat. 13.
10. Bassett, *op. cit.*, p. 634.
11. Act of March 1, 1875, 18 Stat. 335.
12. 109 U.S. 3 (1883). *Ibid.* at 11.
13. *Ibid.* at 13.
14. *Ibid.* at 59.
15. 92 U.S. 542 (1875). In accord with this decision are *Hodges* v. *United States,* 203 U.S. 1 (1906); *Baldwin* v. *Franks,* 120 U.S. 678 (1887); *United States* v. *Harris,* 106 U.S. 629 (1883). See also *United States* v. *Powell,* 212 U.S. 564 (1909), affirming 151 Fed. 648 (C.C.N.D. Ala. 1907); *James* v. *Bowman,* 190 U.S. 127 (1903); *United States* v. *Reese,* 92 U.S. 214 (1876).
16. 100 U.S. 339 (1880). In accord with this decision are *Virginia* v. *Rives,* 100 U.S. 313 (1880); *Strauder* v. *West Virginia,* 100 U.S. 303 (1880).

17. 110 U.S. 651 (1884).
18. United States Constitution. Art. I, Section 4.
19. The vote on the repealing legislation was as follows:
    House: *For:* 193 Dem., 40 Rep. *Against:* 102 Rep., 0 Dem.
    Senate: *For:* 35 Dem., 1 Rep. *Against:* 28 Rep., 0 Dem.
20. Act of February 8, 1894, 28 Stat. 36.
21. Act of March 4, 1909, 35 Stat. 1088.
22. There is also the Hatch Act, 18 U.S.C. section 594 (1952), which prohibits the intimidation of voters in final federal elections; and 18 U.S.C. sections 1503, 1505 (1952), which prohibits the intimidation of witnesses in federal judicial or administrative proceedings.
23. 18 U.S.C. section 241 (1952).
24. 18 U.S.C. section 242 (1952).
25. 325 U.S. 91 (1945).
26. 341 U.S. 97 (1951). For other decisions under section 242 in accord with Williams, see *Lynch* v. *United States,* 189 F.2d 476 (5th Cir. 1951), cert. denied, 342 U.S. 831 (1951), in which police handed Negro prisoners to the Ku Klux Klan for beating; *Apodaca* v. *United States,* 188 F.2d 932 (10th Cir. 1951), in which police used torture in attempting to secure a confession; and *Crews* v. *United States,* 160 F.2d 746 (5th Cir. 1947), in which a Florida constable whipped a Negro farm hand and forced him to jump into a river, where he was drowned.
27. 71 Stat. 634, 42 U.S.C. sections 1971-95 (Supp. V, 1958).
28. 71 Stat. 635, 42 U.S.C. section 1975 (c) (Supp. V, 1958).
29. 71 Stat. 636, 42 U.S.C. section 1971 (b) (Supp. V, 1958).
30. 71 Stat. 636, 42 U.S.C. section 1971 (a) (Supp. V, 1958).
31. *United States* v. *Raines,* 172 F. Supp. 552, 561 (M.D. Ga. April 16, 1959), appeal filed, 27 U.S.L. Week 3328, Docket No. 914 (May 12, 1959); in February, 1960, the Supreme Court of the United Sates sustained the constitutionality of the Civil Rights Act of 1957 and reversed the district court which held the act unconstitutional.
32. *United States* v. *Alabama,* 27 U.S.L. Week 2645 (5th Cir. June 16, 1959), affirming 171 F. Supp. 720 (M.D. Ala. March 6, 1959).
33. *Terry* v. *Adams,* 345 U.S. 461 (1953); *Smith* v. *Allwright,* 321 U.S. 649 (1944); *United States* v. *Classic,* 313 U.S. 299 (1941); *Nixon* v. *Condon,* 286 U.S. 73 (1932); *Nixon* v. *Herndon,* 273 U.S. 536 (1927).
34. 334 U.S. 1 (1948). *Accord, Barrows* v. *Jackson,* 346 U.S. 249 (1953).
35. 347 U.S. 483 (1954).
36. 163 U.S. 537 (1896).
37. 358 U.S. 1 (1958).

38. *Ibid.* at 4.
39. *Muir* v. *Louisville Park Theatrical Assn.,* 347 U.S. 971 (1954), reversing *per curiam* 202 F.2d 275 (6th Cir. 1953) (private association which leased amphitheater in park from city may not discriminate); *Department of Conservation and Development* v. *Tate,* 231 F.2d 615 (4th Cir. 1956), cert. denied, 352 U.S. 838 (1956) (lessee of Virginia public park may not discriminate); *Dawson* v. *Mayor and City Council of Baltimore,* 220 F.2d 386 (4th Cir. 1955), affirmed *per curiam,* 350 U.S. 887 (1955) (enforcement of segregation in public beaches and bathhouses unconstitutional).
40. *City of Petersburg* v. *Alsup,* 238 F.2d 830 (5th Cir. 1956), cert. denied, 353 U.S. 922 (1956).
41. *Holmes* v. *City of Atlanta,* 350 U.S. 879 (1955), reversing *per curiam* 223 F.2d 93 (5th Cir. 1955) (city's refusal to permit Negroes to use white golf courses, and city ordinance prohibiting Negro use of white parks are unconstitutional); *Simkins* v. *City of Greensboro,* 149 F. Supp. 562 (M.D. N.C. 1957), affirmed, 246 F.2d 425 (4th Cir. 1957) (lessee of city may not discriminate in its operation of golf course).
42. *Browder* v. *Gayle,* 142 F. Supp. 707 (M.D. Ala. 1956), affirmed *per curiam,* 352 U.S. 903 (1956); see *Davis* v. *Morrison,* 2 Race Rel. L. Rep. 996 (E.D. La. 1957), affirmed, 252 F.2d 102 (5th Cir. 1958), cert. denied, 356 U.S. 968 (1958). Prior to the Brown case, the Supreme Court had, in *Morgan* v. *Virginia,* 328 U.S. 373 (1946), declared that segregation in interstate transportation was an unconstitutional burden on interstate commerce.
43. Cambridge, Mass., 1954.

Chapter Five

1. Malcolm Ross, *All Manner of Men* (New York, 1948), p. 20.
2. *Ibid.,* p. 19.
3. *Ibid.,* p. 20.
4. *Ibid.,* pp. 21-22.
5. *Ibid.,* pp. 22-23.
6. *Ibid.,* pp. 23-24.
7. Speech by Sen. Richard Russell of Georgia, *Congressional Record,* Aug. 9, 1944, XC, Part V, p. 6803.
8. Telegram by Gov. Ellis Arnall of Georgia to Sen. Harry Byrd of Virginia, in Ross, *op. cit.,* pp. 244-45.
9. *Ibid.,* p. 260.
10. Chavez FEPC Bill, S. 101, 1946.

11. New York State, *Report of the New York State Temporary Commission Against Discrimination,* Legislative Document, 1945, no. 6, p. 21.
12. New York State War Council, Committee on Discrimination in Employment, Report, Mar. 1941 to July 1944 (1944).
13. Monroe Berger, *Equality By Statute* (New York, 1952), p. 111.
14. *Ibid.,* fn. 11, p. 48.
15. N.Y.L. 1945, C.118, N.Y. Exec. Law, Art. 12, SS 125-36, renumbered in 1951 without substantive change to Art. 15, Sec. 290-301, Laws of 1951, Chap. 800. This law now extends also to discrimination in places of public accommodation and publicly assisted housing.
16. Sec. 290. Purposes of article.
17. Sec. 291. Opportunity for employment without discrimination a civil right.
18. Sec. 292, Subdivision 3.
19. Sec. 292, Subdivision 5.
20. Sec. 292, Subdivision 6.
21. Sec. 293. State Commission Against Discrimination.
22. Sec. 294. General policies of commission.
23. Sec. 295. General powers and duties of commission.
24. Sec. 296. Unlawful discriminatory policies.
25. Sec. 297. Procedure.
26. Sec. 298. Judicial review and enforcement.
27. Sec. 299. Penal provisions.
28. Sec. 300. Construction.
29. N. Y. State Assembly, *Hearings on A.I. 883, Assembly Print 1138, by Mr. Ives before the Assembly Ways and Means Committee and Senate Finance Committee,* Feb. 20, 1945, pp. 2, 14, 58.
30. N. J. Stat. Ann. Sec. 18:25-1 to 28 (1957 Supp.). This statute now extends also to discrimination in places of public accommodation and in publicly assisted housing.
31. Mass. Ann. Laws, ch. 151B, Secs. 1-10. This statute now extends also to discrimination in places of public accommodation and in publicly assisted housing.
32. Conn. Gen. Stats. c.371, Secs. 7400-7407 (1949) as amended in Secs. 3034d, 3035d (1955 Supp.); c.417, Secs. 8374, 8375 as amended in Secs. 3267d, 3268d (1955 Supp.). This law now extends to discrimination in public accommodation and publicly assisted housing.
33. Ind. Stats. Ann. Secs. 40-2301-2306 (1957 Supp.); Wisc. Stats. C.490, Secs. 111.31-113.37 (1945).
34. Wisc. Stats. Secs. 111.31-111.36 (1957 and 1958 Supp.).

35. R. I. Gen. Laws, Secs. 28-5-1 to 28-5-27.
36. N. M. Stats. Ann. Secs. 59-4-1 to 59-4-14 (1953).
37. Wash. Rev. Code, Secs. 49.60.010-.320 (1951).
38. Ore. Rev. Stats. Secs. 659.010-.115 and 659.990.
39. Colo. Laws, 1951, c.97, Art. 5A, Secs. 199-1 to 199.8.
40. Kan. Laws 1953, c.249, Sec. 44-1001-1008.
41. Minn. Stats. Ann. Secs. 363.01-.13 (1957).
42. Pa. Stats. Ann. Title 43, Secs. 951-963 (1957 Supp.).
43. Mich. Stats. Ann. Secs. 17.458(1)-(11) (1957 Supp.).
44. Wisc. Stats. Ann., Secs. 111.31-111.36 (1957 Supp. and 1958 Supp.).
45. Colo. Rev. Stats., Secs. 80-24-1 to 80-24-8.
46. Calif. Labor Code, Secs. 1410 *et seq.* (1959).
47. Ohio Rev. Code, Secs. 4112.01-.08 and Sec. 4112.99 (1959).
48. Alaska Laws (1953) c.18, as amended by L.1957, c.114.
49. Mun. Code of Chicago, Chap. 198.7A.
50. Cincinnati Code of Ordinances, Supp. Sec. 308-19, Ord. No. 196-1946.
51. Milwaukee Code, Secs. 106-24 to 106-29, May 13, 1946.
52. Philadelphia Ordinance, approved March 12, 1948.
53. Minneapolis Ordinance, adopted by Minneapolis City Council, Jan. 31, 1947, published and effective Feb. 5, 1947.
54. 31 L.R.R.M. 3021.
55. City of Youngstown, Ord. No. 51948, approved May 15, 1950.
56. *Cf.* Berger, *op. cit.*, fn. 13, pp. 167-69; and Jack Greenberg, *Race Relations and American Law* (New York, 1959), p. 5 and pp. 198-200.
57. President's Committee on Government Contract Compliance, *Report on Equal Economic Opportunity,* p. 102; Conference of Governors of Civil Rights States, *Report on Fair Employment Practices at Work in Twelve States,* 4 (1958). These figures do not reflect the impact of the addition in 1959 of California, Ohio, and Alaska to the roster of states with FEP laws, nor do they include New Mexico, which did not participate in the conference.
58. Greenberg, *op. cit.*, pp. 197-98.
59. *Biennial Report,* July 1, 1954 through June 30, 1956, Fair Employment Practices Division, Wisc. State Industrial Commission, p. 14.
60. See Reports of Division Against Discrimination, New Jersey State Dept. of Education.
61. *Five Years of Progress Under Oregon's Fair Employment Practices Act,* Report of Bureau of Labor, State of Oregon 1954, pp. 14-15.
62. 1956 Report of Rhode Island Comm. Against Discrimination, p. 5.
63. *New York Times,* Dec. 29, 1957, Sec. 10, p. 25.
64. Conference of Governors of Civil Rights States, *op. cit.,* p. 9.

Chapter Six

1. *New York Times,* Oct. 13, 1958.
2. *Washington Post,* July 15, 1959.
3. Harry Fleischman and James Rorty, *We Open the Gates* (New York, 1958), p. 39.
4. 1958 Annual Report, Washington State Board Against Discrimination.
5. Executive Order 10479 as amended by Executive Order 10482.
6. Executive Order 10557.
7. *Washington Post,* Sept. 24, 1959.
8. *Idem.*
9. *Five Years of Progress: 1953-1958.* A Report to President Eisenhower by the President's Committee on Government Contracts (Washington, D.C., 1958).
10. *New York Herald Tribune,* Oct. 7, 1959.
11. *Ibid.,* Apr. 29, 1959.
12. *Third Annual Report on Equal Job Opportunity: 1955-1956* (Washington, D.C., 1957).
13. Executive Order 10590.
14. *Third Report of the President's Committee on Government Employment Policy* (Washington, D.C., 1959).
15. S. 1999.
16. *American Jewish Year Book,* LI, p. 105.
17. *Holland* v. *Edwards,* 282, cited in *American Jewish Year Book,* LV, p. 36.
18. Report of Bureau on Jewish Employment Problems and the Anti-Defamation League of B'nai B'rith, 1957.
19. *Rights,* Apr.-May, 1959, Anti-Defamation League of B'nai B'rith, New York.
20. Anti-Defamation League Report, *New York Times,* Dec. 3, 1959.
21. N. C. Belth, ed., *Barriers: Patterns of Discrimination Against Jews* (New York, 1958), p. 49.
22. *Ibid.,* p. 50.
23. *New York Times,* Dec. 13, 1959.
24. *United Press International,* Sept. 12, 1959.
25. *Associated Press,* Oct. 20, 1959.
26. *Washington Post,* July 28, 1959.
27. Fleischman and Rorty, *op. cit.*
28. *Washington Post,* Jan. 23, 1960.
29. *Ross* v. *Ebert,* 2 Race Rel. Law Rep. 151; *Ibid.,* cited by the *American Jewish Year Book,* LIX, pp. 82-83.

30. *Ross* v. *Ebert*, 82 N.W. 2d 315.
31. American Jewish Congress Report, Dec. 4, 1959. See also *New York Times*, Jan. 21, 1960.
32. *Washington Post*, Sept. 24, 1959.

Chapter Seven

1. *Washington Post*, July 21, 1959.
2. *Ibid.*, March 22, 1960.
3. Published in Sept., 1959. See also *Congressional Record*, Feb. 27, 1960, pp. 3386-95.
4. *New York Times*, March 1, 1960. The Supreme Court unanimously affirmed a lower-court decision ordering back on the voting rolls the names of 1,377 Negroes previously purged.
5. 104 F. Supp. 442, affirmed 201 F.2d 644.
6. Louisiana Revised Statutes, Section 37, Title 18.
7. *Intimidation, Reprisal and Violence in the South's Racial Crisis*, joint report by the American Friends Service Committee, National Council of the Churches of Christ in the U.S.A., and Southern Regional Council. Reprinted in *Congressional Record*, June 17, 1959, p. 10038.
8. *U.S.* v. *The Association of Citizens Councils of Louisiana, et al.*, Civil Action 7881, U.S. District Court for Western District, Louisiana.
9. Press conference, July 29, 1959.
10. Murray G. Lawson, "The Foreign-Born in Congress, 1789-1949," *American Political Science Review*, Dec., 1957.
11. *New York Times*, Aug. 16, 1959; *Washington Post*, Aug. 23, 1959.

Chapter Eight

1. *Where Shall We Live?* Report of the Commission on Race and Housing (Berkeley, Calif., 1958), p. 2.
2. R. M. MacIver, ed., "Education Costs," *Discrimination and National Welfare* (New York, 1949).
3. *Trends in Housing*, May-June, 1959.
4. Gunnar Myrdal, *An American Dilemma* (New York, 1944), p. 627.
5. *New York Times*, Nov. 10, 1958.
6. *American Jewish Year Book*, LIX, p. 3.
7. Robert C. Weaver, *The Negro Ghetto* (New York, 1948), p. 8.
8. *Ibid.*, pp. 42-43.
9. Homer Hoyt, *The Structure and Growth of Residential Neighborhoods in American Cities* (Washington, D.C., 1939), p. 66.

10. Davis, Gardner, and Gardner, *Deep South* (Chicago, 1941), p. 50.
11. Irene B. Taeuber, *Migration, Mobility, and the Assimilation of the Negro* (Princeton, N.J., 1958), p. 2.
12. Morton Grodzins, *The Metropolitan Area As a Racial Problem* (Pittsburgh, Penna., 1958), p. 1.
13. Weaver, *op. cit.,* p. 14.
14. Myrdal, *op. cit.,* p. 196.
15. Edward C. Banfield and Morton Grodzins, *Government and Housing in Metropolitan Areas* (New York, 1958), p. 155.

   Chairmen of ACTION are: Andrew Heiskell, Board of Directors (board chairman, *Time* magazine); Ford Kramer, Research Committee (president, Draper & Kramer, Inc.); Joseph W. Lund, *ad hoc* Committee on the Investor (Executive Vice President, R. M. Bradley & Co., Inc.); Roy W. Johnson, *ad hoc* Committee on the Producer (director, Advanced Research Projects Agency, Dept. of Defense; former executive vice president, General Electric Co.); Ben Fischer, *ad hoc* Committee on the Consumer (International Representative, United Steelworkers of America); Philip L. Graham, *ad hoc* Committee on the Government (president and publisher, Washington Post Company); and Guy T. O. Hollyday, *ad hoc* Committee on the Community (chairman of the board, Title Guarantee Company).
16. *FHA Underwriting Manual,* p. 937.
17. Sec. 980 (1938), *Report of U.S. Commission on Civil Rights, 1959,* p. 464.
18. Housing and Home Finance Agency, *Eleventh Annual Report* (Washington, D.C., 1957), Table III-4, p. 57.
19. *Shelley* v. *Kraemer,* 334 U.S. 24. In this case the Supreme Court held that the right to own, use, occupy, and dispose of property is a privilege guaranteed to a citizen within the contemplation of the Fourteenth Amendment.
20. *Report of U.S. Commission on Civil Rights,* pp. 464-65, citing FHA Form No. 2004C.
21. *Ibid.,* fn. p. 463.
22. *Urban Renewal Project Characteristics,* Housing and Home Finance Agency, Urban Renewal Administration (Washington 25, D.C., Dec. 31, 1958), Table III, p. 8.
23. *Trends Toward Open Occupancy,* Housing and Home Finance Agency, Public Housing Administration (Washington, D.C., 1958), Table 2.
24. *Code of Ethics* of the National Association of Real Estate Boards, Article 34.
25. Luigi Laurenti, *Property Values and Race: Studies in Seven Cities*

(Berkeley, Calif., 1960). See also *Trends in Housing*, Jan.-Feb., 1960, p. 6, and Eunice and George Grier, *Privately Developed Interracial Housing* (Berkeley, Calif., 1960).

26. *Carolina Israelite* (Charlotte, N. C.), July-Aug., 1958.
27. *Trends in Housing*, May-June, 1959; Jan.-Feb., 1960.
28. *Buchanan* v. *Warley*, 245 U.S. 60.
29. The Birmingham racial zoning ordinance referred to was held unconstitutional by a federal court in Dec. 1950 (*City of Birmingham* v. *Monk*, 195 F.2d 358 [1950], cert. denied May 29, 1951.)
30. *Queensborough Land Co.* v. *Cazeaux*, 136 La. 724, 67 So. 641 (1915).
31. *Corrigan* v. *Buckley*, 299 Fed. 8.99 (D.C. Cir. 1924), appeal dismissed, 271 U.S. 323 (1926).
32. *Favors* v. *Randall*, Tasker St. Project. 40 Fed. Supp., 1941, p. 743.
33. *Detroit Housing Commission* v. *Lewis, et al.*, 226 F.2d 180. *Seawell* v. *MacWithey*, 63 A2d, 542 (N.J.).
34. *Ming* v. *Horgan, et al.*, Superior Court of the State of Calif. in and for the County of Sacramento, Memorandum Opinion No. 97130, June 23, 1958.
35. *New York State Commission Against Discrimination* v. *Pelham Hall Apartments, Inc., et al.*, Westchester County Supreme Court, Case No. 8642, 1957.
36. *O'Meara* v. *Washington State Board Against Discrimination*.
37. *Trends in Housing*, Oct.-Nov., 1958.
38. *Ibid.*, May-June, 1959.
39. Report of the Commission on Intergroup Relations of the City of New York on Study of the Attitudes of Real Estate Owners and Managers. See also testimony by COIR Chairman Dr. Alfred J. Marrow, Jan. 27, 1960 before N. Y. State Senate Committee on Public Health, in which he cited twenty-one-month report on experience with the law.
40. Constitutionality of the Fair Housing Practices Law was upheld on Apr. 1, 1960, when State Supreme Court Justice Aron Steuer rejected the suit.
41. *Where Shall We Live?*, p. 51.
42. Testimony of Frank C. Lowe before the Federal Commission on Civil Rights, New York hearing, Feb. 9, 1959.
43. Testimony of James H. Scheuer, before the Federal Commission on Civil Rights, New York hearing, Feb. 9, 1959.
44. *Highlights*, Mar., 1959, Des Moines Commission on Human Rights and Job Discrimination, Des Moines, Iowa.
45. *Trends in Housing*, Aug.-Sept., 1958.
46. *Where Shall We Live?*, p. 53; *The YWCA Magazine*, May, 1959; *Trends in Housing*, Mar.-Apr. and Aug.-Sept., 1958.

47. *Catholic Bishops Speak on Racial Discrimination and the Moral Law,* 1958, Catholic Interracial Council of Chicago; *Interracial News Service,* National Council of the Churches of Christ in the U.S.A., N.Y., "Race Relations—Denominational Statements," Jan.-Feb. and Mar.-Apr., 1959; Resolution on Segregated Housing, Union of American Hebrew Congregations, 44th General Assembly, 1957; Resolution on Housing, AFL-CIO Convention, 1957.

48. Member organizations are: Amalgamated Clothing Workers of America, AFL-CIO; American Civil Liberties Union; American Council on Human Rights; American Ethical Union; American Friends Service Committee; American Jewish Committee; American Jewish Congress; American Newspaper Guild, AFL-CIO; American Veterans Committee; Americans for Democratic Action; Anti-Defamation League of B'nai B'rith; Congregational Christian Churches, Council for Social Action and Race Relations Department, Board of Home Missions; Co-operative League of the USA; Friendship House; Industrial Union Department, AFL-CIO; International Ladies' Garment Workers' Union, AFL-CIO; International Union of Electrical, Radio and Machine Workers, AFL-CIO; Jewish Labor Committee; League for Industrial Democracy; The Methodist Church, Woman's Division of Christian Service; Migration Division, Puerto Rican Department of Labor; National Association for the Advancement of Colored People; National Council of the Churches of Christ in the U.S.A., Race Relations Department; National Council of Negro Women; National Urban League; Presbyterian Church, USA, Department of Social Education and Action; United Automobile Workers of America, AFL-CIO; and United Steelworkers of America, AFL-CIO.

Chapter Nine

1. Benjamin Epstein and Arnold Forster, "Barriers in Higher Education," in N. C. Belth, ed., *Barriers: Patterns of Discrimination Against Jews* (New York, 1958), pp. 60 ff.

2. *Ibid.,* p. 65.

3. Louis Krapin, "The Decline of Fraternity Bias," in *ibid.,* p. 78.

4. Paul Hartman, "State Laws Against Discrimination in Education," in *ibid.,* p. 89. See also Report of the President's Committee on Civil Rights, *To Secure These Rights* (New York, 1947), pp. 66-67.

5. 163 U.S. 537.

6. Louis R. Harlan, *Separate and Unequal* (Chapel Hill, N.C., 1958).

7. Ernst W. Swanson and John A. Griffin, *Public Education in the South Today and Tommorrow* (Chapel Hill, N.C., 1955).

8. Harlan, *op. cit.,* pp. 14-15.

9. *Ibid.,* p. 208.
10. Swanson and Griffin, *op. cit.,* pp. 62-63.
11. 169 Md. 478 (1936).
12. 305 U.S. 337 (1938).
13. *G. W. McLaurin* v. *Board of Regents,* 339 U.S. 637 (1950).
14. *Sipuel* v. *Board of Regents,* 332 U.S. 631 (1948).
15. 339 U.S. 629.
16. 339 U.S. 641.
17. *Time* magazine, Sept. 19, 1955, p. 26.
18. 347 U.S. 483.
19. *Bolling* v. *Sharpe,* 347 U.S. 497.
20. *Brown* v. *Board of Education,* 349 U.S. 294.
21. *Southern School News,* Nov. 4, 1954, p. 15.
22. Don Shoemaker, ed., *With All Deliberate Speed* (New York, 1957), p. 38.
23. Ernest Q. Campbell and Thomas F. Pettigrew, *Christians in Racial Crisis: A Study of Little Rock's Ministry* (Washington, D.C., 1959), pp. 110-11.
24. *Southern School News,* Sept. 1955, p. 11.
25. Report of the United States Commission on Civil Rights, 1959, (Washington, D.C., 1959), pp. 252 ff.
26. Estimated by Gordon M. Tiffany, director, United States Commission on Civil Rights, in letter dated Jan. 29, 1960.
27. *Congressional Record,* Feb. 10, 1958.
28. *Ibid.,* July 1, 1959, pp. 11291-92.

Chapter Ten

1. Report of President's Committee on Civil Rights, 1947, p. 89.
2. *Civil Rights in the Nation's Capital: A Report on a Decade of Progress,* National Association of Intergroup Relations Officials, (Washington, D.C., 1959).
3. Report of the United States Commission on Civil Rights, 1959, p. 175-76.
4. *Southern School News,* cited by the *New York Times,* Apr. 10, 1960.
5. *Washington Post,* Mar. 19, 1959.

Chapter Eleven

1. *Jewish Advocate* (Boston, Mass.), May 14, 1959; *Washington Post,* Aug. 30, 1959.
2. Unruh Civil Rights Act, signed Sept. 18, 1959.

3. 163 U.S. 537.
4. *Time* magazine, June 1, 1959.
5. *U.S. News and World Report,* June 15, 1959.
6. *Washington Post,* July 22; Aug. 1, 1959.
7. *New York Herald Tribune,* Oct. 8, 1959.
8. *Washington Post,* June 10, 1959.
9. *Ibid.,* July 18, 1959.
10. *Ibid.,* Aug. 15, 1959; Jan. 12, 1960.
11. *Ibid.,* July 31, 1959.
12. Letter in the *Arkansas Democrat* (Little Rock, Ark.), June, 1959.
13. June 27, 1959.
14. *Gayle* v. *Browder,* 352 U.S. 903, affirming 142 F. Supp. 707. See also *American Jewish Year Book,* LIX, pp. 87-88.
15. *New York Times,* July 26, 1959.
16. *Ibid.,* Jan. 7, 1960.
17. *American Jewish Year Book,* LIX, p. 89.
18. *Washington Post,* July 30, 1959.
19. *Ibid.,* July 9, July 11, and July 21, 1959.
20. *American Jewish Year Book,* LIX, p. 91.
21. N. C. Belth, ed., *Barriers: Patterns of Discrimination Against Jews* (New York, 1958), p. 27.
22. *New York Times,* July 9, 1959.
23. *New York Herald Tribune,* July 10, 1959.
24. *New York Times,* July 18, 1959.
25. *Ibid.,* July 15, 1959.
26. N. C. Belth, ed., *op. cit.,* pp. 32 ff.
27. Arnold Forster, *A Measure of Freedom* (New York, 1950), pp. 170-71.
28. The Supreme Court on May 25, 1959, upheld a lower-court ruling declaring unconstitutional a Louisana law barring matches between colored and white boxers.
29. *New York Times,* Jan. 29, 1960.
30. *Ibid.,* Feb. 5, 1960.
31. S. 2784, Jan. 11, 1960.
32. In *Williams* v. *Georgia,* the conviction of a Negro for murder in a state court was reviewed by the United States Supreme Court. The state attorney conceded that Negroes had been kept out of the jury panel, thus denying Williams a fair trial. He claimed that since the defense had not challenged this exclusion of Negroes within Georgia time limits, no federal question was involved. The Supreme Court said there was a real constitutional issue but declined to act. The majority of the Justices stated that they could not imagine that the "courts of Georgia would allow this man to go to his death as the result of a conviction secured from a jury

which the State admits was unconstitutionally impaneled" (349 U.S. 375, 391-1955). The Supreme Court remanded the case for further consideration but the Georgia Supreme Court said: "We will not supinely surrender sovereign powers of the State." It reaffirmed the conviction, and Williams died in the electric chair.

Chapter Twelve

1. *Time* magazine, Nov. 9, 1959, p. 17.
2. Quoted in *Congressional Record*, Sept. 9, 1959, p. 17333.
3. On H.R. 8385, 86-1, 1959.
4. Anita Libman Lebeson, *Pilgrim People* (New York, 1950), p. 354.
5. Charles Reznikoff, ed., *Louis Marshall, Champion of Liberty* (Philadelphia, 1957), pp. 102-4.
6. *New York Times,* Jan. 1, 1959.

Index